AF552546

Science, Power and Society

Science, Power and Society

INTERNATIONAL ENCYCLOPAEDIA OF SCIENCE AND TECHNOLOGY EDUCATION 8

SCIENCE, POWER AND SOCIETY

By

Dr. Digumarti Bhaskara Rao

M.Sc., M.A., M.A., M.Ed., Ph.D.
Dean, Faculty of Education
Member, Academic Senate
Ex-Chairman, Board of Studies in Educatioı
Member, Research Advisory Committee
Acharya Nagarjuna University
D-43, S.V.N. Colony
Guntur-522 006 (India)

DISCOVERY PUBLISHING HOUSE PVT. LTD.
NEW DELHI-110 002

First Published - 2000

Reprinted - 2016

ISBN: 978-81-7141-548-9 (Set)

ISBN: 978-81-7141-575-5

Science, Power and Society

Published by:

DISCOVERY PUBLISHING HOUSE PVT. LTD.

4383/4B, Ansari Road, Darya Ganj

New Delhi-110 002 (India)

Phone: +91-11-23279245, 43596064-65

Fax: +91-11-23253475

E-mail: discoverypublishinghouse@gmail.com

sales@discoverypublishinggroup.com

web: www.discoverypublishinggroup.com

Printed at:

Infinity Imaging Systems

Delhi

Preface

Science and Technology have occupied almost all spheres of human life. The wonderful achievements of science and technology have glorified the modern world and transformed the modern civilization into a scientific and technological civilization. Considering the importance of science and technology, they have been incorporated in every stage of education.

This International Encyclopaedia of Science and Technology Education is developed covering a wide range of aspects related to science and technology education for the benefit of all those who are associated with science and technology education. This Encyclopaedia is consisting of eleven volumes, namely:

1. Science and Technology Education,
2. Science Education in Developing Countries,
3. Organizational Structure of Science in Europe
4. Science Education in Asia and the Pacific,
5. Science and Technology Education for All,
6. Values, Ethics, Talent and Girls in Science and Technology Education,
7. Popularization of Science and Technology Education,
8. Science, Power and Society,
9. Information Technology,
10. Teacher Training in Science and Technology Education, and
11. Science, Technology and Society—A Curriculum Framework.

I convey my cordial thanks to UNESCO-PROAP, Bangkok, Thailand; UNESCO-ROSTE, Venice, Italy; UNESCO Paris, France; IIEP, Paris, France; Commonwealth Secretariat, London, UK; UNCTAD, Geneva, Switzerland, Queen's University, Kingston, Canada; and Alberta Education, Edmonton, Canada for their kind co-operation in preparing this Encyclopaedia.

DR. DIGUMARTI BHASKARA RAO
Secretary
Academy of Communication Culture Education
Science and Service
GUNTUR (A.P.)

Contents

Part I

SCIENCE, POWER AND SOCIETY

Genova Forum of UNESCO on Science and Society: International Symposium on Science and Power

Genoa Declaration on Science and Society

Recognizing that the future of humanity depends critically on the continued vitality of science and its applications, representatives of the world's major Academies of sciences and of the international scientific community met together in the city of Genoa, on the threshold of a new millennium, to foster global awareness of science and of its importance for the welfare of mankind.

The last three centuries have witnessed the birth of modern science and its explosive growth. The impact of science now extends to nearly all fields of knowledge and applications thereof, from agriculture to ecology, from neurosciences to psychology, from materials science to information technology, from medical to social sciences, etc.

In this century alone, the conceptual framework of human knowledge and understanding has undergone radical transformation. Determinism has gradually given way to a more open vision, one that offers humanity a growing consciousness of its freedom and of its responsibilities.

Moreover, the progressive transformation of the base of technology from empirical to scientific has generated for science a critical role in all activities, ranging from socio-economic and industrial to philosophical, ethical, cultural and political.

Science has contributed immensely to society, even though its applications can be and have been misused at times. However, it is important to ensure that this positive relationship between science and society continues and is strengthened.

Among the potential threats to this relationship, which may differ from society to society, are irrationality, various constraints on freedom in the conduct of science and dissemination of the results of science, and undervaluation of the role of science.

Universality, freedom and critical thinking constitute basic elements in the scientific process and form as common bond between all cultures. Accordingly, science can make a significant contribution to constructive dialogue between different cultures and thereby act as a powerful antidote to intolerance and ideological and racial barriers.

Moreover, the progress and application of scientific knowledge can offer effective means for solving many of the problems which face humanity, including those generated by the misuse of science.

Recognizing the important and distinctive potential of science to contribute to a better future for mankind, in which the culture of peace prevails, were reassert our adherence to the following principles:

- respect for the diversity of cultures within societies and promotion of science as a distinctive and important contributor to bridging such diverse cultures and promoting peaceful coexistence in accord with the principles of freedom, autonomy and rationality;
- mutual cooperation, reflecting the recognition that the production and utilization of scientific and technological knowledge are decisive for the future welfare of humanity and that science, with its universality, is uniquely positioned to serve as a laboratory in which mankind can work together to achieve a better future in accord with the principles of responsibility, solidarity and respect for the rights of individuals and nations.

Therefore, the Academies and other scientific institutions represented at this meeting reaffirm their commitment to the promotion of:

- the awareness that science, as a product of the history and creativity of mankind, is an integral part of all cultures;

- an increased effort in science education at all levels and in raising the young generations to be guided by a new vision of culture that embraces the scientific "ethos" and the spirit of free inquiry that characterizes science;
- wider dissemination and better public understanding of science and technology;
- balanced development of science and of technology, recognizing that both basic and applied sciences are vital for meeting human needs and for tackling problems such as hunger and disease, environmental degradation, rural and urban decline, and in the long run reducing disparities between rich and poor nations.

International cooperation is a striking feature of the present century. Witnessing the dramatic trend of transition of new socio-economic structure, with the world in search of new goals and approaches, we strongly recommended that particular effort be focused on increasing the scientific and technological capabilities of developing countries.

We are meeting on the eve of the 50th Anniversary of the United Nations and of UNESCO, whose Constitution assigns to it the mandate for promoting intellectual and scientific cooperation within the UN family. We call upon UNESCO to take a lead in implementing the principles and recommendations of this document.

This declaration was approved at the Meeting of the Steering Committee of the Genoa Forum of UNESCO on Science and Society "50th Anniversary of the United Nations and UNESCO: Science for the Dialogue between Cultures and for Development", Genoa, Italy 8-9 October, 1995.

RUBERTI Antonio—President, Steering Committee of the Genoa Forum of UNESCO on Science and Society

BRIAN Luigi—President, Academy of Science and Humanities of Liguria (Italy)

COLLINS Peter—Head of Sciences Advice Section of the Royal Society (United Kingdom)

EBERHARD Franz—Secretary General, International Association of Universities

FORTI Augusto—Secretary General, European Institute for East-West Cooperation

GRUNBERG-MANAGO Marianne—President. French Academy of Sciences (France)

GOTTSTEIN Klaus—Emeritus Member of Directorate, Max Planck Institute for Physics (Germany)

HAIG Frank—Immediate Past President, Washington Academy of Sciences (USA)

HALPERN Jack—Vice President, National Academy of Sciences (USA)

HU Qiheng—Vice President, Chinese Academy of Sciences (China)

JOSHI Shri Krishna—President, Indian National Science Academy (India)

KOSTIOUK Valeri—President, Association of International Cooperation (Russian Federation)

PATON Boris—President, International Association of Academies; President, National Academy of Sciences of Ukraine (Ukraine)

PUPPI Giampietro—Member of the Council, Pontifical Academy of Science (Vatican)

PETROV Rem—Vice President, Russian Academy of Sciences (Russian Federation)

SHAPAK Anatoliy—Secretary General, National Academy of Sciences of Ukraine (Ukraine)

TANDBERG Olof—Foreign Secretary, Royal Swedish Academy of Sciences (Sweden)

VILLEGAS Raimundo—Chancellor, Latin American Academy of Sciences (Venezuela)

KOUZMINOV Vladimir—Fellow of the World Academy of Art and Science

FORTI Augusto—Fellow of the World Academy of Art and Science

PETROV Rem—Fellow of the World Academy of Art and Science

JOSHI Sri Krishna—Fellow of the Third World Academy of Science

BISOGNO Paolo—National Research Council (Italy), Member of the Steering Committee of the Genoa Forum of UNESCO on Science and Society

CLEVELAND Harlan, President, World Academy of Art and Science (USA)

1

Science and Power

AHMED SALEH SAYYAD

President of the UNESCO General Conference

Madame Chairperson of the National Commission of UNESCO, Mr. Mayor of the city of Genoa, Mr. President of the region of Liguria

Ladies and Gentlemen,

It is a great pleasure for me to be here with you at this important meeting, and I wish to express on behalf of the General Conference of UNESCO our profound appreciation for the Italian National Commission for UNESCO, the National Research Council of Italy, the Municipality and University of Genoa and UNESCO Regional Office for Science and Technology for Europe, for their efforts and contribution to organize this important meeting concerning science and power.

Ladies and Gentlemen,

The relation between science and power is essentially based on a complex relationship between scientists and what they represent as knowledge on the one hand and the men and women in command of power in its most apparent forms: political and religious.

This relationship has always its expression in the following formula: men of power lead and scientists follow or as Mr. Winston Churchill said, "scientists were meant to be on tap and not on top". The relation between science and power had its ups and downs: we all remember that the scientist Galileo was killed by the representatives of the religious power when he threatened their control and power they exercised on ignorant masses.

In the old days, representatives of power used the knowledge of their science to consolidate their power by practising magic-like events. Others used the knowledge to manufacture means of destruction: arms, poisons, etc.

All leaders from ancient time until today found it essential to have a science advisor. Some have even a scientific council to advise the president in issues related to technological options for both peace and war.

The misuse of science by political power in this century should not be forgotten. During the period of the Second World War science was used to transform human beings into animal-like creatures, to create arms of massive destruction such as the atomic bomb and to investigate possible justifications for racism through genetic differences.

This horrible human tragedy led scientists and power representatives to conclude that all this should come to an end. They agreed that war starts in the minds of the people and it is in the minds of the people that the edification of peace must be built; they created UNESCO. While prevention may be the least visible of peace-building activities, it is by far the most desirable, and we need, Ladies and Gentlemen, your support and cooperation to reinforce the development of a culture of peace.

I wish you a very successful meeting.

Thank you for your attention.

2

Parliamentary Democracy and the Challenges of Scientific and Technological Development

PEDRO ROSETA

Chairman of the Committee on Science and Technology, Parliamentary Assembly, Council of Europe

Europe is facing a double challenge:

1. It is gaining a new geographic, but also a new democratic dimension: with the fall of the Berlin wall, for the first time it is possible for democracy to spread throughout the continent;

2. It is entering into a new type of society, dominated by a powerful flow of electronic information; some people call it an "information" or "electronic" society. Presumably it is going to be the 21st century reality. The role of science and of its practical implications in that society is going to be predominant. In both fields, there are achievements, gaps and failures.

If the Council of Europe can be considered as one of the most valuable yardsticks for the level of democracy and protection of human rights, one must not neglect the fact that 9 former communist countries have become members of the organization within the last 5 years and that the Parliaments of another 9 countries (Russia and Ukraine are among them) have special guest status. If Russia joins the Council next year, the organization will expand from the Atlantic to the Pacific!

This does not necessarily mean that democracy has been completed continentwide. Important gaps remain in many countries as to the protection of human rights and democratic guarantees. Much has to be done to combat nationalism, racism, xenophobia, which, unfortunately, are gaining ground in Europe. One has also to recognize that a great part of the international action in ex-Yugoslavia has been a failure.

As far as the scientific and technological field is concerned, Europe is continuing to be at the forefront of world research and development achievements. Its competitiveness, however, compared to that of other nations is a matter of concern.

If we try to look at the intersection of both prospectives—democratic and scientific development—a series of problems will arise.

The relationship between scientists and politicians has never been an easy one. On the one side, if scientists examine and try to give a warning on global trends such as the demographic boom, the greenhouse effect and pollution, politicians are much more preoccupied with everyday short term problems like inflation, unemployment, crime. When they have to define political and, before all, budgetary priorities, the next electoral term matters to them much more and, in any case, is closer in time and space than, say, the greenhouse effect.

On the other side, the extraordinary development of new technologies during the last decade has gone to some extent beyond politicians' reach.

A few examples:

The last achievements in the field of biomedicine have reversed the whole concept of human nature. For the first time in history, they give us the opportunity of considering Man not only as the Creator's work, but as a Creator himself. But then one could ask: does one have the right to change the genetical heritage of humanity? Should there be any limits into investigating the human genome? Is it not dangerous that the genetic information could be used against the individual in his professional career or his private life?

These are questions that have not yet received an appropriate answer at a political level. In some countries it is still unthinkable to intervene on human embryo whereas in others, like the US, research on it might be legalized beyond the initial fourteen-day period. There is no certainty on that human cloning might not be legalized one day—and this is something we must never admit! It is very difficult to decide when it comes to evaluate whether a scientific choice contributes to development of humanity or whether it runs counter to some basic human rights.

Another example: electronic information has become so powerful and omnipresent, so penetrating, that it is getting more and more difficult for ordinary people to distinguish between "real" and "electronic" reality. Who has the right to choose what kind of information will be offered to the public? What criteria should be used in selecting information? How to protect people from manipulation and how to protect the protectors themselves? Here is another series of questions which have not yet found an answer. This particular situation is even worse, because it might be very tempting for politicians not to answer these questions and to use ("misuse" would be a more appropriate word) the possibilities offered by the new information systems for their own sake. At the beginning of next year, the Parliamentary Assembly will look more closely into this matter by organizing a conference on the ways of preserving democracy in the electronic era.

Let me just mention one more aspect. With scientific development, new energy sources have become available, but their price is still too high. In the new democracies of Central and Eastern Europe, eager to reach the European Union economic and living standards, politicians are often reluctant to give priority to environmental protection when a huge, Stalinist-time plant can save jobs or when a Chernobyl-style power station can avoid electricity shortages.

Is it better not to comment now on situations where politicians are unable or unwilling to prevent leaks of top scientific and technological information which might lead to massive destruction? When a country's economy is ruined, when most of the people live in misery, how can we prevent scientists from selling their precious and sometimes dangerous knowledge to the highest bidder?

In the new world, the mutual relationship between science/ applied science/technology/economy has changed. As a significant part of scientific research is orientated towards technological innovation, the commercial stake has become very important. As a result, public opinion sometimes considers that science is being involved in certain strategic decisions and economic interests. In people's eyes, science is no longer either "innocent" or "neutral". While some people consider politics as being more and more dominated by science, others suspect that science is being dominated by politics.

This scientific involvement in the economic machinery holds along other disadvantages: commercial competitiveness is based on technological secrecy. That means that some important discoveries and projects are kept secret for a very long time. The point is that it is occuring at a moment when, more than ever, science needs to be persuasive and transparent for the masses. Paradoxically, it has to function behind closed doors at a moment when, more than ever, politicians are open to dialogue and consultation.

Dialogue is probably the best word to describe and the best solution to suggest, to enable science and power to go in the same direction: human development, welfare, prosperity. To provide the democratic background for this development, the Council of Europe has an important role to pay. Its Parliamentary Assembly is the largest European forum where Members of Parliaments can meet, discuss, exchange views and experiences and teach each other the best ways of facing the scientific and technological challenges. This dialogue is not a purely European one; many international organizations such as OECD, the European Bank for Reconstruction and Development, governmental and independent experts, take part in it.

A good example of a fruitful and long-term collaboration is the draft Convention on Bioethics to which the Parliamentary Assembly has been asked to give an opinion. It will be reexamined and, hopefully, adopted at the next Parliamentary Assembly session in January.

Another important area the Committee on Science and Technology is working in, is the role of social sciences in the transition period. After all the years of totalitarian rule in Central and Eastern Euroep, the social sciences' most important task is to help people to perceive today's realities in a free, independent and rational way. It would be impossible for the politicians to reform such a complex society, such a melting pot of not completely overcome disillusions about the past and not entirely realized projects about the future, if it was not for the social sciences to give a realistic analysis of the undergoing processes and to work out models for the future. The challenge is double, because no Western society can be a perfect model for the possible development in the other part of the continent. The situation there is unprecedented.

In the coming years politicians will be faced with scientific and technological options which are likely to nave tremendous impact on our nations' lives. Is the average politician intellectually and technically prepared for making the right choices? If the choices are made instead, by experts and specialists, can we still talk about representative democracy? What does "cognitive democracy"—a notion which is being advocated by some and which I personally dislike—actually mean? How can we reestablish the balance between parliament and government in technical matters, where this latter is much better equipped with high level expertise? Finally, where should the real power lie, in matters that concern the future well-being of nations?

In my view, the scientists, the experts are there to provide for different options, to suggest alternatives, but the final decision, the choice, should rest with the politicians. They should be intellectually and morally prepared to take decisions and to assume the responsibility for the possible consequences. Taking the appropriate decisions is the best expression of their political responsibility and of their democratic mandate. Closer cooperation between scientists and elected members is essential, but I am against the sort of "eliminatory democracy" where it is up to the wise men, and not to the politicians with democratic mandate, to take political decisions

Parliaments for their part, at least some of them, have already realized the stakes, and are organizing their structures in a way to cope with the new challenges. Science and Technology Assessment schemes are being put in place to help them identify the real problems, strategic choices and the right responses. At European level also, both the European Parliament, through STOA, and the Parliamentary Assembly of the Council of Europe are doing their utmost in order to promote this idea.

After the Hiroshima bombing, Einstein said: there are things that are better left undone. But it is sure as well that there are things that must be done. The parliamentarians, who are at the intersection between people and power, have a great deal of responsibility as to defining what should and what must not be done in science.

3
Historical Perspectives

AUGUSTO FORTI

Secretary General, European Institute for East-West Cooperation

Since the beginning of humanity, man has always been looking for rules and methods for placing himself in the context of the planet and the universe. Measuring the distance between the earth, the moon and the sun, studying the sky on a starry night, finding useful ways for counting and linear measuring have been among the first worries and activities of our ancestors.

Mathematics, trigonometry as well as the speculation on the composition of matter have occupied the minds of our ancestors from Babylon to Mexico and in many other places of our planet.

On the other hand, mathematics, geometry, trigonometry, the possibility of forecasting solar eclipses and other natural phenomena gave to the "primitive scientists", who were mainly priests and magicians, an enormous power which was practised since many centuries B C.

It was in the Mediterranean area that science became associated with the conceptual and philosophical view of the world and scientific considerations became part of human speculation for hundred years B C and in the first millennium.

After the first millennium, the development of universities in the Mediterranean area where the culture of the Greeks and the Latins, the Arab, the Christian and Hebrew worlds, created a very lively and fertile environment and background for the rise of philosophical theories which were mainly dominated by the Aristotelian thinkers providing an holistic view dominated by theology and in which science was marginal despite the presence of outstanding scientists during all that time.

But only with Copernicus and Galileo we can consider the birth and rise of modern science which becomes, *per se*, an element, a fundamental element, of our modern civilization through a harsh fight between religious dogmas and intolerance and science.

Since that time, science has played in the history of mankind an independent and fundamental role being used or misused by power and being itself source of a tremendous power.

Let us take an emblematic figure of this time: Galileo Galilei. Galileo is certainly an emblematic figure in the fight between Science and Power. We have already mentioned and flourishing of the ideas and new technological instruments at the beginning of the 17th century and it is exactly in 1609 that Galileo built his own telescope which was a fundamental instrument for his writing the book: "Nuntius Sidereus".

With his instrument, Galileo was able to show the new cosmogonical reality, with the rotation of the satellites and with the observation of the celestial bodies close to us, giving evidence to a new reality which already scientists and philosophisers like Telesio, Bruno and Campanella had foreseen with the critics of the Scholastic and the Aristotelian philosophers.

The publication of the "Nuncio Sidereo", which was basically Copernican in all its implications, gave rise to a harsh confrontation particularly between the new ideas in science, the traditional philosophers and the Church.

Contrary to Thomas Scott or William of Occam and other thinkers (theory of the double truth), Galileo bluntly affirmed that two truths is a non sense. In a period when the inquisition was becoming more and more aggressive. Galileo had the courage to state that the Holy Scriptures often need an explanation which is different from the words and that in any case in the controversy concerning the natural laws, the Holy Scriptures should really have a secondary role.

He was at the same time defending the privilege of human ingenuity and imagination. Who would dare to assert that we already know everything which is to be known and discovered in the world? It is the interpretation of the Holy Scriptures that has to adapt to the conclusions of science which are the result of research, experiments and demonstrations and not vice versa. This is the revolutionary view that Galileo supported and just for this we can say that we owe him the birth of Modern Science, which should be independent in its own merits and inspiration.

However, the revolutionary ideas of Copernicus and Galileo not only gave raise to the fight between science and religion but also inside the Roman Church they provoked a harsh confrontation between the Dominicans, who at that time represented the conservatory and reactionary avant-grade of the Catholic Church, and the jesuits, who were more open to culture and science, also because at the beginning of the 17th century the Jesuit mathematicians and astronomers of the Collegio Romano were recognized among the highest scientific authorities.

But the publication of the "Dialogo dei Massimi Sistemi", the difficult position of Pope Urbano VII, who at the beginning had been one of Galileo's indulgent supporters, the late acceptance by the Prostestants of the Copernican theories and the fight that the Jesuits were conducting against the reform, made inevitable Galileo's trial and condemnation by the Inquisition.

So one of the greatest spirits nearly blind and severely ill, ended his days in the hands of the holy Inquisition on 8 January 1642. Galileo died but, after a very dark period, Science finally won its battle for the freedom of thinking against the dogmatic attitude of the Church.

Other scientists like Lavoisier, during the French Revolution, or Lisenko, paid with great sufferance the freedom of expressing and supporting their scientific theories and ideas against the power of the time. But after Galileo and after the birth of Modern Science, we can say that the battle between Science and

Power gave raise to the new vision of the world where Science became more free from power, as a fundamental, strong and independent element in the history of human mankind.

In some way, science could claim victory on the power of the dogmas against which the battle was won. But now, it is the political and state power which takes over and tries to impose its views on science.

A typical example is the history of the Ecole Polytechnic and of Napoleon. Between 1798 and 1815, we witness to a deep transformation of the Ecole. The scenario changes. From a school devoted to the teaching of mathematics and physics, it gradually became a school for the teaching of the art of war. From an academic school, it gradually became a school ruled by military governors, mainly oriented towards the solution of the practical problems of warfare.

Despite the fact that Napoleon gave medals to Volta and Davy, despite his relying on the advice of Cuvier and Delambre, all his efforts were directed towards making science concur to this own aims which were the expansion of the empire and a successful warfare.

He suppressed many of the scientific institutions which were created by the French Revolution and he conceived science in a strict utilitarian manner. This was the end of the utopias which reigned during the enlightenment and during the revolution.

The restoration policy is also evident in the reform of the Université Impériale, in which the Church managed to re-establish its educational monopoly. Saint-Simon and Comet fought to keep and spirit of the enlightment alive but their influence came about only at the end of the Second Empire and the Third Republic. So during the Napoleon period we see the relegation of science as something marginal whenever people like Comte tried to use it as a weapon to reform the state.

Here, we can, say starts the dilemma of *the two cultures*. "Les belles letters" became again *à la mode,* relegating science as a utopistic and dangerous elements for the stability of the state.

This was the beginning of a time, the time of "La vie de bohème" which came as an antithesis to scientific thinking. An example of this is Claude Barnard who arrived in Paris with high literary ambitions and only after the deception in this literary career, he turned to science.

Nevertheless, we should not forget that at least the Napoleonic period established a very strong link between science, technology and the military system with a good side and also a bad one in the sense that in this way Napoleon derived the French industry and agriculture of important contributions, handicap of which France suffered in the future in comparison with other countries such as England, Germany and Belgium.

This story goes on up to our own with the ideological and political persecution of scientists as happened in the Soviet Union with Vavilov and Sakharov, in Italy and in Germany during the Nazi and Fascist periods with the persecution of Jewish scientists and the consequent damages for the national science which we all know and the loss for these nations of figures like Einstein, Fermi and many others.

Science has now become a widespread constituency of many tens of thousands of individuals. In addition to the traditional academies, after the Second World War, the National Research Councils are established everywhere as well as Minister of Science and Technology.

Scientists become aware of their enormous power. States know that without a lively and free scientific research there will not be industrial and economic development. Without a healthy science, countries will not be able to compete on the international markets.

It is recent history that great influence on the world affairs of the nuclear and atomic lobby and it is history of these days the influence of the life-science lobby which ranges from environmental issues to genetics, to human genome and to other key issues related to our survival on the planet.

It is, therefore, time for a thorough reconsideration of the role of science in our society.

Many are the issues on the agenda for discussion and urgent decisions. I will quote here only a few:

- The structure of the National Research Councils and the Academies which are now bureaucratized and not responding any longer to the objectives for which they have been created and to the present needs.
- the need of a serious confrontation between scientists and politicians to establish a new relationship and a dialogue with reciprocal respect.
- The scientific community has grown enormously and has a great potential power. It has to adopt new ethical and deontological rules in order to block abuses and the potential threates that the new advancement of science and research can provoke to humanity.

Finally, there are sufficient scientific and technical resources to solve many of the problems which are affecting our planet (hunger, overpopulation, environment etc.). It is time for the scientists to the be more engaged in this endeavour, asking to politicians the necessary means to reorient the application of science towards the satisfaction of human needs and towards the preservation of the planet which is the only valid heritage that we can leave to our children.

4

Science and the Quartet of Power

ANTONI KUKLINSKI
Director, EUROREG, Warsaw

Introduction

The Genoa Symposium[1] has created a new brainstorming capacity to look—in an innovative way—at the problem of Science and Power.

It is an old problem in the field of classical universal science as developed in the dramatic and complicated experience of the past—presented in the charming papers of Augusto Forti[2] and Louis Albou[3].

It is a new problem in the field of the emerging global science[4].

The neoliberal vision of the development of this new global science is presented in the bold and controversial paper of Ian O. Angell[5].

It is a highly convincing contribution for those who accept the neoliberal framework of value judgements as the framework which will organize the global scene of the 21st century. This means that the 21st century will be an improved version of the 19th century. This also means, however, that the improved version will create the conditions and motivations for the Second Bolshevik Revolution.

Keeping in mind these very broad issues involved in historical and prospective approaches, I would like to concentrate my attention on research priorities related to the topic 'Science and the Quartet to Power'.

This is the quartet of four institutions: the nation-state, the military industrial complex, transnational corporations, and international organizations.

1. Science and the Nation-State

A well organized programme of comprehensive and comparative historical studies on the role of the nation-state in the development of science should be designed and implemented.

If we restrict our attention to the European scene then, may be, the period from 1648 to 1992 would be most appropriate.

The Peace of Westphali (1648) is widely recognized as the real beginning of the era of the Nation-State.

The Treaty on European Union (1992) may be seen as a symbolic date in the real, or only apparent, retreat of the nation-state.

In the experience of those 344 years, three models of the relation between science and the state can be tested.

1. a model of the positive influence of the state on the development of science
2. a model of the negative influence of the state on the development of science
3. a model of the neutrality zone between the state and the development of science.

In the framework of the models nos. 1 and 2, a place will be seen for different types of science policy[6] defined in broad terms covering not only the experience of the 20th century. It would be necessary to introduce the distinction between the explicit science policy, designed and implemented in a clearly defined institutional framework, and the implicit science policy 'hidden' in other patterns of guided development. These 'hidden' science policies are a very important chapter in the relation between the state and science.

Naturally, this programme should also incorporate the important prospective contributions on the role of the nation-state in the development of science in the 21th century. The question marks, formulated by I.O. Angell, should be considered in this context[7].

It is very difficult to find empirical studies analysing the long-term experiences of different countries. I think, however, that the brain-storming paper of Anatoly I. Rakitov[8] is an excellent inducement for creative thinking in this field.

2. Science and the Military Industrial Complex

In the Genoa Symposium, the problem of 'Military Conversion and its Impact upon Resources Allocation for Sciences' was analysed in the well organized paper of J.H.Proctor[9].

Using that paper as a starting point, I would like to suggest to consider a much broader framework for our discussion arranged along the following questions.

1. How to outline the case studies analysing the positive and negative impacts of different military establishments on the development of science?

Is it possible to develop a sui generis cost benefit analysis in this field?

2. How to analyse the differences between the classical military establishments, developed in the universal historical experiences, and the military industrial complex created by the recent experiences of the 20th century.

3. How to create an objective analytical framework for comparative studies on the structural and behavioural patterns of the two most outstanding military industrial complexes created by the United States and Soviet Union?

We should concentrate our attention not only on the pathology of the Soviet military industrial complex but also on the negative features of the American experience in this field.

4. Is it possible to find and define the common features emerging in the patterns of influence of the military establishments on the development of science?

How to outline the relation of genus proximum and differentia specifica in broad comparative studies moving freely in time and space?

There is no doubt that it is impossible to analyse the general problem of Science and Power without the result of broad comparative studies on science and the military industrial complex. In those studies, we must follow the old Roman rule—*audiastur et altera pars*—and invite the eminent scientists representing directly the philosophy and wisdom of different military industrial complexes. Such an encounter of civil and military science would be a sui generis innovation in the theory and practice of UNESCO activities.

3. Science and Transnational Corporations

The rapid growth of transnational corporations and their involvement in the large-scale promotion of R and D are creating a new type of global science heavily dependant on the financial power and the strategic will of TNC.

This new role of TNC is changing very deeply the field of forces which determine the future of global science. We have to look at the two classical actors of the power scene as related to science: the national state and the military establishments.

The fundamental question is emerging—if the national state—via the classical governmental machinery—is able to define and implement national science policies which do not fully follow the global patterns established by TNC.

We also know that the TNC penetrate very deeply into the structures of the armament industries and, indirectly, into the structures and motivation of R and D promoted by these industries.

So the vision of the classical military establishment, working jointly with the national government in the field of fundamental and applied sciences, may also be outdated.

This reflection is indicating that the classical formulation 'Science and Power' is related to the long era of universal science as a spiritual phenomenon. In this long era of universal science there was an ample place for the classical autonomy of the scientific community and the well, or badly designed intervention of the government representing the national state.

The emerging phenomenon of global science—very strongly influenced by TNC—is quite different.

Following the path-breaking OECD publication[10] a research programme should be established to analyse the transition from international to global science.

The inquiry into the nature of this transition is possible only by joint efforts of interntional organizations and of a representative group of translational corporations.

It is impossible to outline diagnostic and prospective approaches to global science without the active participation of TNC as the main actor determining the future of global science.

4. Science and International Organizations

The international organizations perform a very important role in the development of science.

It would be interesting to analyse the different styles developed by the historical experience of such organizations as OECD, World Bank[11], the European Union[12], and UNESCO.

Each of these four organizations has a different profile of characteristic features in the promotion of the development of science. This hypothesis should be tested in comprehensive empirical studies answering, for example, the question of the relative efficiency of these four organizations in the following fields related to the development of science:

1. the collection and dissemination of relevant information
2. the creation of a new network of cooperation among scientists and scientific institutions
3. the improvement of the efficiency of national science policies
4. the creation of conditions and inducements to accelerate the transition from national to international approaches and systems related to the development of science.

There is no doubt that the international organizations have—especially in the second half of the 20th century—achieved immense successes in the field of the internationalization of science.

This success was achieved via the classical mechanism of cooperation among the nation-states acting as good members of international organizations.

This classical field of forces has been changed by the entrance of a new powerful actor—the Transnational Corporation—which created the conditions for a new stage—the transition from international to global science.

We should look once more at the four international organizations and formulate, *inter alia*, the question—to what extent UNESCO has the capacity and will to deal with the new situation of the emerging global science.

Sometimes, I have the impression that UNESCO is rather more oriented towards the classical pattern of internationalization that was very successful and efficient in the past, and less oriented towards the emerging challenge of global science and the absolute necessity to establish new links of cooperation between UNESCO and the Transnational Corporations as the main actors in the development of global science.

5. The Scientific Community and the Changing Relations Inside the Quartet of Power

We have a classical vision of the semi-autonomous scientific communities[13] with socially accepted and promoted rules of behaviour, principles of competition, cooperation, and solidarity.

This classical vision is now replaced by the near reality created by the changing relations inside the quartet of power.

The role and rank of the scientific community is dependent not only on the external objectives conditions but also on the 'Will to Power' demonstrated by the members of the Scientific Community.

The dilemma outlined by I.O. Angell[14] is a real dilemma.

Conclusions

This paper is a set of Treppengedanken generated by the Genoa Symposium.

I hope that this paper is a modest contribution to the development of the brainstorming capacity of that Symposium.

Science and Power is a fascinating field of research. We are just at the beginning of a long and interesting scientific inquiry and intellectual adventure.

This inquiry and this adventure should be built into a consistent framework of an International Research, Conference and Publication Programme—Science and Power—to be designed and implemented by UNESCO as a contribution to the general reflection on the role of Science in the unique period of history—the transition from the Second to the Third Millennium.

REFERENCES

1. UNESCO Symposium: "Science and Power", Genoa, December 1-3, 1994.
2. A. Forti, *Science and Power. Historical Perspectives,* Genoa Symposium 1994.
3. L. Albou, *Science as a Counter-Power,* Genoa Symposium 1994.
4. OECD, *Technology and the Economy.* The Key Relationships. Paris 1992.
5. I.O. Angell, The *'Will to Power' of Scientific Knowledge Workers,* Genoa Symposium 1994.
6. Compare: N. Rosenberg, *Critical Issues in Science Policy Research.* "Science and Public Policy", Vol. 18, No. 6, December 1991, pp. 335-46.
7. I.O. Angell, op. cit.
8. A.I. Rakitov, *The Prospects of the Russian Science: Past, Present, Future.* (in:) A. Kuklinski (Ed.) *Science Technology—Economy.* "Science and Government Series" Vol. 3, State Committee for Scientific Research, Warsaw 1994, pp. 405-19.
9. J.H. Proctor, *Military Conversion and its Impact upon Resources Allocation for Sciences,* Genoa Symposium 1994.

10. Compare: OECD, op. cit.

11. Compare: F.R. Sagasti, *Science and Technology Policy Research: Some Lessons of Experience and a World Bank Perspective.* "Science and Public Policy", Vol. 18, No. 6, December 1991, p. 379-83.

12. M. Macioti, *The Role of the European Union in Science,* Genoa Symposium 1994.

13. A Kuklinski, *Opinion: Society, Science anu Government,* "Educational & Training Technology International", Vol. 31, No. 2, May 1994, pp. 126-33.

5

Deforms in Science and Studies in Transition Period

BRONISLOVAS KUZMICKAS
Lithuanian Scientists Union

I want to give a short outline of perspectives and contradictions which Lithuanian science and higher education system is facing in transition period.

Along with the upsurge of the Lithuanian national revival in 1988 the scientific community became aware of the necessity to reform the outdated Soviet system of science in keeping with the coming economic and social changes. The first stimulus to start reforms gave the *Lighuanian Scientific Society*[1], established recently as non-governmental organization, joining together scientists of research and educational institutions.

From the very beginning it was obvious that the centralized hierarchical organization of science should be dismantled, the bureaucratic control over science reduced, existing state planning system given up, diminished the separation of the research institutes and the institutions of higher education.

The negative consequences of centralized system are widely known. Centralized research funding and control over resources, exercised by powerful scientists administration, gave rise to favouritism and corruption, restricted initiative and activity, weakened scientific criticism, prevented open discussion of controversial questions. Negative side of centralism was isolationism with respect to the international science community.

Therefore, it was intended to replace the uniformity of the past with an emphasis on autonomy and individuality, to establish and widen self-regulation of scientific institutions, to ensure full intellectual independence at the universities, to increase the role of creative person inside the institution. This was ensured by the *Law on Science and Studies*[2], prepared by the Lithuanian Scientific Society and passed on February 1991, that also provides the possibility of establishing private higher institutions. According to the Law the major institution, accomplishing the independence of science and higher education, is the *Lithuania Council of Science,* provided with vast province.

But the Law whatever it would be works not automatically, its implementation depends on additional factors, particularly, such as common civic and cultural level.

In reality the autonomy is not always brought about in an appropriate way and giving expected results. Sometimes it turns to be the form of strengthening of the self-will of the new administration and dependence of ordinary researcher on it. It happens that in the institutions with weaker potential autonomy is changing into sort of isolation, based on the statute of the respective institution, allowing to tolerate the low quality of work.

Besides that, genuinely self-regulation is hardly possible because of the fact that nowadays no one research institution can keep on it own feet and do without solid budgetary supply.

Obviously the weak and negative sides of autonomization can be avoided by performing appropriate states policy and regulation, by establishing certain governmental bodies.

During Soviet period science and technology has officially been considered to be the field of relatively high priority and received stable financial state support, scientific elite enjoyed certain social privileges. In Lithuania comparatively potent scientific community has been concentrated and brought up, particularly in such branches as chemistry, theoretical physics, semiconductors, molecular genetics, astronomy etc. The humanities and social sciences were in the worse condition because of severe ideological control.

But almost all fields of science developed in Lithuania were thoroughly integrated into the centralized Soviet science system, to large extent served to military purposes and had very weak links with the economy and culture of Lithuania. The results of researches carried out in Lithuania were as a rule applied beyond our country.

When, after collapse of Soviet Union the former science system became disintegrated, entire institutions and branches of research remained excluded or with very poor financing sources.

Therefore, on the way of reforms extremely difficult task arises, namely, to orientate as much as possible the development of science in Lithuania to the economic, cultural, environmental needs of our country, to decide which branches would be considered as priorities. On the other hand, to reform the economy in such way that it could be receptive to science results. Quite definite answer should be given to the questions: what branches of science could really be perspective in Lithuania? What balance could be between long range fundamental sciences and short range applied science? How research and higher educational institutions might function in the transition to market economy, what role will play science in the future of post-communistic society?

Thus, the proper state policy is required, and that presupposes a deliberate concept of the priorities in science and higher education development. But elaboration of such concept is not yet started. One of the reasons of such situation of things is that till now quite uncertain remain the priorities in industry and agriculiture. The second reason consists in the fact that scientific community itself is deeply divided over the issue of reforms, a lot of researchers are interested to preserve the present situation. It seems very likely that because of unwillingness of some authorities international evaluation of the science in Lithuania was not undertaken as it was done with success in neighbouring Latvia.

One of the most important aspects of the reform is the integration of research and educational institutions, in conformity with the practice in the Western world. Abandoning thus the Soviet tradition, when at the universities and other higher educational institutions worked only lecturers, pedagogues as a rule overburdened with lecturing, and in the institutes of the Academy of Sciences researchers were deprived of the opportunity of pedagogical activity.

In principle everybody agrees that integration is indispensable, but practically it is being accomplished more slowly than expected. Efforts to integrate "from above" by means of administrative measures are not giving desirable results and meet with opposition.

Attractive and perspective is the moving towards integration on the basis of fulfilling common programmes. But this way is rather exception than the rule because isolationists legacy will be overcome, when individual researchers working in the same field are isolated from each other. Researchers working in the institutes of the Academy of Sciences are afraid to be incorporated into the structure of universities, because that could bring the prospective of loss of position to many of them. Inside the universities there are also groups, guarding their particular interests, being afraid of competition and practically resisting to integration. Nevertheless in the integrative process universities are given the priority. In the respective committee of the Parliament (Seimes) the legal basis of the sort of research institute within the structure of higher educational institutions is being prepared.

But the major impediment on the way of reforms is sudden decrease of financing. Government funding is quite unsatisfactory, scientific institutions cannot rely on it largely. Within the framework of budgetary financing the payment of researchers and university lectures is very low even in comparison with payment in other budgetary institutions. A lot of researchers are abandoning science, the brain drain is taking place, the generational exchange is turning to be almost impossible. Underestimation or rather disregard of science and education by the governmental power is obvious.

But scientists themselves are also not seeking for the contacts with industry. On the other hand, industry is half dead and simply fighting to survive, therefore there is no demand for new theoretical thinking or highly developed technologies. Unluckily, the competitive grant system is introduced slowly and irresolute. Scientists are unprepared to compete for funding not only with each other, but also with other sectors, seeking for budget financing. Former educational system has been based on collectivistic mentality, suppressed individuality, suggested that no one should think he is better than anyone else. Scientists are unprepared to compete under market conditions or even to tie together science and market.

The transition to open society and market economy requires more technical advices to the government but also more responsibility for the consequences of advices. In reality things are quite the reverse. The declining industry doesn't demand new specialists, remains up to now like a wall between industry and science, between practical action and theoretical thought. The governmental authorities are deaf to the suggestions of scholars and scientists, as well as to the pressing needs of scientific institutions.

Such situation caused numerous manifestations of the professorate and students that took place at the end of November 1994 in several Lithuanian cities, claiming to increase the state budget allotment of science and education.

The execution of reforms are accompanied by growing concern about the continuity of national scientific tradition, survival of the top intellectual potential. Main concern is the survival of fundamental range researches, meanwhile it is doubtful whether applied sciences will be capable of competing with foreign companies on international level. It is quite unlikely that the present power could change its unfavourable attitude towards science and education to take more responsibility about their future. Therefore the adjustment of science system to the current economic realities will be a long and difficult task. It is necessary to learn more about how research and education are functioning in Western countries, how to get access to foreign investments and foundations.

Meantime instead of speaking about the social implications of science development, we can speak rather about the long-term consequences of the crisis of science.

REFERENCES

1. Lithuanian Scientific Society. Information Bulletin, Vilnius, 1994.
2. Parliamentary Record. Supreme Council of the Republic of Lithuania, 1992, Nr. 6, pp. 2-10.

6

Science As a Counter-Power

LOUIS ALBOU

Secretary-General of the World Institute of Science

First of all, we must pay tribute to the discernment of UNESCO and its Regional Office in Venice, and to the Italian authorities, including the National Research Council (CNR), for having organized this symposium on a theme so vital that the very future of making perhaps depends upon it.

To being with, we must examine considerations of two kinds.

The first concerns the very justification for the symposium. Why is the symposium taking place? It is because it states the central issue, namely that there is a worldwide crisis of civilization, probably Western in origin, and that this crisis is influenced by the relationship between Science and Power.

It would seem relevant to show the successive stages through which awareness of this problem has developed by quoting the words of some great forerunners:

- Nietzsche: 'God is dead, everything is possible', and since then the world has been in a state of crisis.
- Oswald Spengler: 'The decline of the West'.
- Paul Valéry: 'We as civilizations now know that we are mortal . . . and that the abyss of history is big enough for everybody'; and; 'Two calamities are threatening the

world: order and disorder', these being in fact totalitarian order on the one hand and moral disorder on the other.

- André Malraux: 'We are a civilization without a precedent because ours is the first civilization capable of committing suicide'.

In reply to his friend Charles de Gaulle who, in 1969, said to him: "The world is in a state of crisis and I am relying on you to say so' André Malraux remarked: 'The crisis of civilization is a crisis of culture, and the crisis of culture is the inability of culture to assimilate a vital part of it, which is Science'.

In another connection, he added: 'There is one thing which cannot continue any longer and that is the failure of intelligence to assume any responsibility. Either it overcomes its failure or it is the West that will fail'.

Finally, in 1974, at the award of the Nehru Prize in New Delhi, André Malraux spoke of the urgent need to establish a pilot institute for research into the crisis of civilization. This institute now exists. It is the World Institute of Science which came spontaneously into being in 1989.

Tribute must also be paid to the two great forerunners in this field:

Firstly, the Pugwash movement, launched in 1967 by Albert Einstein and Bertrand Russell and composed of the greatest American and Russian atomic scientists. They issued document after document about the enormous danger represented by military nuclear might in order to influence the governments of the two great atomic powers. Their efforts were crowned with success.

Secondly, the Club of Rome, founded in 1968, which has devoted itself to the dangers of the misuse of Science.

In this respect, we should mention the Heidelberg Appeal, launched by the World Institute of Science to heads of government at the opening of the Rio Conference in June 1992.

The second kind of consideration concerns the distinctions that must be made about the words 'Science' and 'Power'. A distinction has to be made between:

1. 'Fundamental Science', which is defined as the *need to understand.* Its aim is not utilitarian and in that sense it serves no purpose. It is the sublimate tool of Homo Faber at the present final stage of the evolution of Man. Among its great discoveries are heliocentricity (Copernicus and Galileo), gravitation (Newton), radioactivity (Becquerel and Curie), microbes (Pasteur), relativity and $E = mc^2$ (Einstein), the expanding universe (Hubble), the double helix (Crick and Watson), and so on. It should be understood that fundamental discoveries are not 'programmable'.

2. 'Applied Science', as its name clearly indicates, is concerned with the Applications of fundamental discoveries. Applied Science depends on economic, political and military policy decisions.

One should, of course, remember that fundamental Science and applied Science interact and that some scientists are engaged in both.

One final clarification is needed concerning 'scientism' and the positivism of Auguste Comte. Marcelin Berthelot thought that the physics of his time had discovered everything: 'Science knows everything and will solve everything'. In reaction to this fatal error, the antiscience movement and the upsurge of irrationality are still growing today. Today, however, there is not a single genuine scientist who is confined by these narrow and erroneous views. Science progresses by successive stages but Newton does not cancel out Copernicus and Galileo and Einstein do not cancel out Newton. Each stage recapitulates and integrates the preceding ones at a level of greater complexity. Science proceeds by approximate truths, such that Henri Poincaré said: Science has more ability than knowledge'. Alchemy never found the way to transmute common lead into gold whereas nuclear physics creates gold that is purer than in nature and even creates new atoms like plutonium or americium.

Nevertheless, if Science does not know everything, who knows more about the great secrets of the universe—the infinitely small, the infinitely great and infinitely complex, with its three degrees of inert matter, living matter and thinking matter?

Furthermore, although Science will not solve everything, it is certain that where the major vital world problems are concerned, no further solutions will be founded without Science.

Turning then to 'Power', what 'power' are we talking about? The limited sense of 'political power' has the double disadvantage of excluding the other forms of power and above all of masking what is in fact the chief real power, namely, economic power (industry and banking). In addition, the dependence of political power on economic power is confirmed by the present corruption of the political parties in France and Italy. In France, it is common knowledge that four big firms finance the masjor political parties in power.

In his book entitled 'I'Argent fou', Alaîn Mine, the right-hand man of De Benedetti in France, writes: 'Democracy implies a balance of power. There is, in fact, however, now only one real power, which is economic power, and all the other forms of power have crumbled and disappeared, e.g. religions, parties, trade unions, the independent press and television, and so on'.

Alain Mine aoes not seem to see that there are two possible and necessary counter-powers, namely justice, which is asserting itself in Italy with exemplary courage, and Science. Likely many technocrats, Alain Mine is, in fact, scientifically illiterate and has not gone beyond the scientism of the nineteenth century.

It is said that the media have become the leading power in the United States but this is, strictly speaking, an optical illusion since they depend to an even greater extent on the economic power which pays them for services rendered, i.e. staging the 'political show', which contributes greatly to causing the political world to be held in low esteem.

The hitherto uncontrolled explosion of major discoveries in the fundamental science, which has too frequently been accompanied by irresponsible misuse for civil or military purposes, has thus brought about an unprecedented high-risk situation throughout the world. This realization was what led to the spontaneous formation in 1989 of the World Institute of Science, on the initiative of leading scientists themselves within the world scientific community and, in particular, at the Collège de France in Paris; all were aware of the need henceforth to assume direct responsibility for Science. The members of this Institute are 80 of the most eminent scientists from the five continents, including more than 20 Noble Prize-winners, representing every discipline.

Science is indeed involved at three essential levels of this process.

1. It is the source of all material progress, good or bad. It is the first link in the chain by which its fundamental discoveries are transformed by the applied sciences and by technology. Science thus now has a duty in certain cases to prevent the premature and uncontrolled spread of its discoveries (cf. the moratoria in the field of genetics).

2. Science alone is in possession of vital information about the potential dangers of its discoveries and is thus in a position to make that information known so as to warn those in charge of the economy, political leaders, public opinion and, where necessary, the media.

3. Science alone is in a position to find possible remedies to the disorder that has already been created by the irresponsible misuse of its discoveries, e.g. the population explosion, the exhaustion of natural resources (including energy), civilian and military technologies, various forms of population, and so on.

It is highly unlikely that any spontaneous solution will be found to these major risks at a worldwide level. The worst can be avoided only be genuine and sustained collaboration, on a world scale, between the major economic decision-makers and the great scientific creative minds. This is the objective of the WIS, which constitutes, in fact, a force for providing information and making proposals, one of the essential criteria of which is independence, which alone can guarantee the validity of the scientific appraisal of the world's major problems.

We have provided a summary of the field covered by the new obligations of Science in the annex entitled 'Science and Responsibility'.

Economic power and governments can no longer continue to decide without Science what the future of the world shall be. The social function of Science is obvious but the danger is that

Science will be what men make of it. Science is in no way seeking to take power, only to help it.

Before concluding, I must mention two unconnected but convergent events which occurred on 1 February 1992.

1. In the 'Quotidien de Paris', Elie Wiesel, the winner of the Noble peace prize, stated: 'Tomorrow, world public opinion will no longer turn to the UN and governments but to the great scientists'.

2. On the very same day, the daily paper 'La Croix-Evénement' had organized a symposium on 'Science and Faith', which has followed by a Broadcasting Authority opinion poll based on ten questions. The question which finally gripped the public most was: 'Who does the future of the world depend on?' The choice was between religious figures, philosophers, politicians, artists, etc., but 67 per cent of those questioned, the vast majority of whom were believers, replied: 'the future of the world depends on the ideas of the great scientists'.

To conclude, in this unprecedented state of crisis, Science must not only warn about the risks and propose possible remedies but also play a part in the construction or reconstruction of the values on which any civilization is founded. That is probably an essentially ethnical problem in the etymological sense of the Greek word *'ethos'*, meaning morals or behaviour, which gave the Latin word *'mos, moris'*, with the same meaning. Ethics are thus the necessary code of behaviour for members of group in that every sense in which Spinoza said: 'Freedom is necessity agreed to'. This is also why there exists a science called 'ethology', the purpose of which is to study either animal or human behaviour.

It is possible, if not probable, that the salvation of our societies lies finally in government by intelligence and morality, as seems to be emerging in Italy and France. That represents a vital ethical choice.

That is indeed the conclusion the Jacques Monod borrowed, without acknowledgement, from Albert Camus in the last five lines of his deservedly well-known book entitled 'Hasard et necéssité': 'The old alliance is broken. Man at last knows that he is alone in the vastness of the Universe out of which he emerged by Chance. His duties are written nowhere, any more than is his fate. He nevertheless still has to choose between the Kingdom and Darkness'.

ANNEX

1. The face of the Earth has changed.
2. What has changed the face of the Earth is Science.
3. The environment as changed by Man is compelling Man to change.
4. Being involved at the source, Science can and must assume responsibility for this unprecedented mutation.
5. Science is an integral part of human culture, of which it is, today, a foremost and exemplary part. As such, it must tell people what it is and what it is not, what it knows and what it does not know, what it can do and what it can not do, what it must do and what it must not do.
6. Science is exemplary because of its exacting intellectual and moral approach, accepting as it does, as a permanent exercise, the questioning of its method, its knowledge and its very existence.
7. Science is exemplary because it places in the service of Mankind a unique and living culture heritage—knowledge of the essential processes of the universe, of matter and of life, with the prospect of an increasing, relative and properly reasoned mastery of these processes, which involves the responsibility of Science.

   Consequently:

8. Science can and must now contribute to controlling the chain of activities by which its fundamental discoveries are transformed, so as to prevent any irresponsible misappropriation.
9. Science can and must strive to put right the disorders already caused.
10. Science can and must contribute to the elaboration of the reconstruction of the value systems that are the basis of any civilization.

7

Don't Bother Me versus Everything [Has Its Price]

HARALD GARDOS
Secretary General, Austrian National Commission for UNESCO

"Science" and "power" are two historically incompatible notions.

Power is old, science is young, power always existed in the animal world, whereas science is a genuine human endeavour.

'Power' is a word describing structures, "science" an amalgam of individual and team achievements. "Hierarchy" and "network" could reflect the antagonism between the two concepts, "dependence" express the interference between them—though there are hierarchies in the scientific sphere also, and networks of power on the other side.

The idealistic concept of science, the famous words of Archimedes 'don't disturb my circles" or the so-called ivory tower, is in contradiction with everyday reality, the scientist being paid by his company or his authorities or even abused by an aggressive dictatorship. This controversial situation became apparent in modern times, when the scientist was either in opposition or obedient to power in an obvious way, whereas in earlier ages, he was an integral part of the system, be it in Old Egypt, in Rome, in the Jewish, Christian or Islamic worlds. Like for artists, poets or philosophers, the world—and intellectual professions—became "discernible" only during the periods of Humanism, Renaissance and Reformation, i.e. during the 15th and 16th centuries.

In today's democracies, the scientific world is as pluralistic as other parts of society, its relationship with power is as heterogenous as individual backgrounds, characters, careers or economic situations of scientists can be. Science "power" has got a relatively smooth taste, its interdependence with science has received a touch of "wild marriage" in which children are born and raised sometimes without the control of both parents.

8

The "Will to Power" of Scientific Knowledge Workers

IAN O. ANGELL

Professor of Information Systems, London School of Economics

Introduction

Today we are on the verge of a new social and economic reality, perched on the 'Edge of Chaos'. The Information Age takes as out of the Machine Age, into ... who knows what. We all sense that the changes will be just as significant as those of the Industrial Revolution. The very natures of work, of institutions, of society, and even of capitalism itself, are mutating. These mutations are confronting each other in the political power vacuum left by the fall of communism, and the increasing impotence of liberal democracy when facing the mass unemployment of its citizens.

"History is the natural selection of accidents" (Leon Trotsky) and our world is now full of accidents waiting to happen. In my talk today I will give you my vision of a new order in tomorrow's history. I want to expose you to the fault lines that are appearing everywhere, and the awesome effects they will have on the role of the scientist.

The Superhighways

A new order (which many will call disorder) is being forced upon an unsuspecting world by advances in telecommunications.

(See Barnet and Cavanagh [1]. The future is being born in the so-called *information super-highways*. Very soon these electronic telecommunication networks, covering the world via cable and satellite, will enable everyone in the world to 'talk' to everyone else.

Global commerce will force through the construction of the multi-media highways, and anyone bypassed by the highway faces ruin. Throughout history highways have brought wealth to towns along their length—this was true for the Roman roads, canals, railways, motorways—and superhighways are no different. Wealth is focused in 'strip development', while those off the beaten track are abandoned to obscurity.

We are entering a new elite cosmopolitan age, stemming from the collision of previously disparate technologies of computers, telephones, consumer electronics, television and radio. Information technology, together with speedy international travel, is changing the whole nature of political governance and its relationship to commerce, and commerce itself. There has been a corrosion of national sovereignty: "rapid capital flows can offset, negate or subvert government policies", but you can expect politicians to find novel ways of hanging on to power. All the while citizens are losing their faith in the nation-state, seeing it as a peculiarly twentieth century pehnomenon. For the state is failing to deliver its side of the Fustian pact, where the individual submits to the legitimate violence of the state in return for protection and security.

Whether we like it or not, the world as we know it is changing, it may even be moving in reverse. But this is not a time for despair, quite the opposite. It is a time of great opportunity as well as risk—it is in such times that new empires are made. But it will take claver strategies to succeed; strategies based on totally new paradigms that can deliver a vision that "is the art of seeing things invisible" (Jonathan Swift). What is more, "the difficulty lies not in [just] creating new ideas but in escaping from old ones" (John Maynard Keynes).

Globalization and Localization

One major factor that is emerging in the new order is the *globalization* of organizations, and not merely their *internationalization*. Individuals and companies are setting up large transnational networks that pay absolutely no heed to national boundaries and barriers. The commercial enterprise of the future will be truly global, it will relocate (physically or electronically) to where the profit is greatest and the regulation least. The umbilical cords have been cut; the global company no longer feels the need to support the national aspirations of the country of its birth. Recently this new business paradigm was expressed most forcibly by Akio Morita, causing uproar in Japan, when he announced that Sony was a global company and not Japanese!

But paradoxically, globalization is resulting in a trend towards *localization* or, as Morita calls it, 'global localization'. Global companies are setting themselves up within *virtual enterprises,* at the hub of loosely knit alliances of local companies, all linked together by global networks, both electronic and human. These companies assemble to take advantage of any temporary business opportunity; and then separate, searching for the next major deal. Apart from local products, local companies also deliver local expertise and access to home markets for other products created within the wider alliance. Companies that are part of virtual enterprises have enormous potential, while those outside such networks have no future.

The very presence of these vigorous global enterprises can strengthen national economies, but they can just as easily destroy them; just consider the recent sterling and lira crises precipitated by the money markets, and the likes of George Soros and his Quantum Fund. Global organizations do not identify with any particular country, and they walk away from a country just as easily as they enter it. Benjamin Frankilin recognized this truth over two hundred years ago: "merchants have no country. The mere spot where they stand on does not constitute so strong an attachment as that from which they draw their gain".

Run by an international elite, global enterprises are stalking the world looking for talent and profit; in the Information Age this pairing is indivisible. In particular the products of science and technology are in high demand. International trading now includes new forms of barter and exchange, particularly in superior scientific and technological expertise and knowledge.

Money, which is merely a means of facilitating economic transactions, has itself become electronic information, and what constitutes money can no longer be monopolized by national governments. This inevitably lowers the transaction cost of money, and makes taxation of profits and regulation of the process almost impossible—a real competitive advantage for any virtual enterprise with a moveable centre of gravity; and for the scientists who are willing to trade their expertise in this electronic market.

Knowledge Workers versus Service Workers

Peter Drucker has a very interesting forecast. He says that humanity is polarizing into two employment categories: the intellectual, cultural and business elite (the mobile *knowledge workers*), and the rest (the immobile service workers). In a similar vein, Robert Reich believes there will be three categories: *symbolic-analytic services* (the knowledge workers who are problem identifiers, solvers and brokers), *in-person services,* and *routine production services.* The latter two groups roughly correspond to Drucker's service workers. Routine production services can either be replaced by robots or exported anywhere on the globe, and wages in this sector are already beginning to coverage worldwide to Third World levels. This is having the (slightly less extreme) knock-on effect of dragging down the wages of in-person service workers, a sector which is itself being increasingly automated. Inevitably the slow redistribution of wealth that has occurred over the last century is being reversed, rapidly. Societies are stratifying and new elites are appearing. The future is inequality; at the very bottom of the heap, western societies are already witnessing the emergence of a rapidly expanding underclass.

Now we can see that knowledge workers are the real generators of wealth. These owners of intellectual and financial wealth will be made welcome anywhere in the world; and more so, both companies and countries will be competing with each other to attack them—and to keep them. In May 1994 the UK government offered British nationality to anyone willing to invest £200,000 in Britain. It is only a matter of time before intellectual capital such as scientific expertise will be included on the balance sheet.

On the other side of the coin, there is a growing realization that each service worker is a net loss both to the state and to the company—they cost far more than they generate. Companies will be reducing the wages and staffing levels of service workers, and it is no accident that most Western companies are presently instigating major downsizing programmes. This is all happening against a background of an exploding population in the Third World (95 per cent of the world's population increase is in developing countries: see Kennedy), who through television can see science and technology making 'the rich richer and the poor poorer'. To combat the inèvitable mass migrations, state barriers are being thrown up everywhere to keep out alien service workers; each state has a surplus of its own to support. It is already happening in California. Preposition 187 intends to bar the nearly two million illegal immigrants from schools, welfare services, and all but emergency health care. How long will it be before there are 'differential rights' for 'differentiated citizens', identified in a data base and policed by smart cards? How long before the notion of 'Human Rights' is as outdated as the 'Divine Right of Kings'?

Loyalty, but to What?

It was inevitable that predatory global networks would drive loyalty to the state into a steep decline among the swelling number of would-be 'economic mercenaries'. At a time when their skills are in increasing demand by global companies, knowledge workers feel more and more undervalued and betrayed by the nation-state. Global enterprises will demand that the loyalty of their employees be transferred to the company. But will they get it? Comparies regularly use headhunters and pay substantial 'golden hellos' and 'golden-hand-cuffs' to symbolic-analysts, but how far can a company trust them? It is increasingly easy for knowledge workers to walk away with corporate knowledge—as in the recent 'Lopez Affair' that set General Motors against Volkswagen.

The situation is possibly even more complex, because of the increased reliance of companies on the symbolic-analysts, the owners of intellectual equity. We are witnessing an intensifying a power struggle between the symbolic analysts and the owners of financial equity in those companies, and this is likely to change fundamentally the very nature of capitalism itself. This battle is likely to be at least as significant as that between landowners and industrialists in the early part of the nineteenth century, that was formative of today's capitalism.

Very soon companies will be negotiating preferential tax deals not only for themselves but also for chosen elite employees, including their leading scientists. According to Geoff Mulgan,-14 "the main producers and repositories of wealth—multinational companies—have increasingly been able to adjust their accounts and the prices of their international transactions so that their profits are declared in low tax countries, while they continue to operate in high tax ones." Furthermore, a recent estimate from Karl Ziegler of the Centre for Accountability and Debt Relief (see Mulgan-14) claims that 60 per cent of the worlds's private banking is held in trust in offshore unsupervised tax havens. Through its secrecy laws and minimal regulation, Grand Cayman has become the fifth largest banking centre in the world, with 500 banks; this year 600 billion dollars will pass through the island.

We are rapidly approaching a situation where, in order to attract the (scientific) elite, with their knowledge and money to enliven the economy, *the elite group will be expected to pay less tax and not more!* Examples are everywhere. Eire already gives writers and artists preferential tax deals on foreign earnings. The great majority of governments are lowering top tax rates in line with declining global levels. "Top income tax rates fell an average of 16.5 per cent between 1975 and 1989". (see Mulgan-14).

All the while, the disposable income for most of society will be drastically reduced. When Leona Helmsley said "only the little people pay taxes" she was unwittingly making a prediction. Of course the 'Queen of Mean', as the populist press disparagingly called her, was sent to jail for twenty months by a petty, jealous and vindictive jury of "little people" for non-payment of taxes. But she will have the last laugh. History will mark that shameful judgement as the beginning of the end of the old order of taxation. The tax burden is irrevocably moving onto the shoulders of the immobile; and way from income and onto consumables. This goes counter to every notion of social justice that has been prevalent over the past two hundred years—but in the new order of things it will still happen. "Nature is not immoral when it has no pity for the degenerate" (Nietzsche). This will inevitably lead to massive social unrest and disorder.

A Role for the Nation-State?

The result of these forces is that everywhere the nation-state is in retreat (see Horsman & Marshall [10]). The nation-state is based on the premise that the state owns the individual and that the leaders of the state can dispose of his property as they see fit. But knowledge workers call it social injustice: there is no justice in equality—"all taxation is theft" to pay "for equal division of unequal earnings". They want "the equality to make themselves unequal" (Iain Macleod). They say with derision that the 'Common Good' isn't good, it is merely common! Globalization has shown the James Bond myth, that the state is good and global corporations (Spectre) are bad, to be blatant propaganda on behalf of the nation-state.

Today's trend towards the growing power of knowledge workers is totally undermining the centralized power of the state and its ability to tax and regulate. The very nature of the nation-state itself is mutating; increasingly it will have to behave as merely another form of commercial enterprise; some states are becoming criminal enterprises according to western sentiment.

That the roles of governments and organizations are converging was unconsciously highlighted in the Guardian of 10th December, 1993. They asked the question: *"what's the difference between Zambia and Goldman Sachs"*. The answer: *"One is an African country that makes $2.2 billion a year and shares it among 25 million people. The other is an investment bank that makes $2.6 billion ... and shares it between 161 people. FAIR ENOUGH?"* Of course the 'bleeding heart' liberals of the Guardian 'tut tut' at such gross unfairness and make snide comments about "Goldmine Sachs". Unfairness! They fail to see that the symbolic analysts of Goldman Sachs earned that money. Yes, they earned it, and they earned it fairly.

To the knowledge workers, this call for fairness is the mere wailing of failures and parasites. They say it is time to rid ourselves of that backward looking idea, that work involves physical effort. Of course labour is needed—but there is a world full of labourers out there. It is that rare commodity, human intellect, which is the stuff of work in tomorrow's world. Politicians really must stop playing to the sentimentality of the herd. Governments, like all other organizations will have to survive economically on the efforts of the elite few—no nation has an automatic right to exist.

The role of the corporation-state in the new order is to produce the right people, with the right knowledge and expertise, as the raw material for the global companies that profit from the Information Age, to service these companies, and to provide them with an efficient infrastructure, a minimally regulated market and a secure, stable and comfortable environment. If a state can not produce a quality 'people product', particularly scientists and technologists, in sufficient quantities, then it must buy them from abroad.

If the state can convince the commercially attractive elite of knowledge workers and local entrepreneurial companies to stay, then a virtuous circle of success is ensured. For then, migrating global players and their wealth will also be attracted into that country. If, however, the state maintains a greedy collectivist and populist stance, under the defunct motto 'power to the people', then the entrepreneurial and knowledge elite will move on to more lucrative and agreeable climes, and, in the long-term, leave that country economically unviable, composed solely of the unproductive masses, sliding inevitability into a vicious circles of decline.

As far as global companies are concerned liberal democracy itself will mutate into an irrelevancy. It will be merely the means of governing the immobile service workers. That they, elect their slave masters makes democracy slavery none the less. Global enterprises have no interest in populism, unless it adversely affects their business, when they will simply leave: 'democracy is bad for business'.

Governments will have no choice other than to acquiesce to the will of global companies if they want to attract and keep employment. The Marxist myth that labour creates wealth has been buried once and for all. A large population, particularly an uneducated and ageing population, has now become the major problem facing all Western governments. The masses themselves will put employment and economic well-being before the dubious privilege of electing powerless representatives. Even Karl Marx anticipated politicans becoming ineffective, but for other reasons! Which is just as well since government regulation inhibits trade, a fact that most self-promoting politicians simply refuse to understand.

Because of the need to employ the local masses, the major social problem for politicians in the coming decades is going to be how to attract global employers to partner local companies, and how to keep them attracted. Because of the need to entice global companies and the employment they bring, not only will state be pitted against state, but also area will compete against area, town against town, even suburb against suburb. Tax holidays and reduced regulation aimed at attracting employers will be 'the name of the game' everywhere.

Already different states in Europe have embarked on 'regulatory arbitrage' to tempt financial sector companies away from their 'European partners'. Inevitably this trend will undermine national legislation and taxation policies. Any area with independent aspirations will use economic weapons against its neighbours and distance itself from their legislative oppression. Staten Island recently voted to split from New York. Quebec scrapped local taxes on cigarettes, and people from neighbouring Canadian states such as New Brunswick bought their tobacco across state lines. The result was a collapse of tax revenues from smokers in these neighbouring states, whereas Quebec earned far more from increased spending than it lost in tax. To make matters worse, a recent Toronto produced television programme implied that British Columbia resents what it sees as its subsidy of the rest of Canada. It hinted at independence for Cascadia (British Colombia with the American states of Washington and Oregon), which has a combined GDP of $250 billion and an economy almost the size of Australia. So is there a future for Canada? For as Daniel Bell so eloquently put it, "the nation-state is too small for the big things and too big for the small things".

Some futurologists, such as Heineken (reported by John Naisbitt in his book *Global Paradox*), expect that early in the next century the number of states in the United Nations will increase from the present number of 184 to over a thousand. Perhaps the new self consciousness in Lombardy, and with it the rise of the Northern League in Italian politics, can be seen as part of global trend.

So how can an independent-minded state/area/town/suburb, and its indigenous businesses, succeed. They must develop a good understanding of changes in their external and internal environment, over which they have little influence, but of which that can take advantage. Obviously, the first priority is to attract wealth-bearing global organizations, which necessitates being part of the information superhighway. If they do not, then that locality will lose out to the town down the road. Yet far too many governments still maintain a penny-pinching approach to telecommunications. Their decisions are rationalized away by claiming that cost/benefit analyses fail to justify expenditure on this technology. But comparison with the telephone shows the flaw in this argument.

Business today is totally impossible without the telephone, even though it is impossible to put a financial value on it; tomorrow's business will be impossible without access to the global superhighway. Of course, the real reason why politicians are so wary of these highways is nothing to do with cost, it is that telecommunication open up borders to the knowledgeable elite and to undermine state control; just consider the role played by fax and by satellite television in preventing the Russian coup. No politician will pay to lose power: but they've lost it anyway.

One inevitable consequence of global trade will be the rise of the New City State at the hub of global electronic and transport networks. The non-democratic model of Hong Kong is an exemplar; even though the city itself doesn't yet realize that is has defined the future. Singapore too is a useful model.

What European city will be the first to break ranks with the nation-state mentality holding back progress? A number of European cities can make the leap. Liechtenstein has already started; what about Monaco? And let us not forget Venice, perhaps it will rediscover former glories. It is only a matter of time before Lisbon jumps: it has the singular example of attracting the Gulbenkian wealth earlier this century. The Corporation of the City of London too has enormous potential and could be revitalized, however, the dead hand of the 'Mother of Parliaments' in Westminster will make this is far more difficult.

A new paradigm is upon us, in which the nation-state has mutated into just another form of organization, which will delegate market regulations to continent-wide bodies such as NAFTA or the EU. It will be inevitable that nation-states will fragment: rich areas will dump the poor areas, Such shakeout trends can be interpreted as *downsizing*, a strategy that is being considered by most shrewd major corporations these days. To protect their wealth, rich areas will also undertake a *rightsizing* strategy, ensuring a high proportion of (wealth generating) knowledge workers to (wealth depleting) service workers. Rich areas have to maintain and expand a critical mass of scientific and technological expertise, and use it to underpin effective education system of regenerate the resource. These rich areas will reject the liberal attitudes of the last century, as the expanding underclass they are spawning, and the untrained migrants they welcomed previously, are seen increasingly as economic liabilities.

To be successful, a geographical region needs major cultural and social attractions to entice the global corporations, and it also has to be safe for a company and its employees. Consequently I expect much closer cooperation between local police forces and company security agencies, and the edges between the two groupings will become increasingly blurred. Today in the USA there are nearly twice as many private security guards as there are official police. Furthermore, to protect supportive companies, I expect (sub-)states to impose draconian penalties on the perpetrators of economic crimes and those who betray commercial secrecy, along the lines of the Swiss system.

The region has to have the intellectual infrastructure to generate its own elite. And it has to reorganize if it is to make itself an ideal to do business, while remaining a pleasant place to be. Unquestionably, the first priority is a substantial investment in a centre for global communication, and a control centre at the hub of international cable and satellite traffic. Almost as important is for country and business to support art, culture, science and education, not for reasons of altruism or philanthropy but because it makes hard headed business sense.

An Unholy Alliance: Science and Alchemy

The utopia promised by science and technology has turned into a nightmare for the 'common man': globalization, overpopulation, mass migration, unemployment, poverty pollution etc. etc. The world is full of frightened people, as everywhere the institutions of the twentieth century are foundering. Newly emerging elitist global enterprises are rushing in to fill the economic and political power vacuum, and they are engaged in power struggles among themselves, and with the new corporation-states, to determine who will win the natural selection for dominance. Scientists and technologists can be major power brokers in the struggles to come. Is it any wonder then, that there is growing global competition for these highly mobile symbolic analysts?

Consequently, this is a time of great opportunity for the scientific community. And yet still many in this community feel subservient to their has-been political masters; showing gratitude for the merest crumbs thrown from the tax-payers' table. The 'guild of scientists' really must change its mindest and enhance its status. It must stress the role of 'Science' and 'Scientists' in the dynamic of history, and assert the scientific knowledge worker's 'will to power'.

How can the guild do this? It would seem only natural that it turn to the methods of science when plotting their economic future. But that would be a mistake, for these conventional methods simply don't work in the social arena. The idea of 'equilibrium' that underlies so much of the 'scientism' in modern economics and management theory has been shown to be a fiction—merely a comforting fairytale for those lost in the post-modern world. As George Soros so eloquently put it, there is no such thing as a state of equilibrium, only the question of where we are in the perpetual movement between 'near-equilibrium' and 'far from equilibrium .

The people who succeed in today's dynamic environment are alchemists—they can turn the base metal of socio-economic chaos into the gold of success. They are pragmatists who do not promote false theories of scientific truth, but base their actions on what they believe to be 'procedurally successful' (Soros). Scientists must stop deluding themselves that our world is a rational causal system, in which problems can be viewed *ex post*, and then treated 'scientifically', predominantly as sequence of technological tasks.

The sheer scale of complexity and uncertainty requires that they must develop an adequate strategic understanding of the socio-economic properties that emerge from the reflexive interaction between science and its social context. They must throw off the shackles of the 'One-Dimensional Man'. The effectiveness of these strategies will depend on the vision of the community, the sense of identity and trust within it, and how it deals with change.

As the old power bases collapse all around, science and scientists can be the new power-brokers, who create a new order of things, through novel, imaginative, and often opportunistic and simplifying interpretations of complex situations. The guild of scientists must promote itself to be among the elite of symbolic-analysts. But to do this they must develop their own alchemy, which is not a science. They must learn to be less dogmatic when contemplating the future, but more productively, identify the issues and trends that will be of far more fundamental use. They can then broker the identification and solution of scientific problems delivered by their community, and then turn these into organizational procedures and technological applications that can succeed in the midst of social, political and economic upheaval.

With a loyalty to science and to their fellow scientists, they can realize the power in the group, organize that power to demand economic and political power; and then let the natural selection of history take its course. But can the alchemists of science make the best of it? Is the scientific community up to it? Can it mutate? Scientific knowledge workers have the power if only they would recognize it. But do they have 'the will to power'; and will they use it?

REFERENCES

1. Barnet R. & Cavanagh J. (1994), *Global Dreams: Imperial Corporations and the New World Order*, Simon & Shuster, London.
2. Barker J. (1993), *Paradigms*, Harper Business, New York.
3. Baudrillard J. (1994), *The Illusion of the End*, Polity Press, Cambridge.
4. B.B.C. (1994), 'Dirty Money', broadcast 20th September.
5. Bell D. (1976), *The Coming of the Post-Industrial Society: A Venture in Social Forecasting*, Basic Books, New York.
6. Drucker P. (1992), *Post Capitalist Society*, Butterworth, London.
7. The Economist (1994), 'Welcome to Cascadia', 21 May.
8. Heilbroner R. (1986), *The Worldly Philosophers*, 6th edition, Penguin London.
9. Herrnstein R. & Murray C. (1994), *The Bell Curve*, Free Press, New York.
10. Horsman M. & Marshall A. (1994), *After the Nation-State*, Harper Collins, London.
11. Kennedy P. (1993), *Preparing for the Twenty-First Century*, Fontana, London.
12. Marcuse H. (1991), *One-Dimensional Man*, Routledge, London.
13. McRae H. (1994), *The World in 2020*, Harper Collins, London.
14. Mulgan G. & Murray R. (1993, *Reconnecting Taxation*, Demos, London.
15. Murray C. (1994), 'Underclass: the crisis deepens', Sunday Times, 22 May.
16. Naisbitt J. (1994), *Global Paradox*, Nicholas Brierly, London.
17. Nietzsche F. (1968), *Will to Power*, Vintage, New York.
18. Ohmae K. (1994), *The Borderless World*, Harper Collins, London.
19. Reich R.B. (1991), *The Work of Nations*, Vintage, New York.
20. Soros G. (1994), *The Alchemy of Finance*, Wiley, New York.
21. Turner L. & Hodges M. (1992), *Global Shakeout*, Century Business, London.
22. Wendt H. (1993), *Global Embrace*, Harper Business, New York.

9

Selection of the Priorities for the Development of Russia

NIKOLAY G. MALYSHEV
Adviser to the President of Russia on Science and Higher Education

Complex and balanced development of the economy of Russia should obviously be based on the scientific, technological and industrial potential of the country, inward and outward sources of accumulaton, the cultural wealth of peoples of Russia, taking into consideration the variety of national goal and tasks. It is possible only in conditions of attracting means from the enterprises of all ownership forms, financial institutions, funds and citizens.

We must consider that such scenario is to be realized stage by stage. It is expedient to single out two main stages: short-term one, aimed at stabilization of economical, political and social situation in 2-3 years; and the stage of large-scale structural and institutional long-term reconstruction (about 10-15 years). According to this division the goals of economical and social development of the country are determined and the priorities for scientific and technological development are selected.

The priority tasks of economical and social development at the stage of stabilization are as follows:

- to put a stop to the recession and to begin further upsurge of production;

- selection of "the break-through zones" allowing to overcome negative tendencies and to reach socially valuable results (house building, "folk car" production, road construction, solving problems with food-stuffs and medicines etc.);
- stabilization of financial situation, gradual inflation reduction to the level, acceptable at this stage;
- saving the potential of revival and economic development (scientific, technological and labour potential, advanced technologies, unique research etc.).

At the stage of the large-scale structural and institutional reconstruction the following targets must be realized:

- restoration of the pre-crisis scale of industrial manufacturing, structural reconstitution of the economy, final forming of subjects and infrastructure of market economy;
- active penetration into the foreign markets of the processing industry's products;
- increase of the consumer goods production and provision on this basis labour motivation to the population; decrease of resources-intensity of national economy;
- technological alignment of different sectors of economy in order to reduce spending of resources and raise quality of final products;
- re-distribution of capital investments into consumer goods industry and accleration of retirement of ineffective part of assets;
- attracting military machinery-producing to the structural reconstruction of national economy.
- analysis of the economical, social and political development targets also shows that it needs reorientation and structural reconstruction of scientific, technological and industrial potential of the country.

Analysis of the possible scenarios of the economic development of the country shows that upon present conditions of economic recession and inflation concrete guiding lines for scientific and technological development are as follows:

In short term:

- provision of acceptable (in conformity to the economic situation) level and quality of life;
- stabilization of the ecological situation, first of all, averting ecological accidents;
- economy of resources and power;
- increasing of the industrial potential of the raw materials branches—main exporters of raw materials and sources of hard currency;
- stimulating of development of defence branches of industry, having high export potential (in particular, in the sphere of armaments' systems) and providing high efficiency of services;
- development of the economy sectors providing fast return of capital investments;
- supporting and reorientation of scientific and technological personnel towards main tasks of structural policy.

Strategic social-economic guiding lines of scientific development priorities' selection are as follows:

- supporting of national security;
- support to market structures and relations establishing;
- integration in the world community (in order, in far outlook, to occupy adequate place in the world labour division and to obtain a new quality of life);
- reconstruction, technical renewal and creation of new, ecological effective, large scale (in tons), extremely secure manufacturing processes especially in oil processing and petrochemical industry;
- support to the "break-through" (critical) technologies giving opportunities to obtain leading position at the world markets and based, first of all, on using own scientific and technical potential and having both military and civilian applications (so called "dual-use" technologies);

- conversion of military industry, which main target is to refit up the civilian machinery-producing industry, and to manufacture not separate items, but complex machines systems;
- support to the technologies, stimulating obtaining positive results in other technologies' development, production or sales.

Analysis shows that during the last decades the task of selective structural reconstruction hasn't been solved. The problem of selection and realization of the scientific and technological development priorities still cannot be considered resolved.

For example, in August 1993 the Government formulated the priority direction of structural policy, embracing the following branches of economy; fuel and electric power complex; oil processing and petrochemistry, food and medicines supply; transport and different means of communications (including telecommunications); house building; science; urgent questions concerning social sphere. However, above-mentioned priorities of the governmental programme cover all main branches of national economy, attracting 90 per cent of total capital investments to the economy of Russia.

More selective approach towards selection of the scientific and technical policy priorities presupposes using the general objectives of the country's economic course, selected development scenario, main directions of structural reconstruction as well as social-economic guiding lines of scientific and technical progress.

- According to it, research and development first of all must be aimed at the following objectives:
- creating technical premises for maintaining existing level of raw material and power resources producing and its limited increase;
- wide implementation of the basic technologies, providing increasing of the products quality and reducing deficit at the domestic market due to the wide use of Russian R&D achievements and active purchases of foreign licences;

- changing technology, providing necessary economy of resources that can compensate growing prices of raw materials;
- increasing Russian products' competitive standing at the domestic, and in some cases—at the foreign markets.

On the basis of these targets and tasks the key scientific and technological direction must be selected and ranged in accordance to their importance from national economy. These directions must be legislative adopted and serve as a basic for the state support of projects and programmes.

The results of the researches conducted by large group of scientists and specialist and the data of the first large-scale expertise by the prominent scientists in Russia show that it is possible to determine two groups of priority directions from the prospective point of view:

For the short-term outlook—the directions which are of vital importance for the country in the conditions of economic crisis:

- conversion and stimulating of the export production of military industry (including services);
- increasing technical level of the primary links of the technological structure (extraction and processing of mineral resources, raw materials and agricultural products);
- maintaining potential and creating premises for further development of Russian science, obtaining own high level scientific results as well as learning and practical implementation of achievements of the world science and technology;
- further development of those sectors of economy that can provide the fastest solutions of social problem during transition period.

For the long-term outlook—the directions, connected with the progress of the abovementioned first group. Their development depends in many respects on the hard currency resources and on maintaining existing scientific and technological potential;

- raising quality of nutrition products; elimination of harmful substances and food additions; satisfying demand for protein-rich products; providing stableness for agricultural industry;
- improvement health of the population, raising quality of diagnostics, prophylaxis and treatment; developing and manufacturing of medicines and medical preparations;

  realization and stimulation of measures preventing ecological accidents and improving ecological situation;
- reconstruction, technical renewal and creation of new, ecologically effective, large scale (in tons), extremely secure manufacturing processes especially in oil-processing, petrochemical, metallurgical, provisional and allied industries;
- support to the "break-through" (critical) technologies giving opportunities to obtain leading position at the world markets and based, first of all, of using of own scientific and technical potential;
- material, technical and informational provision of the transition to the market economy; informatization of the society;
- raising quality of education and specialists training; transport and communications development;
- strengthening defence capacity of the country on the basis of the accepted military doctrine.

Comparisong of the directions of scientific and technological development of Russia with the critical basic technologies in the most industrially developed states shows that at present in our country not all technologies, that are the most actively stimulated abroad, can be considered to be of top priority, due to the substantial economic limitations.

- In this case the most important for Russia are:
- new basic technologies—development of new materials and software;

- basic technologies supplying manufacturing process—development of production technologies and increasing efficiency of energy using;
- basic technologies having social significance—systems of satellite communication, communication nets, aerospace industry and shipbuilding, space using technologies;
- technologies aimed against environmental pollutions—only those preventing deterioration and some sanitation of environment.

Thus, we can speak about possibility and necessity of selective approach towards structural policy of reconstruction of Russia economy on the basis of development, production and using of progressive technics and technology.

Thus, substantial state support is necessary for successful development of high technology sectors of economy (especially nuclear power and defence industries, shipbuilding). Simultaneously, development of high technology production will be also induced by investments from national and foreign oil, gas and power companies. On the other hand, taking into consideration lower wages of industrial personnel in Russia, the special importance is attached to the allocation at the Russian enterprises of the orders for technological equipment manufacturing for extractive industries according to the foreign technologies. Financial support to such import-substituting projects must be given by governmental structures as well as by enterprises-consumers.

Concrete priority directions of state scientific-technological policy for the nearest short-term outlook. According to the conducted analysis, in the high technology sectors of economy, first of all in the defence industry, from the point of view of experience transfer from military into civilian branches, the most important directions are those, noted for manufacturing of specialized, small-serial or unique products, connected with developing of new materials and rendering special services.

Among them, first of all, there must be:

- space technics, passengers and transport aircrafts and engines for them;

- rendering services on deliveries to space of scientific equipment; cargo transportation by aircrafts and other similar tasks; satellite communication systems;
- special means of transportation, including those for northern parts of the country and regions with difficult weather conditions; specialized passengers and cargo ships;
- nuclear power plants of natural security with lead heart-carrier; gas-turbine plants for electric power industry; compressors for gas pipe-lines; boring equipment;
- new materials and technologies;
- specialized computer systems and software, automated systems of technological processes management;
- special and unique scientific devices based on the achievements of fundamental science.

In the extractive industry of fuel and power complex the selection of priority technologies must be conducted, taking into consideration new possibilities aroused from the conversion of military industry, international cooperation and attracting of foreign capital. In particular, in oil extracting, the priority directions of the development must be the following:

- developing oil resources, difficult for extracting;
- systems of deposits development with the help of horizontal and branched bore holes;
- developing and using new methods of increasing oil output.

Reducing losses of agricultural raw materials and food stuffs sufficiently depends upon implementation of progressive technologies and increasing of capacities for products processing and conservation. Developing technologies for small businesses and equipment for farmers must be induced. The specific role of importing new technologies is determined by the lag of national machinery-producing for light and food industries, lack of experience in developing and producing equipment for agricultural products processing. Foreign equipment and technologies are needed practically for all agricultural products manufacturing and conservation.

The main direction of the large-scale (in tons) manufacturing processes development also must be determined according to the results of defence industry conversion and possibility of foreign capital attracting. In this respect in oil processing and petrochemical industries the following must be of top priority; technologies of deep oil processing; technologies of oil products' extracting from gas raw stuffs; technologies of large-scale manufacturing of petrochemical basic products from gas raw stuffs. In metallurgy industry special attention is to be paid to stimulating of progressive mental products manufacturing.

One of the important directions of solving social tasks should be the development of consumer goods industry. It can change labour motivation of the employees. The main condition here, after prices liberalization, will be saturation of the market with products affordable to all groups of population. The priority item is the sufficient increase of autocars manufacturing, especially of cheap models such as "folk car". For this purpose it's necessary to use the possibilities of defence industry and agricultural machinery-producing, as well as to attract foreign investments into automobile (including assembling) plants construction.

Also top priority is to be given to manufacturing of agricultural machines and equipment for tenants and country house owners.

All this will require sufficient efforts from the state system of management, especially in selection and realization of concrete objectives and priorities of social, economic, scientific and technological development.

10

Relationship Trend between Science and the State in Latvia After 1991

JANIS FREIMANIS

Full member of the Latvian Academy of Sciences

As it was mentioned before at the Erica Seminar in Italy (August 19-24, 1994), the science development now frequently was lost a very strong driving force: after the Cold War and the collapse of USSR in the most well-developed countries their State Power now lacks the feeling of fear before any threat outside. Therefore, the science is no more considered as a defence tool for the state security, and tends to be regarded as less valuable, less advising and deserving less financial assistance. Such a situation is especially disappointing in the small countries which have restored their real independence recently, and where the science never can be treated as an argument in favour of state security and, as a consequence, as a matter of priority in the state budget.

Science Pattern in Latvia

Some of our analysts explain many of science's shortcomings, or a negative science development with the ongoing science reorganization as a whole. In Lativa we also have passed some profound science changes: the science now is financed only according the State covered Grand Project system, the Latvian Academy of Sciences has become a personal Academy, and scientific institutes now are free and completely independent from any previous centralizing ties. But, I insist that also our State Power attitude towards science might be a serious source of the existing problems. I feel that certain governments definitely may have no idea what to do with their own science and their scientists, instead of solving, say, winter survival challenges, border control problems or dealing with the rise of criminalty. Let us look on the science financing pattern in Latvia since 1990, see Table 1, because here money is attitude.

Table 1. Science Situation in Latvia, 1990-1995

Index	1990[a]	1991[a]	1992[a]	1993	1994	1995[a]
GDP, Mln Lats	3347	3070	1814	1433	(1984)	(2300)
Sci. budget expenses, Mln Lats	53.55	n.e.	5.44	5.09	5.66	(8.60)
% to GDP	1.60	n.e.	0.30	0.33	(0.29)	(0.35)
% to total State budget expenses	n.e.	n.e.	n.e.	0.72	(0.92)	(0.91)
Number of scientists (N)	17730	13270	7230	4000	3900[c]	?
N/1000 inhabitants[c]	6.631	4.97	2.72	1.53	1.52	n.e.

(a) recalculated in national currency, Lats (0.54 Ls = 1 USD) on a comparative standard
(b) or data in parentheses—estimated or planed.
(c) data on January Ist of the current year.
n.e. not estimated yet

On the one hand, the science decrease trends—easily seen from the Table 1—can be directly explained due to the fact, that the old, soviet-style and oriented-to-East industry have collapsed. Therefore, also the main source of state budget income vanished, as well as any possibility for an additional science contract financing. As you see, all this manifests in a dramatic drop of Gross Domestic Product (GDP).

Consequently, we are facing also a considerable science support decrease, and great losses in scientific personnel. Only starting from the current year we can count on a small absolute rise in science financing, and in the coming year expect a relative increase of GDP expenses for science. I guess, only today we can speak also about a passed maximum point of brain losses in science. To be not too optimistic, but some stabilization may be foreseen also in the supply of modern scientific literature in Latvia, see as an example the data of Table 2.

Table 2. The Supply in Foreign Scientific Journals in Latvian Academic Library

Money ordered-	1991	1992	1993	1994
spent-	1992	1993	1994	
Amount, USD	300.000	110.000	none	100.000
Number of subscribed sets[a,b]	500	n.e.	none	100

(a) taking into consideration the subscribing rate increase is 10 per cent annually

(b) excluding items, obtained on exchange basis

n.e.- not estimated

Unfortunately, during these dramatic times the Latvian scientific community frequently experienced incomprehension from the side of Power circles, say, about the mental importance of the scientific intellect to be saved, or its potential role in the State future at all. A superficial, sometimes even illiterate attitude of certain state officials towards a scientists is completely odd, because simple, human understanding does not need any money at all. I'm convinced many of us could survive easier and maintain a better mood, having a little bit more attention and some care.

Owing to the fact that various already operating international financial aid programmes (Soros foundation, PHARE or TEMPUS programmes, EC organized E-W scientific joint projects, etc.) can cover only the annual inflation losses in our science expenditures, it is clear, that the scientific community in Latvia .will face serious development challenges in the near future.

Some Possible Solutions

The first way-out to a sufficient survival of Latvian scientific community might be its penetration into various state-power, or any enterprise advisory boards, consulting commissions and committees, for the sake of the best decision-making in any, but first of all, state level afterwards. This means a wide use of informational or technical skills of a scientist by the state official, and—on the other hand—a serious responsibility increase of a scientist in his activities. I'd say: no decision in power circles should be made without adequate consulting aid from the scientist!

The second way-out—especially for Latvia as a state, that lacks huge energy or strategic raw-material resources—should be the scientific evaluation of local natural resources which, nevertheless, are present and may cover a considerable portion of material hitherto imported. For instance, here I could mention a thorough evaluation of the existing oil deposits—for the filling of the local market with the everyday chemical products (solvents, waxes, some lubricants, detergents, etc.).

The third way should be a massive participation of scientists in different energy saving projects and technology applications, as well as in ways of utilization of reusable waste products, e.g., in activities, which could liberate more funds for the state assistance, say, for basic science projects. Perhaps, this would be the time when our science must become more open for urgent practical needs, and when—with a regret—some basic research projects might be postponed to 'better' times.

Seeking a perspective on a state level, very important, of course, is the fulfilment of wide scope existing educational programmes—making the young specialist mentally more flexible and more adapted to market economy principles also in science. BUT. It isn't sufficient to bring up a young scientist for a modern research formally. More important is to teach him to find out his own scientific way both **realistic and scientifically valuable**. Frequently a young man, especially after some praxis in advanced Western scientific centres, is able to manage either with the first, or only with the second necessity. Exactly such a kind of 'thinking shift' aid, as a part of any educational programme and within any international training assistance, would be greatly appreciated in my country.

But for all that, good relationships between science and power is urgently expected. I'd like to offer even a somewhat technocratic concept—no power without a scientific approach to a State problem, and no Science without frequent, efficient and responsive advisory aid in State decision making. I suppose such a mutual interaction between science and power in Latvia çould only facilitate the desired progress of events, and, what is more important, would raise the science prestige before the state power and vice versa, and for both—also their prestige before the people.

Thank you for your attentiona!

11

Public Attitudes Towards Science and Technology in Estonia

ARNO KOORNA
Estonian Academy of Sciences

Sociologists in Estonia accomplished comparative study of public attitudes toward issues including education, science and technology in Estonia. The aim of the study was to get the information on public attitudes toward science and education, how public evaluate effects of science on their lives, and on development of young Estonian society after regaining independence. Data have been collected for international comparison about public knowledge of basic scientific concepts and other issues of public attitudes towards science and technology.

Estonians' Knowledge about Science and Technology

The survey shows that within the last couple of years access to information has become more limited. This has happened in spite of the fact that the number of information sources has increased. Quite a large portion of the population has simple no money to buy newspapers and magazines.

Ten years ago only about 4 per cent of Estonians did not watch TV and 1 per cent of Estonians did not listen to the radio. The average Estonian family regularly read 3-4 newspapers. Now the situation has changed dramatically.

Newspapers are read regularly by 54 per cent of the population of Estonia (64 per cent of Estonians, 37 per cent of non-Estonians). Reading of magazines has decreased even more drastically. Only 9 per cent of population are regular magazine readers (11 per cent of Estonians, 5 per cent of non-Estonians).

People are not very interested in the problems of science either listening on the radio or on TV. News broadcasts are followed regularly by 79 per cent of respondents (81 per cent of Estonians, 75 per cent of non-Estonians), but broadcasts about science are followed only by 1.3 per cent of the repondents (1.7 per cent of Estonians. 0.7 per cent of non-Estonians). 47 per cent of population has no contact with any (popular) scientific journal at all.

Science and nature museums are regularly visited by only 3.6 per cent of respondents. 3/5 of population never go there.

In Estonia people have only a vague sense of different spheres of Science. In America during last 10 years an interest in new scientific discoveries has been very high (37-48 per cent) of population have been very interested in it), in Estonia only 9 per cent of population were very interested in scientific problems in 1993. From 5 per cent to 19 per cent of the respondents had a great interest in medical discoveries, environmental pollution, policy of armed forces, defence policy, foreign policy, nuclear energy, new discoveries in cosmology and space exploration. Estonians' interest towards different spheres of science is 1.5—4.2 times bigger than that of non-Estonians.

We have probed the quality of basic knowledge which the Estonian population has.

By this we mean knowledge that does not depend on everyday information so much as on the quality of formal education. To test this we used questions like "Does the earth go around the sun, or does the sun go around the earth?" etc.

The results of these tests show that the population of Estonia (especially Estonians) is a bit more informed than the population of the US. Out of 13 questions Estonians gave 8 correct responses, non-Estonians 7 correct responses. The analysis showed that the more established knowledges, explained by the scientist, was, the more correct were the answers given. Modern discoveries were given less correct answers. E.g.: "Lasers work by focusing sound waves" was correctly answered by 27 per cent of respondents. "Antibiotics kill viruses as well as bacteria" was correctly answered only by 15 per cent of our respondents.

It is the lack of modern scientific knowledge that determines people's overall attitude towards science. Six statements concerning science were given to respondents to evaluate (these statements have been asked in 14 developed countries in Europe and in North America, too).

53 per cent of Estonian respondents agreed to the statement "It is not important for me to know about science in my daily life". We do not meet such a low evaluation of the role of knowledge in any other country. "Science makes our way of life change too fast" was supported by only 33 per cent of the respondents. This shows graphically that science and its achievements have up until now remained so removed from our daily life that people have no reason and even no basics upon which to evaluate their influence.

Public Attitudes Towards Science and Education in Estonia

Science and education are highly valued in Estonian society. This is proved by the models of development that are suggested for Estonia's future. Among the respondents 64 per cent are of the opinion that Estonian science has an important role to play in the fields of production which rely upon high technology. 69 per cent of the respondents support the viewpoint that science must become more important.

Only 1.2 per cent think that we should primarily sell our cheap labour. 22 per cent think that Estonia's main role is to be a mediator between West and East. It is remarkable that this last position is equally supported by people of different ages and education.

Will Estonian scientists be able to manage the mission they are expected to carry out? Public opinion does not hold Estonian scientists' contribution to solving current problems very high. Only 28 per cent of respondents consider it great (5 per cent very great), 45 per cent as small. Does this mean that Estonian scientists are not sufficiently competent or is the reason the kind of policy of science?

In the survey the following question probed the issue: "Are Estonian scientists able to work out the development programmes needed in Estonia, or are only foreign scientists able to do this?" 20 per cent were of the opinion that Estonian scientists would manage with these tasks. Only 2 per cent thought that only foreign scientists could do so. Most respondents supported the position that Estonian and foreign scientists would do it best together. Such an attitude reflects the high esteem in which Estonian scientists are held.

It is interesting to note that those people whose knowledge of scientific theories was the highest, evaluated the potential of Estonian scientists most highly and that of foreign scientists at lowest level.

State Scientific Subsidies

The rather reserved evaluation of scientists' ability to solve the problems of Estonian society is partly explained by the Government's "reserved" attitude towards science.

Only 3 per cent of the respondents are of the opinion that science is strongly supported by the Government. Educated people thought the Government gave little support to science. Dividing the opinions into two main groups: a) Government supports science, and b) Government does not support science, we get two indexes: 35 per cent take a positive stand towards the Government's, 38 per cent have a negative attitude.

The scientists' wages are lower than Estonian average wages. They are absolutely minimal compared to Western scientists' salaries. According to the official exchange rate in Estonian crowns, scientists's wages in Estonia are about 1/25—1/100 of those of Western scientists.

About 67 per cent from the money given to the science institutions in 1994, goes to salaries and social taxes. It is a great problem to buy expensive instruments and installations necessary for experimental researches as very much money is needed for heating, communication and other material spendings. The scientists are living in a poor way, though there work many internationally recognized scientists and they have achieved good scientific results in these fields.

Public opinion expects growing of the role of the science in society. "Even if it brings no immediate benefits, scientific research which advances the frontiers of knowledge should be supported by the government" was approved by 75% of the respondents.

In order to understand general attitudes better, we asked a question about attitudes towards financing concrete branches that could show us all possible different variants on most general level. National sciences that should be of great importance in Estonia were separately brought out.

Answering the question "Which branch of science would you prefer to give money?" the respondents had to make the first and the second choice (only one branch at the same time). The most preferred branches of science were economics (29 per cent) medicine (28 per cent) and agriculture (19 per cent). These branches were dominant in summary of two choices as well. National sciences gathered only 10 per cent of supporters in the result of two choices. The least amount of money had been decided to give to theoretical and applied sciences.

The similar results were not from the question "Which branches of science would you not give any money?" These branches of science which were less supported in the previous question, were at the leading position here

For background information we have to emphasize that 65 per cent of people could not give any answer to this question. Besides, we can ever that the essence of theoretical and applied sciences is grasped quite vaguely by public opinion. This kind of comprehension belongs to specific knowledge. That is why the public opinion first of all supports these branches of science which have direct practical value: medicine, agriculture and economics.

Analyzing the results of this research we reached to an interesting contradiction. On one hand, public opinion finds that Estonia should base on production which relies upon high technology in its economic development. On the other hand, these branches of science which could be the basis of its direction of development (theoretical and applied sciences), are not supported.

This contradiction is mainly related with specific scientific problems, which are as research showed us—very difficult to understand on the level of mass conscious of today.

Attitudes to Education

Estonian public opinion believes in science and wishes the increasing of its role in the development of Estonia. The level of science is closely connected with education. The science is considered to be one of the keys to solve the problems of society, and it is also found that by raising the level of education (among Estonians education has been assigned a great value throughout centuries), many problems could be solved as well. There are 30 per cent among the respondents who think that raising the level of people's education will improve the situation in social sphere remarkably. 48 per cent of the respondents believe that better education enables essential improvement of competitiveness. 59 per cent of the respondents believe in Estonia's greater success in science and technology if people were more educated.

Science and education are like two whales the flourishing of which brings along the improvement of Estonian economic and social life. This is the opinion of the greater part of Estonian society that supporting of science and education is necessary. Though public opinion might be incompetent in certain questions, in the limits of its competence it supports science.

We have to recognize the competence of Estonian public opinion because compared to several foreign countries the population of Estonia is better informed about fundamental scientific theories. But there is still a problem in Estonia: people should have better access to modern scientific discoveries.

12

International Association of Academies of Sciences as a Regional Factor

ANATOLIJ SHPAK
Chief Scientific Secretary of the National Academy of Sciences of Ukraine

During many decades the scientific cooperation between the scientists of the Academies of Sciences of the republics of the former Soviet Union achieved the extremely high level. This fruitful cooperation brought quite a few outstanding achievements and discoveries to the world science.

The processes of spontaneous reorganizations and consequent deep crisis in the national structure, in the national and mainly, economic relations which are taking place at the moment on the territory of the former Soviet Union couldn't but affect the sphere of scientific activity.

The current course of events which is characterized by ceasing the joint fundamental research and breaking the traditional links among scientists presents an indubitable threat to the intellectual potential of the new states which have appeared on the territory of the Soviet Union. It's quite natural that the scientists are greatly interested in the united scientific space which is based on the community of a number of scientific schools, close cooperation in training scientific personnel, joint use of unique research complexes.

The creation of the International Association of Academies of Sciences in September 1993 reflected this interest. The Academies of Sciences of 15 sovereign states have become the members of the Association: Azerbaijan Republic, Republic Armenia, Republic Byelorus, Socialist Republic Vietnam, Republic Georgia, Republic Kazakhstan, Kirgiz Republic, Republic Moldova, Russian Federation, Republic Tadjikistan, Turkmenistan, Republic Uzbekistan, Ukraine and also Slovak Republic and Czech Republic which have the observer status.

The President of the National Academy of Sciences of Ukraine B.E. Paton was elected the first President of the IAAS. At the last sitting of the Council of the Association on 11th February 1994 his powers were extended for 2 years more. It should be noted that in Ukraine IAAS was officially recognized by the state. According to the Decree of the President of Ukraine "About the International Association of Academies of Sciences" from 25th May 1994 N 252/94 IAAS is recognized as an international non-government self-governing organization that is a juridical person carrying out its activity on the territory of Ukraine according to Ukrainian laws.

At the Constituent Assembly of IAAS members the Regulations about the Association were adopted which include non-payment of its executive elected posts (President and Vice-President) and the absence of its own research Institutes. This makes IAAS to a greater extent similar to the famous international academic scientific societies.

The Association does not carry out the general supervision of the research work, it only facilitates the preservation and development of the links which were historically established. The main work of IAAS is carried out in the permanent Committees on some fields and directions of sciences and the most important problems. Such Committees are established in different countries at those research centres which hold the leading part in the particular field. In these Committees the most important trends of scientific development are considered, appropriate expert conclusions recommendations and proposals on international cooperation are prepared.

The Association Council confirmed the main principles of organization and activity of IAAS Committees, their members in natural, social sciences and humanities, information provision of Academies of Sciences—IAAS members and appointed the Chairmen and their deputies of these Committees.

It is to be noted that the IAAS Council obliged that Academy of Sciences where the Chairmen of the Committee works to provide organizational and technical work of each Committee.

It has been decided to create 7 more Committees: on technical sciences; ecological problems; space exploration; energy problems; problems of law and economic provisions of the activity of Academies of Sciences—IAAS members; rational use of unique equipment, expedition ships including regional science and technical programmes.

It is necessary to underline that the Agreement on establishment of IAAS is open for signing by Academies of Sciences of other countries which wish to take part in the Association activity.

During the first year of the work of the Association the main thing was to find the practical forms and methods of implementation of those noble goals which were proclaimed in the Agreement and the Regulations of IAAS. It is important not to substitute the effective bilateral links among the Academies of Sciences—IAAS members but to develop multilateral cooperation where it is necessary, where one can't do without joining the efforts just on the multilateral basis. Such directions include, in particular, the whole complex of ecological problems connected with Chernobyl and the fate of the Aral Sea and also with the nuclear polygon near Semopalatinsk. It is only by joint efforts that one can provide, for example, further development of research in the field of physics of high energy space rays. Quite a few proposals of this kind have already been advanced by the scientists.

The practical value of joint efforts of this kind has been confirmed by the mutual understanding about cooperation in the field of certification of scientific personnel, the creation of the appropriate inter-state association of HCK—IASC.

The headquarters of IAAS which is in Kiev organized publishing of bulletin of IAAS and references about the Association and the Academies of Sciences—its members. Under the aegis of the Association quite a number of international conferences and symposia have been held during the year.

Speaking of IAAS perspectives it is necessary to note that its Committees intend to pay special attention first of all to supporting young scientists. At present the process of establishing of the Association is going on and, as the international experiences shows, it will continue during 3-5 years, that's why the possibilities of IAAS are quite limited. However one can find the forms of such support relying on the potential of the participants of IAAS. For instance, the Committees could annually prepare the collections of the best scientific works of young scientists for publication and publish them in the Academy of Sciences which carries out the organizational and technical provision.

Having the regional character the International Association of Academies of Sciences aims at establishing close links with different international scientific communities: Academy of Europe, International Council of Research Union, Permanent Conference of European Academies of Sciences, German Research Society, Third World Academy of Science and others. This direction of IAAS activity is a primary one. One of the possible ways of establishing stable contacts may be signing the Memorandum about the scientific cooperation between IAAS and the corresponding international research organization which would allow for coordinated directions of interaction, for example, constant exchange of information.

We should point out the practical steps of IAAS aimed at getting the status of the consulting member at UNESCO; the fact that the International Association of Academies of Sciences tries to exert its influence on pursuing scientific policy at the government level. In particular, at the last sitting of the Council the Address to the heads of states and governments of the Commonwealth of Independent States about the necessity to re-establish the united scientific space.

13

Science and Power: Past and Present

JOAO M.G. CARACA
Calouste Gulbenkian Foundation, Lisbon

Knowledge-based activities were implemented ever since the first human societies acquired the capacity to use fire. The attitude of dominance over nature was certainly overwhelming and the acceleration and deceleration of social and economic development processes (in fact, the whole thickness* of the history of mankind) can be thought of as being the result of technique and ingenuity.

What are the relations between knowledge and power?

The employment of power always involves the constitution of a domain of knowledge, from which its own legitimation and cultural identity can be derived; concurrently, the rules that govern the operation of this body of knowledge induce a set of power relations**. Therefore, we can say that knowledge and power mirror each other, to the extent that the conditions for the enactment of both spring from their mutual coexistence. In the epochs and communities, each one also set its indelible mark of the other.

---

* Fernand Braudel—in "Les Structures du Quotidien", civilization materielle, Economie et Capitalisme XV-XVIII siècle, Armand Colin, Paris 1979.

** Michel Foucault—in "Resumés de Cours", quoted by M.M. Carrilho, ltinerários da Racionalidade, Dom Quixote, Lisboa, 1989.

The birth of modern science in the 17th century and the formidable impact of the transformations brought about by the industrial revolution led to the constitution of a body of scientific and technological knowledge that plays a central role in the performance of contemporary economies and societies. Scientific and technological research is thus a crucial process both for the generation of technological innovation and for the construction of the meanings that embody the cultures of today (which, ultimately, enable the diffusion of innovation in society).

Therefore, in the relations between science and power we must distinguish between "power" and the "power of science" on one hand, and between "power in science" and "scientific power", on the other.

And what is power? Power, the prime mover of human populations, can no better be described in today's language (using the concept from the theory of dissipative structures) than by saying that power is self-organization.

We can not pretend to understand better the essence of power as long as we don't perceive what is beyond the principle of self-organization. We have to accept that our best vision of the universe entails irreversibility and self-organization. And we should not attempt to understand power better than we today understand matter or knowledge. But we must not feel discouraged by this: we now see why power is everywhere and prevails in every aspect of life.

Power has to be conceived as being expressed through two components. Successful self-organization is the one who commands a system (a dissipative structure) through the operation of its material and immaterial variables towards bond-term survival. Successful self-organization is the one who is able to enforce both action and communication in its own system for that purpose.

Power exhibits, thus, a mixed character: it is a composed device of both violence and authority. We define violence as the forced physical action over a system and its interfaces, and authority as the corresponding forced process of communication, which ensures that individual elements are convinced (i.e. accept a meaning). Power works through the combination of both its material and immaterial attributes. Power is inherent to the command of the activity of a system. This is why it is so obsessively sought.

Human societies are highly organized dissipative structures; they survive due to their capacity to maintain a flow of matter and energy, and this capacity has to do with both material (physical) and immaterial (cognitive) aspects.

The power of science (meaning the command by science of societal matters) is directly related to its influence on aspects that are deemed of relevance by society. Thus, the power of science is not dictated by the strength of science and technology but rather by the perception of its importance for the consolidation and survival of (the system of) power itself. The status of eminent scientists and the "proximity" to power of scientific advice are, thus, indicators of the social value of science and tools of its invigoration.

Power in science (which means the command of power relations inside the system of science and technology) serves the important objective of securing the standards and competence of the scientific establishment. Of course, sometimes a degree of immunity of research laboratories and science centres to the vices of other existing societal institutions is seen. But that is also frequently not the case.

Finally, let us consider scientific power, meaning enlightened power, the goal of so many good souls and minds. Here, we must recollect that science and technology is just one of the domains of knowledge (an expanding and very pervasive one, if we look at modern societies) that embody our culture. The exercise of power, to be viable, needs thus to be based upon scientific knowledge. By that doesn't mean that decision-making is a scientific process, nor that other non-scientific aspects concurring to an issue should be discarded. Science doesn't have the monopoly of meanings in our culture and power knows it. That is why we must strive, consistently, towards sounder scientific bases in decision-making.

The making of present decisions genuinely characterizes us and the times we live in. In the past, when the future was supposed to be pre-determined (or written) the search for meanings through oral tradition or history was complemented with the recourse to divination—a way of mobilizing the unknown to minimize the consequences of uncertainty. In our century, the growing weight of science and technology in society led mankind to view the future as a construction, as the embodiment of present decisions. Decision have, thus, to be evaluated in relation to their time horizon.

In fact, the growing role of immaterial factors in our society contributed to clarify the differences between the values at the heart of the scientific practice—the search of plausibility—and those underlying the administration of science—the search of utility. From the tension between these values, from the continuous process of reconciliation between these two activities, emerges the motivation for generating elements that enable better choices.

Finally, how can we thus briefly formulate comments towards a better Policy for Science also towards better Science for Policy?

First, we must admit that the essence and logic of power and even of "scientific power" lies outside the aspirations of science; power maintains an ambivalent relationship with science, allowing sufficient "power of science" for its own legitimation purposes but inducing necessary "power in science" to be able to supervise on competence issues. Of course, all this network of interactions evolves in time and is subject to constraints and conflicts. But choices are, ultimately, the attribute of governance.

Second, we feel that scientific advice should be close to policy-making and that the impact of the opinion of eminent scientists, of respected scientific unions and of learned societies should not be underestimated. Active support should be explicitly dedicated to this purpose.

Third, we think that priorities should not be set systematically under the majestic dominance of resource scarcity but rather be primarily directed towards the detection of opportunities. The issues of development are not solved, but managed, as goals and targets continuously evolve, by virtue of the actions launched to meet them.

Better policies for science will bring sounder scientific advice and awareness to the sphere of government. No modern society will survive without sound scientific attitudes, that press both for excellence and for the recognition of others, as well as for the need of assessing long-term perspectives.

14

Military Conversion and Its Impact upon Resources Allocation for Science

JOHN H. PROCTOR

Secretary General, World Academy of Art and Science

We are still in the midst of momentous changes begun in the late 1980s which are continuing principally in Europe and the former Soviet Union, as well as in the rest of the world. These changes will have great impact upon political, economic and social conditions of most of the people of earth. For many of us, the impact upon the present state and future development of science is the issue.

Introduction

My presentation today will summarize principally the work of the Round Table on Military Conversion and Science convened in Venice last week by the UNESCO Regional Office for Science and Technology for Europe (ROSTE) and conferences preceding that Round Table. This contribution is intended to underscore how scientists from many scientific disciplines and national ameliorate negative consequences and generate positive opportunities for society though cooperative study.

In November, 1990 a two-year project of UNESCO-ROSTE was initiated at the Working Party meeting in Lisbon, Portugal alarming trends in the migration of scientists—"Brain Drain"—principally in Eastern Europe. In April 1992, UNESCO-ROSTE convened the International Seminar on Organizational Structures of Science in Europe. In 1993, I was honoured with an invitation to the International Seminar on Brain Drain Issues in Europe, also convened by UNESCO-ROSTE in Venice. So, to me, this International Symposium on Science and Power is building upon the work of these preceding conference, the shared thinking of scientists from many nations. A deep debt of gratitude is owed to those in ROSTE's Scientific Council and those in co-sponsoring organizations who developed and implemented this vision for producing these influences upon society. In my view, it is international symposia like this that provide a rapid means of developing and disseminating the thinking of those engaged in science about the role of science in problems and opportunities in today's society.

Background

In Russian and Eastern European science, much of the state support of sciences has disappeared. Newspapers tell us it is because of a great economic crisis. But my visits there strengthen my belief that profound reconsiderations are underway of the place science is to have in the former Soviet states and countries of Eastern Europe. Civilian and military leaders of massive military oriented programmes were lavish in their support of basic hard science, key technologies and supporting disciplines. After the political and economic collapse of the Soviet state, hard science lost support; "Big Science" Projects stopped, and as for the soft sciences, they appear to be struggling and gasping for credibility and support. [I. UNESCO-ROSTE Seminar, 1990]

The Russian Federation's funding of the Russian Academy of Sciences with its over 300,000 employees, dozens of institutes, libraries, test sites, observatories, publishing houses, research ships and planes has been cut from 3 to 5 times in comparable terms according to S.P. Kapitza. [2.S.P. Kapitza, 1994] Coupled with inflation of over 4000 per cent in the last two years, the compensation of scientists, technicians, architects and medical doctors is ridiculously low. Youngsters are not entering science and technical careers; scientists are leaving science. Some say. "Fine. Science in the USSR was top heavy and overstaffed. Let the dismantling continue." Others say the pillaging of the former USSR and Eastern Block science is ridiculous, sadistic or downright stupid in the face of possible nuclear proliferation, not to mention chemical and biological threats. Ignoring the promises of their science in bio-technology, advances in rocketry, mathematics, optics, and lasers is simply irrational.

The United States Department of Defence Budget for Research and Development in 1991 was $30 billion in 1995 dollars. In 1995, it is $26 billion and by 1999, it is budgeted at $21 billion in 1995 dollars, a minus 30 per cent change from 1991! (3, U.S. Congress, Congressional Budget Office, 1994) The private sector will have to increase its financial support of science and technology and that in turn, depends upon controlled economic growth. Having to depend upon market forces to provide financial support for science and technology is risky indeed.

Brain Drain and Military Conversion

The problems of defense conversion and brain drain provides a uniting global issue for learned societies, academies of art and science, and organizations advancing technology around the world to maintain pressure on decision makers to raise science and technology in their scheme of priorities. The open market economies can not be expected to support basic science research and the education of scientists. Governments must continue to provide this support.

Let's examine some of the key recommendations of the UNESCO-ROSTE conferences over the past four years, many of which have been put into practice.

Report of the Working Party on "Brain Drain Issues in Europe", 1990:

- The phenomenon of massive intellectual migration should be considered as a positive process in the context of the development of mankind. The right of peoples to migrate in search of appropriate living and working conditions, free of any political prejudice, was confirmed at the Helsinki Conference on Security and Cooperation in Europe.
- The Scientific Council recommended that ROSTE suggest courses of action that should be undertaken, at national and international levels, so that the outcome of the flow of

expertise is more beneficial to both native and receiving countries. These actions are meant to avoid the additional socio-economic problems that may appear in the course of European democratization, and thereby adversely affect East-West cooperation in all areas of human activity, particularly in science and technology.

- The participants in the Working Party recommended UNESCO in collaboration with governments and institutions concerned, as well as potentially interested European organizations (e.g. EEC, Council of Europe), at the regional and national levels, to evaluate and to monitor this new situation within Europe, and to propose concrete actions and emergency measures in order to prevent losses of intellectual and cultural potential there. In this connection, it was strongly recommended that UNESCO use its contact with major regional governmental and non-governmental organizations working in the field of science and technology, in order to mobilize financial resources to create a "Science Stability Fund for Eastern Europe." This fund would be used to maintain centres of excellence in research and training in the countries of Eastern Europe, at a level of operation that would be of mutual benefit for all of Europe. UNESCO's traditional European programmes and projects should give certain priority to the involve-ment of individual specialists and research centers from Eastern Europe.

Proceedings of the International Seminar on "Organizational Structures of Science in Europe", 1992:

- Finding: It was recognized that each country has its own historical and cultural traditions reflected in the individual organizational structures of science. Practical solutions for restructuring the S&T system in Central and East European countries should respect national socio-political, cultural, and historical context, at the same time adopting where relevant input gained from international experience. Indeed, the West is in a position to offer suggestions or recommendations to Central and East Europe with regard to the transformation of science in Europe, as a result of its

- Finding: It was very evident that there are vast variations from country to country in organizational structures. While science may be truly international, the scientific structure should not be expected to follow a single model or constrained to a single mould.
- It was recommended that ROSTE bring to the attention of UNESCO the idea of studying the individualism of nations. This is the basis of the case for 'anthropological psychoanalysis' of individual nations in the area of R&D.
- It was recommended that urgent and well coordinated efforts should be undertaken at governmental and non-governmental levels to eliminate or at least diminish the negative impact of massive intellectual migration both direct and intersectorial which could lead to serious intellectual losses in the region, especially in Central and East Europe.
- It was suggested that the international organizations and UNESCO in particular, continue their studies and monitoring of this phenomenon in order to work out recommendations addressed to governments and national and international funding organizations on this issue.
- All participants stressed the importance of international and regional co-operation in science as a necessary and desirable aspect of the present environment. Many organizations and foundations in Europe are currently undertaking tremendous efforts to aid scientific communities in Central and East Europe by providing direct financial support, organizing large-scale research projects, promoting staff mobility.

Proceedings of the International Seminar on "Brain Drain Issues in Europe", 1993:

- It was recommended that European governments should unite their efforts in working out national and regional science and technology policies based on democratic approaches to the organization and management of the R&D process.
- The main efforts should be undertaken at national levels to work out attractive stimuli for young people to join the intellectual spheres of life, in particular science and technology.

- International organizations and UNESCO in particular might be interested in arranging a "Peace Corps" that could use researchers from central and eastern European countries and university staff for research and teaching in developing countries.

Round Table on Military Conversion and Science, 1994

Defence Conversion

Military conversion or defence conversion, is taken to mean the management of change in the military and its supporting industrial base that has resulted from the problems in the current global political and economic climate. Today's military system are extremely complex and have become too expensive to maintain: as a response, governments worldwide envisage a conversion to simplified and cheaper systems. But in all systemic environments, the switching from one stable state to another will require the consumption of energy. With social system, this means the expenditure of effort and funding. Piecemeal reduction of a stable but undesirable system always results in chaos, and not stability. In this context, in the absence of specific defence conversion, military capability disintegration will ensue. In fact, what we are seeing at the moment is military contraction and not military conversion. We must consider the long term vulnerability that is a consequence of such action.

There are 3 major inter-related aspects to be dealt with 1) the maintaining of a "minimum" state-of -the art capability military readiness to deal with a politically chosen part of the threat spectrum which must be preserved; 2) the doing away with redundant capabilities and capacities; and 3) absorption of products and personnel into the general economy.

Issues to examine include science and technology, human resource dislocations, incentive strategies, socio-economic phenomena such as brain drain, the transformation of educational and scientific institutions and of culture in general. The machinery of conversion is to be driven in parallel with the new culture of peace being promoted by UNESCO.

The process of military conversion has the by-product of unemployable or unfunded and underfunded military personnel and of scientists and technologists. Strategically driven military conversion aims to minimize waste of intellectual resources and maximize the exploitation of existing technologies for civilian use.

While global war is now less likely, regional threat to security has increased and the probability of *local,* tactical wars remains unchanged or even increased by the need of ethnic and religious groups for self-protection.

The UNESCO Culture of Peace programme aims to use transdisciplinary education to teach tolerance, overcoming, resistance to change, and encouraging openness to the idea of learning to learn. Increased worldwide employment of women in science and their greater role in peace-keeping policy generation implementation and evaluation, could lead to a softening of masculine aggressive decision-making. A great deal of thought must be given to the effects of the change on future generations. We are already experiencing a disillusionment with science among school children who perceive little reward for years of effort needed to become qualified scientists. It is nevertheless clear that science is one of the most important aspects of society, and should be given stronger promotion and made more accessible to non-scientists.

Science

Within the military-industrial complex is a high proportion of the world's science and scientists. Conversion will therefore mean a new outlook for science itself as well as the absorption and redeployment of scientists. In this new science, there will be reduced R+D expenditure, which prompts the question of who is to pay for basic science.

Cost

High capital investment is required, at least in the short term, to create an efficient and stable long-term solution. It will be at least as costly as maintaining the status quo.

A few governments may benefit from military conversion by investing in dual-use technologies. In addition, some cost benefits may arise from international agreements or exchanges of commodities or capabilities. But on the whole, there will be no profit from military conversion itself. The anticipated benefits of redirecting military budgets into civilian welfare are as much a myth as the peace divided.

Timing

Medium to long term planning is essential not only for decision-making process but also bearing in mind the inertia of industry. It must be recognized that there are no "quick fixes" to military conversion—20 years of patient effort may be needed for conversion to the civilian sphere, and even then the likelihood of success is uncertain. Constant monitoring should be written into any proposal for measuring the overall success of conversion and non-conversion. Through time, it must be remembered that defence conversion is strongly context dependent.

Legislation

New legislation coupled with normative economic measures are required by individual nation states to enable them to meet their individual requirement for military conversion and science preservation, including safeguards for the protection of new technologies and attendant intellectual property rights.

Personnel and brain drain

Care must be taken to absorb discharged military and civilian personnel employed by government to minimize potential conflicts within the general employment market. Attention must be given to maintaining jobs for the employable and incentives for retraining should be established. The talented scientist should not be left adrift in the wrong environments or given cause to seek satisfaction or remuneration in undesirable situations, or to be lured away from science into more remunerative employment in the business world.

Types of conversion

Military establishments should be involved. While some three quarters of military structures can convert easily (buildings, some jobs, some equipments), the rest (laboratories and the brains of some types of science) will not convert either quickly or cheaply.

Care must be taken with the speed and degree of military conversion, achieving as nearly as possible, a workable balance between the military industrial complex and the rest of the civilian economy. Unrealistic expectations could destroy the military industrial base and produce very costly dislocation in civilian industries. This suggests that regional, continental and international joint ventures or consortia could produce less costly, more sustainable solutions.

Closing Remarks

The world's industrialized nation states are now in a post industrial, information processing, post cold war reconstruction phase and are entering the 21st century with humankind ever more dependent upon science and its many technological off springs.

The sciences and technologies they spawn help shape and define the societies that sustain them; affecting every aspect of culture, language, law, economies, generating methods of destruction and peaceful solutions to the wide ranging problems of the human condition from food and water, to energy and space exploration. But acknowledging that there are limited resources, investments in science and technology must compete with demands for resources from every segment of society.

The World Academy of Art and Science is pleased to be associated with these conferences demonstrating the finest form of scientific cooperation and is reporting the outcomes in its Newsletter to member Fellows in 55 countries.

REFERENCES

1. UNESCO-ROSTE (Regional Office for Science and Technology for Europe, 1261/A Dorsoduro, Venice, Italy 30123) 1990. Report of the Working Party on Brain Drain Issues in Europe, Lisbon, Portugal, 26-28 November 1990. I. O. Angell and V.A. Kouzminov (eds.) technical report no.3.

2. Kapitza, S. P., The Future of Russian Science and Science In Eastern Europe, a paper under preparation, Spring, 1994.

3. U. S. Congress, Congressional Budget Office, "Restructuring and Consolidating Defence Support Activities", Table 2 Department of Defence Funding by Major Program, Page 8, July, 1994.

4. UNESCO-ROSTE (Regional Office for Science and Technology for Europe, 1261/A Dorsoduro, Venice, Italy 30123) 1992. The Organizational Structures of Science, Venice, ZItally, 27-29 April 1992. Susan Biggin and Vladimir Kouzminov (eds.), technical report no. 11.

5. UNESCO-ROSTE (Regional Office for Science and Technology for Europe, 1261/A Dorsoduro, Venice, Italy 30123) 1993. Brain Drain Issues in Europe, Venice, Itally, 25-27 April 1993. Susan Biggin and Vladimir Kouzminov (eds.) technical report no. 15.

6. UNESCO-ROSTE (Regional Office for Science and Technology for Europe. 1261/A Dorsoduro, Venice, Itlay 30123) 1994. Round Table on Military Conversion and Science, Venice, Itlay, 27-29 November 1994.

15

Culture of Peace and Interrelations between Science and Power

BORIS BORISOV

First Councillor, Permanent Delegation of the Russian Federation to UNESCO

Since wars begin in the minds of men, it is in the minds of men that the defences of peace must be constructed.

These are the first words of UNESCO's Constitution, written and adopted almost fifty years ago, just after the Second World War was over.

Ever since, the United Nations Educational, Cultural and Scientific Organization, as the whole UN system, has witnessed drastic and sometimes dramatic developments in the world post war history.

Today a unique convergence of historical facts has put the abolition of war on the agenda. This certainly does not mean an end to the violence of war, it means rooting out the culture of war that has come to dominate our institutions and therefore our everyday lives.

Today, more than ever it is necessary to seek positive ways to resolve conflicts, specifically local and ethnical conflicts, by working out our behaviour and attitudes.

Today with the end of the Cold war and the dissolution of the superpower blocks it is necessary to involve everybody in the peace building process.

Today new peace-building structures are needed to help transition from a culture of war to a culture of peace.

It imposes a re-ordering of global priorities—financial, educational, scientific, cultural, social, human to tackle global problems—from social injustice to the environment that threaten our security and well-being.

In response to the challenge of peace-building, UNESCO, who has always undertaken long term actions to build the foundations of peace through its fields of competence, is to assume a new and dynamic role, aimed at encouraging rind reinforcing a culture of peace.

As Federico Mayor, UNESCO Director-General, said, "it is time to get history to lay down its arms. To teach our children the history of power, but not of knowledge, the history of war but not of culture . . . Therefore, change we must. We must learn to pay the price of peace just as we had to pay the price of war. We shall have to set fresh priorities".

It is, therefore, no surprise that UNESCO's Culture of Peace Programme puts so much emphasis on the ability of each individual, each community, from the grass roots up, to build and enhance peace. What is even more important is to persude policy makers rind leaders of states to adopt the attitude of culture of peace.

It is no surprise that UNESCO has been designated as the leading UN agency to implement the programme of the International Year of Tolerance proclaimed by UN for 1995.

One of the documents that the Executive Board examined at the 145th session in October-November 1994 was entitled: "The culture of peace programme:" from national programmes to a project of global scope. The very title speaks of the necessity to start from a given country. It supposes that any process becomes the object of national policy only if the state is interested in it.

If this is the case, the state should formulate an objective. A system of measures and activities planned and implemented, represent the state should formulate an objective. A system of measures and activities planned and implemented, represent the state policy towards this process.

Take the concrete case of Russia, in particular the actual state policy towards science.

Let us start from positive results. Undoubtedly since the years of perestroika science has become more open and democratic. The state has removed all artificial ideological and administrative obstacles which seriously hindered international scientific cooperation.

At the same time in the changing social and economic formation science in Russia has faced dramatic difficulties, which could be overpassed only with a resolute and active support of the state and society in general.

Economic and social difficulties could be overcome. We have examples in history when the recession of production was replaced by quick progress—take as an example postwar Germany, Japan and quite recently China and Chile. With more difficulty but could be overcome demographic problems.

However, destruction of science, if it reaches a critical level, is becoming irreversible.

At the beginning of the twenties Germany, in spite of the lost war and of enormous economic difficulties, still had the best basic science in the world due to a well founded governmental policy. In fact the German government was wise enough to create a system of foundations (to cite German foundation of support of poor professors), and thus succeeded to keep the best scientific brains in the country. And only when, with arrival of A. Hittler, G. Himmler was appointed responsible for science in the thirties, Germany lost best scientists and consequently had been ruined even earlier than Germany was ruined itself.

Today's prospering Germany is making important efforts to restore its basic science, but the process is advancing slowly. It is known that to create a national scientific school a country should have two or three generations.

Therefore, science even to a greater extent than art is based on a tradition and on a severe professional school. In each discipline a number of leading scientists is extremely limited and could be easily counted. Their loss would lead to degradation of scientific school in different disciplines. A similar danger exists today in Russia.

Science in Russia was developed in its own way and mainly with the help of its own resources. By the beginning of the twentieth century Russian Fundamental Science gained recognition in the world.

It is important to note that Russian science in spite of many difficulties and losses (emigration, arrests, ideological cleanings, etc.) has succeeded to rise during the post revolutionary period and the time of Stalin dictature.

The rise of Russian science coincides with the period of Khrouschev when its rating was extremely high in the country and in the world. It was prestigious for sons of party leaders to choose scientific careers. The sixties were the period of "lyrics and physicists".

The situation changed during what we call "stagnation period", under Brezhnev's rule, when strategic decisions of the development of science were taken by non competent administrators. At this period we witnessed the creation of many secret scientific institutions (so called "boxes") with numerous scientific staff but with very low input. Practically all of these boxes were oriented towards research in one way or another linked with military utilization.

It is sufficient to say that seventy per cent of the total budget of the country went to military purposes at that time.

On the other hand there was a state policy under Brezhnev to cover the whole spectre of sciences to show to the world that we had leading schools in all branches of science. Instead of concentrating on major disciplines there was evident waste of money, scientist's energy and output without visible results.

That was the reason why scientific and technical revolution in the western countries occurred in the late seventies and in the eighties left the Soviet Union scientifically and economically far behind.

At the same time I must stress that science has become one of the most active social detonators which led the country to the collapse of the communist system and to the democratic revolution of 1991. Let us remember the role of Russian scientists in opposition to the official regime, just to cite academicians Pyotr Kapitsa and Andrei Sakharov.

To sum up, many difficulties we experience now are in many respects connected with military oriented science and its extremely heavy burden to the national economy and with the abandon of so called "defensive conception", which swallowed enormous financial and human resources.

Where are we now? I consider that after a sort of "catastrophism" to use the expression of Russian Ambassador to France Academician Ryzhov, a depressive feeling which was characteristic for the years 1991-1993 not only for simple citizen but also for many politicians and specially scientists, we are coming now to the understanding of the necessity of psychological stabilization. To achieve the stabilization it is absolutely vital to launch a national programme of culture of peace.

I think it is symptomatic that the main theme during the meeting of Mr. Mayor, Director General of UNESCO with President B. Eltsin was culture of peace in the minds of men. As President B. Eltsin stated, Russia is willing to cooperate in the development of the Programme "Culture of Peace". Russia is interested in the creation of a national programme, which would include an all embracing system of education of the entire population for peace democracy and human rights, which, I believe, should include an important science component.

All this gives us an optimistic view for the future.

The Meaning of Science

Science is regarded by everyone as one of the most fulfilling activities for both individuals and society. The knowledge "discovered" by the scientist is an immediate addition to humanity's heritage of knowledge and becomes a symbol of universality.

At the same time the history of science reveals the relativity of each discovery, so that it can be considered as a sort of antidote to all forms of "fundamentalism".

If we consider science from a philosophical aspect we should certainly remember that scientific knowledge does not constitute truth, even though one scientist's discovery may become a universal law but is only a milestone in the continuous process of trials and errors, regulation and further experimentation. The humility of science is in no way a contradiction of its ambition for progress.

From a point of view of ethics, science which has become increasingly applied in practice, is in danger of being used as an instrument of domination, an instrument of power over things and what is much more important of people, namely as an instrument of people's death.

And finally from geopolitical point, science becomes increasingly complex and expensive and we look into the other side of the coin, science becomes less and less accessible to those deprived of resources. The "knowledge gap" is constantly widening between major scientific centres and less developed countries (Africa, South America, some countries in Asia).

If we consider the role of science with regard to cultures and societies we may certainly admit that science is synonymous with modernity and is a source of material and symbolic power.

We may also recognize that science opens up great prospects for development. At the same time science must preserve a balance between the cultural past and the unpredictable future. If imported, science runs the risk of being rejected. Therefore, the perception of the role of science and scientists is decisive for the establishment and development of a scientific culture and for the teaching of science.

16

Marriage between Information Technology and Genetic Engineering

CARL-GORAN HEDEN
Biofocus Foundation Stockholm

Introduction

When talking about science as a source of power, it is important to remember that research is the sum of collective endeavours which are governed by rules of behaviour that go a long way towards explaining the unique power of science for finding "truth".

Those values include independence and originality, often expressed in dissent, and they thrive on free thought, enquiry, speech and publication. It has been noted that those values are also characteristic of democracy (Bronowski, 1967), and this of course gives the scientist an important function as a role model. In my view this is particularly true in egalitarian and secular societies, where there is little fear left, either for the hard hand of a dictator or for punishment in hell, and where rewards in heaven no longer seem to be particularly strong incentives. When, in areas like "Big-time Biology", money then takes over as the prime incentive an infectious erosion of the basic values might easily occur (Beardsley, 1994).

As a role model a scientist may exercise considerable power, for instance by playing an active part in organizations and commissions which reflect links between knowledge and responsibility. However, responsibility must of course be expressed in action, and this often requires time consuming transdisciplinary outlooks, which easily interfere with the demand for excellence which underlies the competitive element in all scientific work.

However, it is only when research become superficial and opportunistic, or when "competition ceases to be a means, but acquires the status of an universal credo, an ideology" (Petrella, 1991), that society as a whole will suffer. From this point of view, the dramatic and very rapid advances in biotechnology provide much food for thought, because competition in this field leaves little time for its laboratory champions to participate actively in badly needed trans-disciplinary dialogues. In my view, the best way to achieve this is to make effective use of information technology (Hidden, 1994a).

On the basis of five years of experience as director of the Biofocus Foundation I have come to the conclusion that the democratic character of the "civil society" provides the backbone for mechanisms that can both produce generally agreed action-plans and neutralize excessive competition within and between nations. In this paper I will underline that those mechanisms, and particularly electronic networking, should now be fully utilized as a means to reduce the gaps between the "haves" and the "have nots".

In the context of the growing importance of economy of scope, and of employment generation, I will then also discuss the potential for use, or misuse, of the powers released by the marriage between biotechnology and information technology. After stressing the potential of computer conferening as a means to stimulate trans-disciplinary dialogues, I will finally make some observations on the power of visions, generated by scientists and engineers.

The Power of the Civil Society

The civil society is composed of global networks of concerned individuals, non-governmental organizations, academies and foundations, as well as of powerful multinational enterprises which are now the subject of considerable pressure from various professional groups that are also components of the civil society. The struggle for influence is natural, since the firm has become the main "global" actor for producing objects and technology and this of course gives it a key role for generating wealth and employment, and consequently also for producing individual and collective well-being.

This role of the business community is not very well captured by world trade statistics, because this does not reflect its numerous, often electronic, linkages (currency exchanges, partnerships, equity agreements, cross-licensing, franching, joint ventures and R&D-programs) which give the business world its power and flexibility. As noted by the UN Center for Transnational Corporations, this flexibility is well illustrated by the fact that one-third of world trade is represented by transactions among subsidiaries of a firm.

In this "nebulosa" of influences, ad hoc groups are often formed in order to address general issues like global governance (Cleveland, 1993, Lisbon Group 1993) or sustainability (Schmidheiny, 1992), and they normally produce very significant reports that add a sense of urgency to the points raised at various UN-conferences and in over-views like "Earth with Balance" (Al Gore, 1992) and "The First Global Revolution" (King and Schneider, 1991). The recommendations may have global aims (Brown *et al.* 1991) or more regional targets such as the Baltic rim countries (Heden, 1992), or they can have a thrust towards key actors like the "Triad" (= North America, Western Europe, Japan and SE Asia).

In an extensively documented report entitled "Limits to Competition", 19 individuals from the last group of countries has for instance recently suggested that the Triade should take the lead in a major initiative (Lisbon Group 1993). They expressed this in the form of four "global contracts" which can serve as a reminder of the magnitude of the tasks which mankind now faces: 1. providing, within the next 25 years, the essential means of survival and development to some 2 billion people, 2. ensuring that Agenda 21 (Rio Summit, 1992) is implemented, 3. developing a new generation of economic, financial, political and military mechanisms as well as institutions designed as an accountable form of global economic governance, and 4. fighting all forms of absolutism and integrism, while promoting all froms of dialogue among different cultures.

The civil society has also produced a number of reports from independent commissions chaired by prominent politicians like Brandt, Palme, Brundtland and Nyerere. They demonstrate that the predicament of Mankind is well understood at the pinnacles of power. However, no report has had such an operational thrust as the most recent one "Uncommon Opportunities" which has just been issued by the International Commission on Peace and Food (ICPF). It is also the first commission report which has been chaired by a scientist (Swaminathan, 1994).

This report notes that a consciousness of One World is now emerging above the din of individualistic and nationalistic self-interest, and the Commission interprets this to mean that we have now arrived at a great creative moment, when the political leadership has a unique opportunity to launch an effort to promote jobled economic growth, based on the principles of ecology and equity.

Genetic Engineering—A Subject for Transdisciplinary Dialogues

The need for transdisciplinary dialogues about the dilemmas caused by the applications of scientific knowledge is nowhere more obvious than in the case of biotechnology and genetic engineering. On the one hand its tools are essential for the building of an equitable and sustainable society, with food for everyone and free from such diseases as AIDS and Cancer. On the other hand the same tools can also further deepen the gaps between the rich and the poor.

Future historians may well decide that the current myopic concentration of economic power in biotechnology (Beardsley, 1994) may be one of the factors which mark a bifurcation point between two roads—one leading to starvation, mass migrations and social conflicts, and the other to a redirection of economic and human resources towards the development of ecotechnologies that will gradually stablize the global situation by introducing the "unreached" (landless farmers, poor women and unemployed youth) to a sustainable market economy. However, the trends of strategic alliances in biotechnology indicate that industry has not yet embarked on the second road, in spite of many good intentions (Schmidheiny, 1992). Between 1980 and 1989 there were 846 biotechnology alliances involving developed economies, but only 0.1 per cent of those were between Triad-firms and developing countries (Freeman and Hagedom, 1992).

As recently pointed out by Jessica Mathews, the mapping of the human genome—"a towering achievement" as she calls it—might quickly become a Pyrrhic victory if a broad public conversation is not launched very soon. Only in that way can we lay the foundation for the new institutions, law and regulations, as well as for training the large body of genetic councellors that will be needed to guide the applications of the new knowledge wisely or even safely (Mathews, 1994).

The reason for such a major effort is the challenges which the detailed knowledge about the human genome poses to personal values, religious beliefs and public policy. We must, for instance, now address the question of how much genetic screening that an employer, an insurance company or a future spouse can demand from an individual. And does he really want to know if he, or his unborn child, is likely to become mentally handicapped or to die young or in pain, simply because the cost for the only available medical intervention is economically prohibitive?

No doubt, science will come up with new forms of therapy, but Mathews points out that, in some cases, mass screening can be very expensive. An example is cystic fibrosis, where avoiding one death has been estimated to cost around US$ 22 million. Also in vitro fertilization, as a means to ensure that a parent does not pass along a dangerous gene, is so costly that it is hard to visualize very wide-spread use. However, in a way this is fortunate because—as our knowledge about the genetic basis for "desirable' traits, like intellectual capacity and longevity, grows—widespread applications might lead to social and demographic consequences which are just as unacceptable as the use of biological weapons designed on the basis of knowledge about genes that determine ethnic differences. Incidentally, biological warfare happens to be a field where governments, as indicated by Article X in the Biological Weapons Convention, have committed themselves to a redeployment effort. However, this still remains to be seem (Zilinskas and Hedén, 1991).

Mathews reminds her readers that, since much of the research on screening tests is done in for-profit laboratories, there is little time to think about a measured response, for instance about the psychological and legal consequences of 'false positive' tests:

> "Each new bit of genetic information will be rushed—is already being rushed—into the commercial medical marketplace. Within weeks of the discovery of the colon cancer gene, 10 companies had bought the rights to develop a screening test for it—In just the last year, genes have been identified that confer varying degrees of predisposition to breast, uterine and ovarian cancers as well as to osteoporosis and male homosexuality".

Fortunately, the basis for a broad public debate about matters such as those mentioned, is, however now emerging in the form of papers (medical, legal ethical and social implication of genetic engineering), which have been solicited within the framework of the "Human Genome Project". This whole effort is actually a good example of the powers of science, when its resources are well coordinated. However, it can also serve as a reminder about the responsibility of scientists for bringing about an internationally balanced dialogue involving also poor countries outside the mainstream of molecular genetics.

Re-engineering and Biotechnology

Developing countries also need help to monitor the developments in modern agriculture, since this is an area that will not escape the "re-engineering" of the industrialized world. "Re-engineering" is a term which not only encompasses just-in-time inventory control by means of data processing, but also the reorganization of human resources with the help of empowerment arrangements, work forces, outsourcing etc.

Since re-engineering normally involves job losses, it fuels a lively debate about job-sharing arrangements, reduced working hours, life-long training and other ideas that definitely are of global significance. As the Lisbon Group puts it (1993): "The issue is how to balance process innovation (that is rather job-saving) and product innovation (that is rather job—creating)". However, as the Lisbon Group also notes, there is also an environmental side to the paradigm shift that we now face:

> "It is physically no longer possible to externalize the environmental costs and damages outside the production process, and allow them to be borne by nature and future generations. One has to redesign the industrial processes and products in order to internalize such costs and damages within the production and consumption process."

This is a very tall order indeed, and it provides a special challenge for those bio-engineers who can help to develop the ecotechnologies that will be needed by future human settlements. Here, "industrial clustering" seems to be the logical answer to recycling for emission control (Pauli, 1994), but I fear that such rearrangements call for a new dimension in international cooperation, where the technology—based arrogance of the West must be tempered with some of the ancient values that have survived modernization in the East.

This might be regarded as the first acid test which faces the world's democracies during 1995: the UN Year of Tolerance.

Agricultural Biotechnology—Uncommon Opportunities and Problems

One of the problems which plague the World's agricultural system is that it is supply-driven, which means seasonal storage and transport problems, as well as plantation economies which are vulnerable both to climate stresses and to depressed prices during periods of glut. However, some experts feel that we might well be on the verge of a second Green Revolution. This might well have both ecologically positive and economically negative effects.

Micropropagation for instance provides developing countries with the basis for exploiting their biological diversity through the export of flowers and other plants that can be guaranteed to be free from diseases and pests. However, on the other hand, concern about pesticide residues and recent advances in controlled environment agriculture (CEA), coupled with biological control methods, might also rob those countries of some of the advantages which a favourable climate and cheap labour now gives them.

Since genetic diversity and photosynthetic potential are important resources for many poor countries, the Biofocus Foundation, which was created in 1989 to stimulate entrepreneurship and indigenous creativity in such countries, early focused attention on CEA (Opici, 1994), as a means to save water and to find cheap ways to optimize cultivation conditions.

Those aspects provided arguments for stimulating poor countries to pay close attention to a field which they ought to monitor closely in order to brace for a possible "technical decoupling" that might prove to be just as negative as economic ones, like farm subsidies and non-tariff barriers. The impact on sugar producing countries of high-fructose industrial sweeteners produced from corn starch via enzyme engineering, and the current advances in the biotechnological modification of vegetable oils and fats, might serve as a memento.

In 1991 the industrial nations spent more than US$ 180 bill. on agricultural subsidies to protect their farmers, and it has been noted that this corresponds to three times the total world overseas development assistance (Swaminathan, 1994). However, as a consequence of the GATT-negotiations North American and Western European countries have agreed to cut agricultural subsidies by one-third before 2005, and this is expected to give developing countries a US$ 20-60 bill. share in the boost which this agreement will give to the export of agricultural products and processed foods.

However, no similar share in the expected gains from agricultural biotechnology can be foreseen. Rather, agricultural decoupling might be accelerated by the use of plant genetics, artificial seeds and new plant tissue culture methods. Such developments might for instance reach the stage when large-scale production of plant organs will become profitable in rich countries. After all, plants are vulnerable, and their care requires much labour. Also they are certainly more difficult to transport than the basic ingredients of tissue culture media which is sugar and water. Since only a fraction of the fertilizers, which are normally said in agriculture, end up in commercil products, environmental considerations, based on energy analysis (carbon dioxide and nitrogen fixation, mining, transport and waste management), might also produce arguments for high-tech decentralized production and recycling systems.

Citing the work of Brent Tisserat from Pasadena, who has successfully propagated orange juice vescicles or sacs in culture, Truett-Andersson has suggested that factories for turning out orange juice, tomato sauce and fruit jellies might actually be closer to being realized than an AIDS vaccine (Truett-Anderson, 1990). Such developments, and the possibility to produce also starches, cotton fibers and cherry tissue in culture, has stimulated strategic planners, like Martin Rogoff and Stephen Rowlins, at the US Agricultural Research Service, to look at the food production system as, whole. This for instance gives large-scale cultivation of hardy trees and bushes a new dimension, since they might become important chemical feedstock in the face of conceivable events such as a cut-off fossil-fuel supplies or desertification of America's "bread-basket".

Thinking along those lines obviously makes the development of environmentally friendly fractionation methods for lignocellulosic materials a high priority target for research. Its importance, particularly for countries with an abundance of bagasse, actually explains why the Biofocus Foundation has given the Tigney Technology steam decompression technique the same attention as the CEA-field (delong and Klyosov, 1994). After all, it seems likely that the variety of products that could be derived from the total utilization of the lignin, hemicellulose and cellulose in bagasse (lignin-based adhesives, plastics and dyes, xylitol, industiral alcohol, microcrystalline cellulose and cellulose acetate etc.) would produce more jobs than bagasse used as an energy source.

The Unemployment Challenge

Among various agricultural residues bagasse is particularly interesting, both because it accumulates in facilities that are suitable for steam-explosion upgrading to chemical and microbiological feedstocks, and also because the amounts available are both very large and expected to increase. In fact, the sugar consumption in developing countries is currently less than half the average of industrial nations.

In India, ICPF points out that the sugar consumption is projected to generate a demand for a 100 per cent increase in sugar cane production, and this calls for the establishment of 300-400 new sugar mills and the creation of 3 to 4 million new jobs in that industry alone. World-wide the increasing sugar consumption could generate tens of millions of additional jobs (Swarminathan, 1994).

The ICPF also notes that many other agricultural sectors in India will need labour. The production of fruits and vegetables must for instance double within the next decade, and many East-Asian countries have, in fact, pointed the way by demonstrating that crop-intensive and labor-intensive agricultural methods can make it possible to achieve greatly increased levels of employment and productivity. It is for instance noted that advanced methods for micronutrient management can double or quadruple fruit and vegetable yields in most developing countries. In addition, imitation of the intensive aquaculture methods, which are common in Taiwan and Singapore, might rase the average fish yields in South Asian, African and Latin American countries 25-fold. In "Uncommom Opportunities" it is also noted that Thailand, which still employs 70 per cent of its workforce in agriculture, has attained high rates of production and rural employment through diversification from the cultivation of rice and rubber to high-value crops and agro-based industries (Swaminathan, 1994).

Land reforms seem to be a key requirement for success, even if some observers feel that the self-reliant puritan ethic in the non-Christian countries of the Far East also plays a very significant role (Macrae, 1993). In Taiwan and South Korea the incentives associated with land reforms not only led to dramatic increases in the number of owner cultivators, but they also stimulated diversity, improved productivity and created many new jobs in the post harvest and processing sectors—in the case of Taiwan 100.000.

However, PR China has provided the most dramatic demonstration of what determination can achieve. Here no less than 101 million jobs were created between 1985 and 1991, 70 per cent in township and village enterprises, nearly half of them privately owned.

Such enterprises offer an attractive alternative for preserving the small-scale decentralized pattern of production which is still common in developing countries. They may also play an important role in paving the way for future technology-intensive small firms which would be flexible in meeting specific customer demands and capable of generating more skilled and better paying jobs. I am of the opinion that such firms are also of great importance for the industrialized world, since this now faces demographic and employment problems which force it to explore if the seducing "economy of scale"- philosophy might perhaps not be replaced by an "economy of scope"- approach (Hedén, 1994b).

I have not been able to find a definition of the latter concept, but since it is important for my view on genetic engineering and modern biotechnology as catalysts for moves towards a zero-emission clustering of industrial activities (Pauli, 1994), I have tried to make my own definition. I started out by studying Webster's unabridged dictionary, which states that the word SCOPE comes from the greek "SCOPOS" which means "a watcher" or "aim" ("the range within which an activity displays itself—room or opportunity for free outlook, aim or action—that at which one aims or to which the mind directs its view"). This lead me to the following definition and to a related view on the economy of scale.

Economy of scope: A purpose is achieved via a long-range synergistic design of individually targeted events.

Economy of scale: A purpose is achieved by basically shortsighted but coordinated mass events.

Just as informal private service enterprises in commerce, food catering repair and transport have shown an impressive growth potential, so innovative agri-business ventures no doubt represent a large, often untapped, resource (flowers, processed fruits and vegetables, mushroom cultivation, agriculture, production of hybrid seeds and microbial starter cultures, biological nitrogen fixation, food and beverage fermentation, bioremediation etc. as well as fresh and salt water aquaculture).

Economic liberalization actually opens a door to a learning process which can pave the way for a democratic infrastructure where private enterprise works with small producers in a wide range of agro-industries. Such efforts could in fact play a very important role by combining the social benefits of small holdings with the economies and masrketing expertise of corporate management. Since slightly more than half of the world's workforce is still engaged in agriculture, it is easy to accept such ICPF-arguments for an agro-industrial road to development, particularly since almost a third of this cadre is women, for whom improved food processing, nutrition, hygiene and child health might seem to be more important goals than tribal wars and ethnic cleansing.

The second acid test for the world's democracies is to give priority to the development of technologies which will help to meet goals such as those just mentioned.

Technology Transfer

ICPF has noted that wherever land reforms have resulted in the division of farms into small parcels, farmers need to be supported by well-organized services, particularly for post-harvest handling, provided either by companies or cooperatives. This pinpoints both a political target and a challenge for the world's scientists and engineers.

The ICFP also notes that the world possesses the technology, resources and organizational abilities needed to eradicate poverty from the globe. However, transfer of technology requires that the firms in developing countries discover what is available, which is certainly not easy. Consequently, the Biofoucs Foundation arguments for the need of an "honest broker' in biotechnology (a "Biofoucs Corporation", cf. Fig.1), which was also reflected in the discussion about a Biotechnology Development Corporation at the Rio Summit, runs parallel to ICPF's observation:

> "The process of identifying and commercially transferring technology can be vastly simplified and accelerated by the establishment of international technology transfer corporations, sponsored by UN agencies such as UNESCO and UNIDO, specializing in all the major fields of technology. These corporations should be operated on a commercial basis, though governments of developing countries could become shareholders in order to promote their formation. Each corporation could undertake a detailed study of available technologies in its field

and offer to assist corporate customers in developing countries in selecting the most appropriate technology to meet their needs. The corporations could also acquire the rights to important technologies with large-scale applications and then market them widely" (Swaminathan, 1994).

Activities such as the small-scale agro-industrial activities that were mentioned above might become significant catalysts for economic development, and they should, in my view, be accelerated by means of innovative management techniques such as for instance the Biofocus Foundátion's "Develease"-concept (Hedén 1994a). This combines leasing, as a means to provide the necessary hardward (payment in the form of product!), with franchising as a mechanism for on-the-job training in environmental management and quality control.

An important goal of this approach is to stimulate entrepreneurship by the establishment of small enterprises based on three ground rules: 1. the firm must be owned to at least 50 per cent by the locals, 2. new processes, developed on the basis of international cooperation, should be patented, but the licence fee must be based on the GNP/capita in the country where the industrial property right is exercised, and 3. 10 per cent of the profits, after tax, should be deposited in a local fund aimed at stimulating new ventures. Those are stipulations that have been accepted by the firms which hold the rights to technologies which the Biofocus Foundation has pin-pointed for special study.

The basic consideration of the approach, is of course that jobs, in poor as well, in rich countries, are created by our innate human resourcefulness and ingenuity, expressed in invention, innovation and social imitation. The ultimate determinant for the number and quality of jobs in the future will in fact not be physical or even financial constraints, but rather 'science, technology, values and social organization—in word, the human imagination' (Cleveland, 1989).

"Electronic Zooming" as a Means to Pinpoint Significant Ecotechnologies"

The developments in any high-tech field depends on synergistic interactions between different sciences. Our everyday life for instance gives a multitude of examples of how solid state physics has interacted with many other sciences to yield the communication technologies, information management and process control systems on which we all depend. A modern laboratory devoted to molecular biology is also full of reminders about the feedback links which exist between scientific discoveries and the development of research tools. The breakthroughs in genetic engineering, which we have seen in the last twenty years, are for instance the fruits of a very successful marriage with information technology; on-line accessible aminoacid -, DNA - and vector databases, numerical taxonomy and culture collections, computerized analytical systems etc.

Biotechnology is a word which covers a large number of approaches and techniques which have a profound influence on agriculture, industrial practices as well as on plant, animal and human health. Modern bio-technology is based on our vastly improved understanding of evolution, human ecology and biological diversity, but in order to translate this knowledge into planning for sustainable human settlements, a new class of ecologically oriented technologies—ecotechnologies—is now emerging as a subset in the large family of biotechnologies.

Since half of the world's population lives in cities, which also cause much of its environmental problems (Hedén, 1994c), the planning of future human settlements seems destined to become a focal point for many of the major UN conferences that will take place in the next few years. In 1995 there is the Social Summit in Copenhagen and the UN 50 Year Anniversary in San Franscisco, and in 1996 Habitat II takes place in Istanbul.

However, such intergovernmental activities hardly provide an optimal setting for the selection of defined targets for international cooperation in biotechnology. This presupposes an efficient interaction between specialists who normally move only in the restricted orbits of their specialized congresses and symposia.

Very early in its development the Biofocus Foundation gave special attention to coastal biotechnology with the aim of pinpointing efforts that might help to alleviate some of the negative consequences that are seen in dense human settlements. As a consequence, the Foundation started to experiment with methods that would make it possible to "pick the brains" of its 200 people strong panel of experts which are spread all over the world. This led to the use of computer conferencing in a "zooming mode" involving the various transdisciplinary groups. They started out by discussing fairly general themes which were then gradually narrowed down around topics like CEA and bagasse utilization, where it seemed likely that entrepreneurial activities might be fostered.

The computer conferences activities were carried out in close cooperation with UNESCO's Microbiological Resource Center (MIRCEN) in Stockholm (Foo, 1994), and they concentrated on areas like biological nitrogen fixation and lactic acid fermentations (Foo, 1993) that obviously fitted the Develease- approach mentioned earlier.

In 1993, I visited Madras both to discuss a project for translating the Biofoucs Foundation's interest in cross-flow microfiltration (Martin 1991) as a catalyst for entrepreneurial activities, with the head of the Biotechnology Center at Anna University, professor K. Jayaraman, and also in order to participate in a conference organized by M.S. Swaminathan. At that conference I touched upon the Foundation's communication experiences (Hedén, 1993), and I also had occasion to meet the Minister for Science and Technology and a former Agricultural Minister from PR China. We agreed that both industrialized and developing countries might gain much from an exchange of experiences with various recycling methods, and this led to an agreement to study the feasibility of an electronic zooming effort.

This started on Ist January 1994 in the form of a computer conference entitled "Ecotechnologies for Sustainable Development" (ECOTECH 94). This was managed by the director of MIRCEN/Stockholm, E.L. Foo in cooperation with the head of the Special Committee for Sustainable Development of the Chinese Society of Science and Technology for Social Developments, Li Wenhua. Via a process involving also inputs from face-to face meetings in France and Australia this eventually led to a string of field trips in China which provided material for a regional conference in Beijing (Fig. 2). This was concluded with a three hour video-dialogue between experts from the Chinese Academies, meeting in Beijing, and representatives of Engineering Academies, meeting in Stockholm to celebrate the 75 year Anniversary of the Royal Swedish Academy of Engineering Sciences. This session was entitled "Ecotechnologies for Sustainable Villages and Cities", and it led to the establishment of a formal "Network for International Education and Research in Ecotechnology". Thanks to the ECOTECH 94 preparations this now has an outreach to several thousand people.

It can safely be stated that this whole effort would not have been possible without a systematic utilization of Internet lists and the latest digital technology for two-way video-conferencing (ISDN—first satellite link Paris-Hong Kong second satellite link Hong Kong-Beijing).

The possibility to establish e-mail communication even with the most remote locations in developing countries, with the aid of portable transceivers using low level polar orbiters, means that no significant actor needs to feel that technical barriers make him an outsider to any global biotechnology dialogue (Clements, 1993).

The barriers to easy communication left are financial, but they are so miniscule, in relation to overseas development assistance, that their fate can be regarded as a third acid test for the world's democracies.

The Power of Visions as Signposts for Democracy

Particularly in poor countries there is a need for technology to improve productivity, but there is also a need for organizational know-how that can help to establish effective administrative and political systems. But above all, there is a need for a new vision, a new perspective and a new attitude to "growth", because as the Secretary General of the UN has put it: "growth which is not accompanied by the improvement of the social fabric of society will be only a hollow shell" (Boutros-Ghali, 1994).

This is why scientists and engineers must assume some of the responsibility for generating "operational visions" that can help nations to "navigate between technocratic illusions and theocratic hopes" (Lisbon Group, 1993). Not least must this involve the economists who obviously need to forge new tools, like an improved "Human Development Index" (Parikh, 1994) and a useful "Sustainability Index" (Moser, 1994, Saleth, 1994) in order to develop a long-range economy of scope.

The type and magnitude of the initiatives which are now needed are comparable to President Roosevelt's New Deal during the Great Depression, to the Indian government's decision to achieve self-sufficiency in food grains by launching the Green Revolution, and to Mikhail Gorbachev's initiatives to end the Cold War and to transform Soviet society. Vice President Al Gore's proposal for a Global Marshall Plan falls in the same category (Al Gore, 1992) as does also the Spark-programme in China and the Prosperity 2000 Plan for creating jobs in India. The latter was proposed in 1991 by ICPF, and it is now implemented by "the Small Farmer's Agribusiness Consortium" as part of the Government's Eight Five Year Plan.

In this paper the word paradigm shift has been used, and I have also echoed the view expressed by ICPF that we are at a bifurcation point, when the choice is between two roads: one leading to misery and confrontations and the other to a more mature civilization. And "our future is not a question of fate, it is a question of choice".

The first road, with totalitarian governance in an environmentally decaying consumer society, is certainly not new to utopists, and it was actually described quite vividly in a recently discovered manuscript to a book by Jules Verne. He wrote it in 1863, at the age of 35, in order to sketch a crowded and overindustrialized Paris in the 20th Century (Hedlund and Frangsmyr, 1994). However, it is interesting to note that the same author in a later book ("Begum's 500 millions", 1879) not only talks about an overexploited society run by a dictator, but also about a "green" and democratic alternative, where people live in houses with their own gardens, and with all the chimneys connected to a master exhaust pipe in order to reduce air pollution.

However, Jules Verne's technical utopia of 1863, with driver-less trains, electrically illuminated streets and fax machines, needed 100 years to emerge as a reality. Now the speed with which technical inventions emerge leaves the social innovations that are needed for adaptation far behind. Scientists and engineers working at the frontier of discovery must obviously make up for this by taking the time it takes to paint visions that will stimulate political dialogues about questions, rather than debates about answers.

A redeployment of military resources towards ecotechnologies for sustainable development would seem like a good starting point where "Science Cities" in the industrialized could provide very helpful signposts. I have argued for such a concentration of effort in the Stockholm area, and I have then been fortunate in being able to use Italy as an example. The Science City in Trieste, with its aim to combine national interests with support to developing countries (The Third World Academy for Science and the International Center for Genetic Engineering and Biotechnology—ICGEB etc.) should indeed be replicated in many parts of the world.

This is the fourth acid test for the world's democracies, which might well start out by giving their wholehearted support to ICGEB.

REFERENCES

Beardsley, T. "Big-Time Biology'. Scientific American, pp.72-79. Nov. 1994.

Boutros-Ghali, B. "Mesage from the UN Secretary General" In Uncommon Opportunities", Ed. M.S. Swaminathan, Zed Books, London and New Jersey, 1994.

Bronowski, J. in The Sciences, 7/67. Nov./Dec. 1967.

Brown, L. Flavin, C, and Postel, S. "Saving the Planet". W.W. Northon, New York, 1991.

Clements, C. Paper presented at Pugwash meeting 193: Workshop on "Brain-drain and International Cooperation" Stockholm, Febr. 11-13, 1993 (also newsletters: Healtnet News, Satellite, 126 Rogers St., Cambridge, MA.02142 USA), 1993.

Cleveland, H. "The Knowledge Executive, Leadership in an Information Society". E.P. Dutton, New York, 1989.

Cleveland, H. "The Birth of a New World—an open moment for international leadership". Jossey—Bass Publ. San Francisco, 1993.

DeLong, E.A. and Klyosov, A, "On a novel ecologically safe technology of producing cellulose and of the biotechnology of its conversion into useful products". Paper presented for the ECOTECH 94 Computer Conference. Tigney Technology Inc. 439-22560 Wye Road, Sherwood Park, Edmonton, Alb. T8A 4T6, Canada.

Foo, E.L. "Use of electronic mail in ECOTECH 94". Abstracts etc. from Asian Regional Conference on Ecotechnology for Sustainable Development", Beijing ct 19-26 1994.

Foo, E.L., Griffin, H. G. Mollby, R. and Heden, C. G. "The Lactic Acid Bacteria". Proc. I: st Lactic Acid Bacteria Computer Conference, Horizon Scientific Press, 1993.

Freeman, C., and Hagedorn, J. "Globalization of Technology". Report for the FAST-programme, EC, p. 41, June 1992.

Goe A. "Earth with Balance-Forging a New Common Purpose", Earthscan Publ. Ltd. London, 1992.

Hedén, C. G. "What's next on the rim". Paper presented at the Club of Rome Meeting, Hannover, 1992.

Hedén, C. G. Bioinformatics for Development", pp. 4-9 in "Reaching the Unreached—Information Technology". A Dialogue edited by M.S. Swaminathan, McMillan India, 1993.

Hedén, C. G."Incentives, Integration and International Support", pp. 246-254 in "Ecotechnology and Rural Development", Ed. M.S. Swaminathan, McMillan India 1994a.

Hedén, C. G. "Introduction to video-dialogue, Stockholm-Bbeijing, October 26, 1994. Biofocus Foundation, Drottninggatan 120, Stockholm, 11360 Sweden, 1994b.

Hedén, C.G. "The Metabolism of Cities", Paperpresented at video-dialogue, Stockholm-Beijing, October 1994. Biofoucs Foundation, Drottninggatan 12, Stockholm, 11360 Sweden, 1994c.

Hedlund, B. and Frangsmyr, T. Discussion about Jules Verne on Swedish Radio, Nov. 20th, 1994.

Jonas, H. "Das Prinzip Verantwortung. Versuch einer Ethik fur die technologische Zivilisation". Insel, Frankfurt, 1985.

King, A. and B. Schneider, "The First Global Revolution", A Report from the Council of the Club of Rome. Siman and Schuster, London, 1991.

Lisbon Group, "Limits to Competition". Preliminary Report 1993. Gulbenkian Foundation, Lisbon, Portugal.

Martin, I. "Cory puts the squeeze on heavy metals", Industrial Waste Management, Febr. 1991, Description of cross flow microfiltration system (Exxflow Ltd. 11 Charles Street, London, WIX 7HB, U.K.)

Mathews, J. "Here Comes a Confused New World of Gene Shopping". Article for The Washington Post reporduced in The International Herald Tribune, November 9th, 1994.

Moser, A., "Ecosustainability", p. 280-286 in "Ecotechnology and Rural Development", Ed. M.S. Swaminathan, McMillan India, 1994.

Opici, M. A., "Un tetto dinamico di luce e d'energia". Description of O.J. Gunnarshaug's "Climate shell", Trondheim, Norway, No.3. 1994.

Parikh, K.S. "Human Development Index", pp. 274-280 in "Ecotechnology and Rural Development". Ed. M.S. Swaminathan, Mcmillan India, 1994.

Pauli, G. "The Industrial Cluster of the 21st Century: its Role in Sustainable Development of Cities and Regions", Abstracts etc. from Asian Regional Conference on Ecotechnology for Sustainable Development", Beijing ct 19-26, 1994.

Petrella. R. "Le Evangile de la Compétivité". Le Monde Diplomatique. Paris, Sept. 1991.

Rio Summit, "UN Conference on Development and Environment", Rio de Janeiro, June 1992.

Schmidheiny, S. "Changing Course—A Global Business Perspective on Development and the Environment". MIT Press, Cambridge, Mass. 1992.

Swaminathan, M.S. Ed. "Uncommon Opportunities", a report by the International Commission on Peace and Food, Zed Books, London and New Jersey, 1994.

Truett-Anderson, W "Food without farms". The Futurist, Jan/Feb. p.16, 1990.

Zilinskas, R.A. and Heden, C.G. "The Biological Weapons Convention - a vehicle for international cooperation!". pp. 71-97 in SIPRI Report 12: "Views on Possible Verification Measures for the Biological Weapons Convention" Ed. JJ. Lundin. Oxford Universtiy Press, 1991.

Fig. 1—Objectives of a Bioresource Corporation

To serve the altruistic aims of the Biofuture Foundation by the creation of value through the development of new, judiciously selected, private enterprises in poor countries.

To optimize the sustainable utilization of untapped agricultural, mineral and human resources by providing incentive for indigenous creativity in developing countries.

To practise an "everybody-win" strategy in the process of linking the entrepreneurial tradition biotechnologies that are available in industrialized countries, with the resources and potential business opportunities that exist in developing countries.

To provide venture capital and to participate in holding companies and technology transfer bodies that are set up to use biotechnology as a tool for sustaining the integrity of the global environment.

To make full use of the expertise and world-wide contacts of the Biofuture Foundation in the search both for investment opportunities and for synergistic liaison with various international and local organizations active in the development field.

Fig. 2

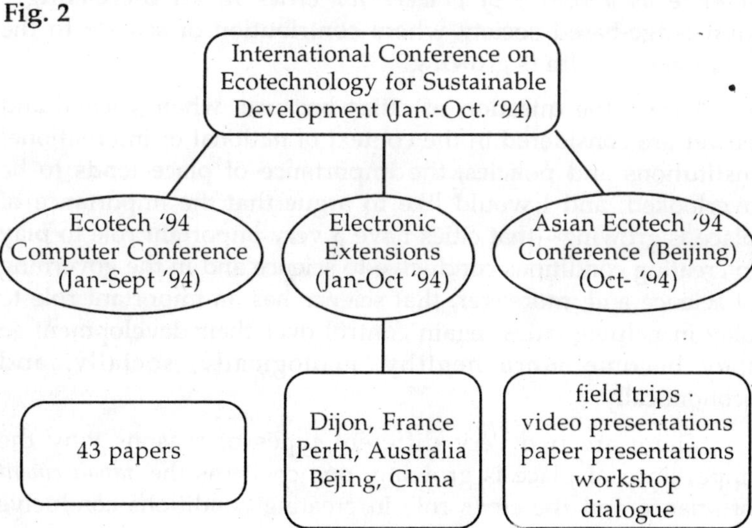

17

Science and Power: The Role of the Cities

RICHARD KNIGHT
Faculty of Architecture, University of Genoa

Since science, like most knowledge cultures, has evolved and remains concentrated primarily in cites, I would like to raise the question of the role of cities in science and power. There are two principle issues, the first concerns *the role cities could or should play in science* in an increasingly global society, and the second, science *as a source of power for cities* in an increasingly knowledge-based society where contribution of science to the creation of wealth is growing.

I raise the question of cities because, when science and power are considered in the context of national or international institutions and policies, the importance of place tends to be overlooked; and I would like to argue that the importance of place is growing—that cities have a very important role to play in creating conditions conducive to science and in the governing of science and, moreover, that science has an important role to play in helping cities regain control over their development so they become more healthy, ecologically, socially, and economically.

There are two very different types of reasons why the importance of place is growing, one concerns the *advancement* of science and the city's role in creating conditions conducive to innovation, to the development of talent and for transforming knowledge into local development, and the other reason has to do with the *governance* of science and the city's responsibility for integrating science with other types of knowledge cultures so that synergies are realized and insuring that development follows paths and takes forms which are sustainable and ecologically sound.

The second part of the question concerning science as a source of power also needs to be raised because cities are in crisis, their economic base is being transformed and since cities do not understand the implications of the changes that are occurring, they are unable to mobilize resources needed to shape their own future. The basic problem is that traditional employment opportunities in production are declining as wealth creation shifts from commodity-based activities in the production sector to knowledge-based activities in the knowledge sector.[1] And since cities do not understand the nature of these profound social transformations, they continue their business as usual; instead of formulating policies for enhancing and volorizing their knowledge cultures and transforming knowledge into local development, they continue to implement policies which reflect the needs of the production sector even though they are ineffective.

Cities do not see science or, more generally speaking, any type of knowledge as a resource and, therefore, do not invest in their developmènt and this places their whole future in jeopardy. Most city development policies are reactive of defensive in nature, oriented towards production and direct public investments towards improving the physical infrastructure for industrial production. These types of policies do not build confidence in the future of cities because industrial production is declining everywhere and such expenditures do not create new employment possibilities, they are, in fact, unable even to arrest the secular decline of increasingly competitive production activities or to attract jobs from other places.

Even the State is unable to lean effectively against ever changing market and technological forces. National governments and trans-national governments such as the European Union also follow traditional development and trade policies aimed at making industries more competitive globally but, by increasing their competitiveness, reduce the number of persons engaged in production jobs. Some national governments have begun encouraging cities to focus more attention on their strengths as knowledge centers and in France, based on the positive results from involving regions in formulating national science policies, cities are also being encouraged to participate. More forward-looking policies are urgently needed at the level of the city so their resources can be reinvested in ways which will enhance their position in the growing knowledge-based society and thereby create new opportunity for their citizens. Increased understanding of the economics of knowledge, of how knowledge resources are developed and how they can be transformed into local development is needed; this would increase both awareness about the importance of knowledge resources and confidence in knowledge-based development.

New impulses are emerging in places where knowledge resources are actually based but these endogenous efforts need support from local, regional and higher levels of government. If the development potentials of locally-based knowledge resources are to be more fully realized, cities will have to take more initiative and reassert their role as actors in science and technology and science along, with other types of knowledge cultures, will have to learn how to work with the city and make strategic choices about what role(s) the city could best play in the growing knowledge-based society. This is in fact, not a new role for cities but it is a competence that cities have not exercised for the last two or three generations.

Up until the Second World War, cities were important actors in science and the principle patrons of culture, education and medicine, Centralization of science, of universities, of medical services and research, and of cultural activities is primarily a post-war phenomenon. Now, science tends to be defined almost exclusively in terms of 'big science' and as being the responsibility of the State, Science Foundations and very large enterprises—as something organized at a very high (national and international) level, as being top down in nature.[2] Cities do not view science or other types of local knowledge cultures as a source of power, of new opportunities, or even as a form of power which they can influence.[3] Cities have been intimidated by 'big science' and no longer support or make demands on science; this role has been ceded to the State and to other power centers such as multi-national corporations. As a consequence, 'small science' and other types of localized knowledge cultures such as crafts and local ecology, which have been passed on informally (through apprenticeships) over the centuries and have not been supported by the State, are gradually disappearing. Diversity is being forfeited to basic research which is become increasingly concentrated and is clustered in very few places.[4]

Although science remains concentrated in cities, it is becoming increasingly isolated from other local knowledge cultures and knowledge resources are not being transformed into local development; synergies are not being realized locally and cities are no longer able to mobilize science to address local needs—science addresses universal values rather than the needs of everyday life in the city. The situation can perhaps best be characterized as proximity without propinquity. Instead of making demands on science, cities now allow big science and technology to drive development. In short, cities are no longer cities in the full sense of the term.

To be a city means having sufficient power and knowledge to shape the city's development. If growth is more accidental than intentional in nature, the city is only a city in name. And today most cities simply react to market the technological forces; they do very little either to help shape them or to protect local values which are being undermined by these external forces. This is not good for citizens, for cities or their surrounding regions nor is it good for society, for science or for the environment. Market forces do not create a good city and certainly will not create a healthy or ecological city. If cities are to shape their own destiny and to maintain their special character, they will have to reassert their role as a civilizing forces and learn how to protect those which give the city its distinctiveness.

Cities are in crisis world-wide; this is a crisis for civilization. The rise of the so-called megacities represent the breakdown of traditional village-based society rather than the emergence of a new civilized order. The US has been characterized as anti-city and there the decline of manufacturing in major metropolitan agglomeration has been particularly traumatic social disparities between the declining central cities and affluent suburbs continue to widen.[5] Even European cities are beginning to lose control over their development as problems of congestion, pollution, unemployment, social exclusion and public finance intensify.[6] European cities, however, have the advantage of having evolved slowly over several centuries and they have greater access to resources than cities in developing countries but they have yet to realy learn from their experience. When the reasons for the declining quality of life in cities are closely examined, we find that many contemporary urban problems have been self-imposed and can be traced to urbanistic concepts and ideologies imposed on cities such as the planning philosophies propounded by the Charter of Athens and written into laws and practices governing modern city planning.

Historically, cities were formed through the agency of the civic process and citizens devoted a great deal of time to articulating local values, collective interests and collective intentions. Citizens invested in their future by investing their time in shaping their cities future and developing its culture. Today citizens have little voice in their governance; Switzerland is perhaps the exception.[7] Refounding the city in the full sense of the term means that more attention will have to be given to the culture and values of cities and, once these values are articulated, cities will, once again, have to begin making demands on science in order to advance their own values. The State could certainly facilitate this process by establishing a policy framework for cities and by having cities participate in formulating national science policies. In short, the power of science should remain closely linked to its source and close to other types of knowledge cultures pasrticulasrly in places where they evolved. This means that science should continue to play an active role in city development especialy in those places where is roots are deepest. Science should not be allowed to become detached, uncoupled or isolated from the local cultures that nurtured them.

These comments are premised on the idea that knowledge is culturally based, that knowledge cultures evolve organically and need to remain deeply rooted in the places where they have evolved. At each stage of development, science has to re-integrate its knowledge at new levels of complexity. Perhaps science has to go back in order to go forward; to become better integrated and to be in greater harmony with its home environment before spreading its influence over the planet. Symbiosis between knowledge cultures and place is important for all types of knowledge cultures, from the culinary arts and medicine to opera and software, orgware and sportswear but particularly so in the domain of scientific knowledge because of its potential misuse for commercial and military purposes. Detached from its roots, science can be like a loose cannon on a ship and do much damage as in Seveso, Love Canal, Bhopal or Chernobyl.

If science is to serve civilization, it must be a good citizen in its home city and in the region where it is based. It is not by accident that knowledge cultures evolve in some places and not in others. Integration at the local level of the city and at the regional level is particularly important because that is where its roots run deepest and where its integrity can best be maintained. That is where its memory is longest, that is where the public is most familiar with its values and thus can be most demanding and least forgiving. However, most cities have become detached from their science base and they are not very demanding on science. They have grown apart, there is no dialogue between the city and locally based science, their presence is taken for granted - the city accepts the benefits which accrue from their presence without questions. That is until something goes wrong as in Basel, where an accident caused chemical pesticides to spill into the Rhine poisoning the river all the way to the North Sea, or until a community finds one of its core-competencies weakened by a brain drain, as in the case of international finance in Amsterdam or lack of apprenticeships in crafts as in the case of goldsmiths and musical instruments in Vienna.

Cities are in a weak position because they do not understand the nature of knowledge-based development and they are not aware of the development potentials of their knowledge resources. Moreover, cities are not aware of the impact that the valorization of these knowledge resources could have on the city or of the role the city could or should play in their governance. When the advancement and regulation of science is left to the State and international conventions, cities and their citizens feel less and less responsible and thus less need to remain well informed about what scientific knowledge is present locally or about how scientific knowledge is beirg advanced or exploited even when it involves taking risks which could directly affect local citizens. Moreover, some types of local knowledge cultures are being allowed to atrophy because, being difficult to organize or exploit commercially, are unable to compete with the demands lobbies for big science lobbies make on science budgets. Most of the knowledge required for sustainable development such as knowledge about the local ecology and crafts has already been lost because there have been no policies for conserving them and these cultures are no longer being passed on to succeeding generations.[8]

As science has advanced, the gap between science and the public has been allowed to widen and science has become a stranger even in its home town. Citizens today have no way of learning about important aspects of their city's development and have very little influence on the way the city develops. There is very little real citizen participation. Basically, the State distrusts the cities and cities distrust their citizens. The nature of local knowledge cultures, for example, is not part of the school curriculum, in fact, local knowledge cultures probably have not been identified or mapped and are not being monitored. Moreover, communications between science and the city are problematic particularly when they cross disciplines or sectors. The academy has difficulty communicating with the municipality, the public secotr has difficulty talking to the private sector, industry has problems communicating with the academy, etc.[9] Moreover, citizens have difficulty communicating with their own city because local and regional governments have also become increasingly complex and bureaucratic making communications between departments and between different local government and regional authorities increasingly difficult.

Science needs to become part of the city's culture but, clearly, this will not happen spontaneously. The breakdown of communications among knowledge cultures at the local level is normal and if the reasons for this were better understood, it would be clear why maintaining such relationships should be the city's reponsibly. Science advances by becoming more specialized and by developing networks of relations concerning very specific branches of scientific knowledge. Each science develops its own culture, its own values, its own language and lines of communications and its exchanges become increasingly specialized, internationally and vertical in nature. As this happens, communications of a local or horizontal nature weaken.

Proximity without propinquity is now the norm in knowledge-based activities in most cities. The gap between what. C.P. Snow called the two cultures continues to widen even in the very places where scientific knowledge is based, even in small university towns such as Delft.[10] This breakdown in communications is not inevitable, it is a form of benign neglect and rectifying the situation can be very beneficial to the city. There are, in fact, some interesting approaches being taken by some cities that specifically address this problem.

Looking back, we can see that cities worked well when the linkages between science and cities were strong—when cities were important actors in science—but the politics of cities has changed and these relationships have been allowed to atrophy. With rapid industrialization, cities shifted their attention to the needs of the expanding production sector, to improving the physical infrastructures, building social housing, highways, power plants, airports, etc., knowledge-based activities were seen as being able to take care of their own needs. And now many cities are in crisis because their production sector is in decline and they do not understand the nature of wealth creation in the knowledge sector.

The problem is not a lack of knowledge resources, the problem is basically a communications problem. If a city does not understand the nature of its knowledge cultures or core competencies, it will not be able to enhance them or to realize development potentials. Knowledge cultures in a city need to be integrated, as they were historically, through the agency of the civic process; their collective interests, intentions and needs have to be articulated and used to form a compelling civic vision.

The consequences of the breakdown of the civic process in cities became very evident during a recent study on the future of European cities conducted for the European Community for DG XII Science, Research and Development. The aim of the study was to assess the impact that science and technology would have on European cities with the advent of the Single European Market. The study, undertaken by an European network of urban research institutes, URBINNO, considered a wide range of science-based developments from high-speed trains and telecommunications to innovation processes and the ageing of the population.

As part of the research, strategic diagnostics of knowledge-based development were undertaken in selected European cities using a methodology elaborated in Delft and Amsterdam.[12] Qualitative data on knowledge-based development were gathered in Barcelona, Genoa, Lille, Lyon, and Milan during open-ended interviews with forty decision makers in each city. The basic finding was that although knowledge resources were viewed as being very important in all of these cities, there were no strategies for knowledge-based development.[13] Moreover, cities lacked mechanisms required for thinking regionally, for thinking in an European context, or for thinking long-term. City planning and economic development at the city level continues to be oriented primarily towards territorial planning—to land-use plans and to physical infrastructure improvements required for activities in the production sector—very little attention is being given to non-material aspects of development such as creating conditions conducive to activities in the knowledge sector or to building a knowledge-infrastructure.

Decision-makers in cities readily acknowledge the importance of knowledge resources but there is very little awareness about the special nature of their knowledge cultures, of their core competencies or of their development potentials. And these potentials are not being realized because cities lack a knowledge-infrastructure, they do not understand how knowledge resources are transformed into local development and the knowledge resources are allowed to become very isolated from each other so synergies are not realized locally.

What is lacking is a framework or a mechanism for articulating collective interests and needs of the knowledge sector, especially needs of a cognitive, intellectual or cultural nature. One of the principle recommendations of the study to the EU was that a policy framework for cities be established at the European level and that cities be encouraged to develop science policies as a critical element of their development strategy and as part of their overall cultural policy. One of the results of the diagnostics of knowledge-based development was that some of the cities studied actually initiated actions to strengthen their knowledge sectors. The City of Delft is now implementing a development strategy which envisions the city as a knowledge city. The Amsterdam Chamber of Commerce has created knowledge circles for selected knowledge cultures.

A more comprehensive way of addressing knowledge-based development developed in Vienna is now being applied in Genoa. The first phase of a systematic study of a city's knowledge base, the design of an approach, sponsored by the City of Vienna Planning Department, has been completed and institutionalization of the process is now being considered. The approach involves creating a high—level, collective learning process about knowledge—based development in the city and engaging decision-makers from all the principle types of knowledge cultures in the city in a duologue about strengthening the city's knowledge base. It is a form of action research; decision makers assist in the design and then participate in a series of dialogue seminars about specific themes concerning the enhancement of knowledge cultures in the city.[14]

Such a dialogue requires extensive preparations, bringing people together in a forum or even around a table is not sufficient. There are several steps to the process. First of all, all the principle types of knowledge cultures in the city need to be identified; in Vienna, for example, over fifty were considered.[15] Then, a decision maker from each of the principle types of knowledge culture has to be identified and interviewed in depth in order to identify the principle themes, issues and topics which need to be addressed. In Vienna, interviews were summarized in the form of briefings for distribution to other study participants so they could be well informed about each other before the actual dialogue.

Once the key themes have been identified, study participants need to be bought together in small preparatory meetings focusing on particular themes where they can decide how the themes can best be introduced during the dialogue seminar. These meetings are particularly important because, by meeting in small groups, they begin identifying common interests and taking over the process. In Venna there were six focus groups, each hosted by study participants and all of the persons attending these meetings participated in the dialogue.

When all the participants came together to discuss the themes they had helped to select, the level of engagement and intensity of interest was very high. During the inteviews, there had been a great deal of scepticism about the success of such an approach but these doubts were completely overcome when the themses were introduced at the initial dialogue seminar. In Vienna, the first dialogue seminar was help in the city hall, was well attended and the participants found the process very productive and expressed strong support for its continuation.[16]

The approach could certainly be applied in other cities but it should be stressed that, if a city intends to stimulate a real dialogue process and if the dialogue is to serve as a mechanism for a high-level, collective learning about the nature and needs of knowledge-based development in the city, there must be a commitments to the process—appropriate preparations will have to be made and the process will have to be institutionalized. Stimulating a dialogue about strengthening the city's knowledge cultures provides the city with a way to begin articulating the collective intentions and needs of its knowledge sector, air is a way of re-establishing the age-old agency of the civic process and applying it to new types of development.

The crisis of cities calls for a new approach to development. Present practices of reacting to external forces or imposing national policies are to little avail, city development needs to became more intentional and driven more by forces of an endogenous nature. The present crisis, when viewed in an historical context, has a lot to do with the breakdown of the civic process. This breakdown began several decades ago when city planning was first becoming professionalized, i.e. when rapid urbanization called for regulation, for territorial, sanitary and physical planning. Until then, cities had developed slowly as centers of knowledge (mercantile, administrative, crafts, etc.) and they served as the primary civilizing agents but, with industrialization and rapid urbanization, cities and their citizens gradually lost control over their destiny. Some places with locational or political advantages became sites for major-production or administrative complexes and grew rapidly, others were left behind and went into decline.

Urbanization has been very unbalanced, some places have been under great stress to accommodate expansion and this, combined with the introduction of new technologies such as motor vehicles, telecommunications, air travel and high-speed trains has caused them to spread out beyond their municipal boundaries. Rising affluence and public investment in highways simply accelerated the suburbanization process and intensified the problems of metropolitan growth. As cities grew they became increasingly fragmented, geographically administratively, sectorally and socially, and they lost their power, their autonomy, and their ability to manage urban growth effectively.

In recent decades, city development has become increasingly accidental in nature and increasingly unsound environmentally and socially. This is not because cities lack power but rather that the nature of their power is changing. These changes in the nature of their power arise from the fact that the nature and way wealth is created is changing. Society is shifting from a commodity-based to a knowledge-based economy with knowledge becoming the strategic resource and the knowledge-base becoming the new economic base of cities. The crisis is not the decline of production jobs but rather the lack of understanding of how wealth and new types of opportunity are being created in the knowledge sector.

With globalization, new possibilities are opening up for cities and, with the lowering of national borders and trade barriers, the market for their knowledge is becoming more and more world-wide.[17] Unlike commodity-based production which is founded on geo-political advantages, knowledge-based development is not as affected by location, it is founded more on the integrity of its knowledge cultures and on the liveability of the city.[18]

An approach specifically addressing knowledge-based development must be treated as a new initiative, independent of traditional, sectorialized, planning because the approach requires anticipating and facilitating societal changes and cultural development and calls for a holistic approach; it is more of a learning than a planning process and does not conclude with the design of specific projects. For example, the process outlined above is basically a collective learning process focusing in on qualitative, cognitive and cultural aspects of the city's development and its impacts are of a cumulative and long-term nature.

Whether cities will take an active role and call on science to help regain control over their destiny and shape their development in ways that are ecologically and socially sound or whether they continue to react to external forces remains an open question. Cities have many options opening up in knowledge-based development but they will need to make some choices. They will have to invest in their future and they will have to begin investing more in developing a knowledge-infrastructure, in talent and in creating conditions conducive to creativity and innovation. Cities should begin by building on their existing knowledge-base and, as a first step, systematically identify and define those special competencies which are already present in the city and then begin positioning the city in the emerging global society by strengthening and valorizing them.

Cites have to learn how to enhance their knowledge cultures and how to valorize their knowledge resources and they can do this by improving relations with those persons and organizations in the city who are already doing this. In an increasingly open and knowledge-based society, every city, regardless of its size or geographical location, can play a role. As the saying goes, no city can be competent in everything but any city can be competent in something.

Society is entering a new era and the question of the role of cities should certainly be on the table and perhaps should even be a central issue in any discussion about science and power. The challenge for society, now, is to humanize and democratize science, which means advancing and valorizing science in ways which are socially and ecologically sound. Integrating science and universal values with other types of knowledge cultures and values particularly those of an informal or local nature would help meet this challenge. The impulse would, of course, have to come both from science and from the locally and their convergence will take time. This is certainly in accord with the subsidiarity principle and with the goal of sustainable development but it also implies greater responsibilities for cities and for science and would help restore the city as a principle civilizing force. If, for example, the ecological city is to be realized, there will have to be a new balance established between science and power—all types of knowledge cultures will have to be bought into play. But science, in the service of the city, will enable cities to respond more effectively to major societal needs such as creating new types of opportunities, preserving diversity, increasing social cohesion and improving the environment.

FOOT NOTES

1. Urbanization, the shift of population from rural to urban settings was driven primarily by the industrialization of agricultura production and the shifting of work from the field to the factory and, more recently, by the shift from factory to office type settings in the service sector. Now, however, the nature of work is undergoing a more fundamental change, traditional types of work are diminishing, cities now have to begin creating new types of opportunity.
2. The costs of 'big science' now dictate international co-operation. Even the US Senate recently determined that increasing its participation in CERN was more feasible than continuing the construction of a new linear accelerator in Texas.
3. Over the last century, the concept of knowledge as a source of power has changed, knowledge is now thought of as reflecting the power of the state; as knowledge acquired through basic research which requires huge public investments as in nuclear physics, space and medicine. Francis Bacon's oft quoted adage that "knowledge is power" has quite a different meaning from '*Nam et ipsa scientia potestas est*' or 'knowledge is more than equivalent to force' (Meditationes Sacrae, De Hoeresibus).

4. Anders Hingel, *Science, Technology and Social Cohesion in the Community—A long term analysis. Overall synthesis report,* (June 1992) FOP 300, Commission of the European Communities, DG XII, Science, Research and Development, FAST MONITOR Programme, Prospective Dossier No.1, Vol. 1.
5. Richard V. Knight, 'The Advanced Industrial Metropolis: A New Type of World City, in Hans-Jurgen Ewers, John B. Goddard, and Horst Matzerath (eds.), *The Future of the Metropolis.* Berlin: Water de Gruyter, 1986.
6. The Future of European Cities was one of seven themes considered during *Les Carrefours de la Science et de la Culture,* organized by Cellule Prospective of the Commission Europèene: *En Quete d' Europe,* 1994 Editions *Apogée, Rennes, distribué par l' Office des publications officielles des Communautés Européenes, 2, rue Mercier,* L-2985 Luxembourg, CM-85-94-591-FR-C English edition available in 1995.
7. In Zurich, citizens were able to vote on the desirability of a new metro system proposed by the planners and their opposition led to a reformulation of plans and the development of what is regarded as the best public transportation system in Europe. Light-rail trams have been used to integrate suburban rail, bus and cars traffic and has incorporated many innovative features such as the control of traffic lights by tram drivers.
8. Henrik Sinding-Larsen,'Information Technology', in Bo Göranzon and Magnus Florin (eds.), *Dialogue and Technology: Art and Knowledge.* london: Springer-Verlag, 1991.
9. Similar types of communication problems exists in universities between different departments and faculties and other large organizations such as hospitals and corporations. Corporations use annual reports and house journals to keep their stakeholders informed about changes, but very few cities publish annual reports.
10. *Economische Beleidsvisie. Zicht Op Delft,* Kennisstad (Oktober 1990), Gemeente Delft, Dienst Beheer & Milieu, Afdeling Economische Zaken.
11. The Future of European Cities: The Role of Science & Technology, Commission of the European Communities, DG XII, Science, Research and Development, FAST MONITOR Programme, Prospective Dossier No. 4. Roy Drewett, Richard Knight and Uwe Schubert. PART I, *Synthesis,* (March 1992), FOP 306.
12. *Amsterdam Knowledge City: Knowledge-based Development with Recommendations and Actions* (May, 1991), Amsterdam Chamber of Commerce and Industry, Transferpoint Amsterdam, Innovation Center Amsterdam-Haarlem.

13. Richard V. Knight, *Cities as Loci of Knowledge-based Development* PART IV. The Future of European Cities: The Role of Science & Technology (March 1992) FOP 379, Commission of the European Communities, DG XII, Science, Research and Development, FAST MONITOR Programme, Prospective Dossier No. 4.
14. Richard V. Knight, *Enhancing Vienna's Knowledge Cultures,* Progress Report on Phase I of the Study of Vienna's Knowledge-base. Vienna Department of City Planning, 1995.
15. For a typologies of knowledge see: Fritz Machlup, *The Production and Distribution of Knowledge in the United States*. Princeton: Princeton University Press, 1962. A series of volumes on *Knowledge and Knowledge Production* by the same publisher followed beginning in 1980.
16. The proceedings were video taped and a summary video titled 'Who Met Who' with exerts from the contributions given has been prepared. A computer presentation on the nature of knowledge-based development and the rules of dialogue has also been prepared. These are available from the author.
17. Richard V Knight with Gary Gappert (eds.), *Cities in a Global Society*. Vol. 35, Urban Affairs Annual Reviews, London, Publications, 1989.
18. Richard V. Knight, "Knowledge-based Development: Policy and Planning Implications for Cities", Special Issue, *Urban Studies,* March 1995.

18

International Organizations and their Role in Modern Science

VLADIMIR KOUZMINOV

Chief, UNESCO, Venice Office

Before opening the third session of our Symposium devoted to the discussions of the role of international organizations in contemporary science, I would like to emphasize the exclusive importance of international cooperation in all areas of human intellectual activities including sciene as a unique phenomenon of the 20th century.

The intellectual cooperation in science was started long ago through the exchange of students, professors and researchers between European universities and scientific institutions but the real understanding of potentialities of international cooperation came to the mind of national scientific communities and consequently to governments only during this century and particularly after the dramatic events which happened on our planet known as "world wars".

After the First World War, some initial steps were taken by different countries to unite their efforts in the peace keeping process and in intellectual life. During this period, the League of Nations was created which could be considered as the major international initiative of a number of countries belonging to different regions of the world and which established a certain type of background for the United Nations Organization which was initiated during the Second World War.

In the period between the two World Wars some important international scientific organizations were established, firstly the International Council of Scientific Unions (ICSU) and the World Energy Conference now better known as the World Energy Council.

Great impetus was received by the international cooperation after the Second World War with the creation of the United Nations System and a wide range of non-governmental and governmental organizations related to the major areas of human activities.

It should be mentioned from the very beginning that international organizations should be considered as one of the most effective instruments in initiating and implementing international cooperation.

Currently we could group international organizations in two major categories: governmental and non-governmental.

The governmental ones include first of all, the United Nations Organization and its family of specialized agencies which work in the major areas of human concern and activities. The UN and its family are approaching their 50th Year Anniversary which will be celebrated in October-November 1995.

The United Nations Educational, Scientific and Cultural Organization (UNESCO) born shortly after the Second World War (its Constitution was signed in London on 16 November 1945) is one of the major UN Agencies responsible for intellectual cooperation of member-states and also includes science. The scientific components are also included in the activities of some other specialized UN Agencies such as the World Health Organization (WHO), the World Meteorological Organization (WMO), the United Nations Industrial Development Organization (UNIDO) etc.

Among the UN family some funding organizations and programmes were also established which contributed substantially to the promotion of scientific cooperation on national, regional and international levels. They are the World Bank for Reconstruction and Development and the United Nations Development Programme (UNDP) and others.

An important role in regional scientific and technological cooperation is being played by the United nations regional economic commissions which were established by the UN Organization in all major regions and are part of this organization.

The regional governmental organizations and treaties are also contributing to the development of scientific and technological cooperation among nations belonging to particular regions. In Europe there are some important governmental organizations with strong scientific components namely, the European Union, the Council of Europe, NATO, the European Bank for Reconstruction and Development and some other European programmes and projects which have proved their effectiveness and visibility.

Under the category of non-governmental scientific organizations we can find a wide range of professional and learned scientific societies and unions. Some of them have been established recently but some of them have a longer history than major governmental organizations.

Many of them cooperate successfully with the latter and produce very visible and useful impact on the scientific life and on cooperation between scientific communities. In this connection, the exclusively important role of ICSU should be underlined, the international organization which unites 92 national scientific academies and research councils and some 23 international scientific unions.

Among non-governmental scientific organizations we should also mention international professional unions and societies which constantly contribute to the development of cooperation between research institutions and individual scientists within the fields of their competence.

International learned societies and first of all international and regional academies of sciences have started to play a remarkable role in scientific communities.

International funds and foundations have become recently more and more involved in promoting international and regional cooperation in different areas of science and technology. Some of these funding organizations are especially active at national levels and provide substantial financial support to basic and applied research in some countries which are currently facing economic problems. This century gave the birth to international and regional research centers which are joint research facilities financed by governments and basic research institutions of mainly European countries.

Among these research facilities we should mention CERN located in Geneva (Switerland), the Joint Nuclear Research Institute located in Dubna (Russian Federation), IIASA located in Luxemburg (Austria) etc.

Having listed the principle categories of international organizations we should identify the role which these institutions play in the scientific life of modern society.

As I can see, one of the major goals of all types of these relevant organizations is to promote the international cooperation in the areas of common interest for the majority of nations.

Another important objective of scientific international organizations is the identification of problems of global nature and the elaboration of common approach in their resolving. The interantional organizations also create a certain background for launching multinational scientific enterprises in the kind of international and regional programmes and projects. They help different nations to elaborate more properly their national policies in the field of R&D. The international organizations finally can be considered as a very solid mechanism for the scientific exchange between nations and individual research centers and scientists. They provide a ground for meetings between scientists, for intensive discussions of scientific problems inside and outside scientific communities.

In other words all kinds of international organizations occupy a very powerful position in the human society and this factor should be taken into account during our discussions concerning the relationships between science and power.

Moreover, it should be noted that science today is considered as a very powerfull element of international action and science has penetrated into almost all international organizations, in comparison with 50 years ago when only UNESCO of the UN Family and some other scientific unions had a strong scientific component in their activities, now almost all organizations have a visible impact on science policy at international and national levels.

That is why, the role of all types of international organizations in modern science and their influence on scientific life should carefully studied with a view of eliminating possible conflicts and undesirable consequences in the relationships between these institutions and the world scientific community.

19

The Support of Science by International Foundations

JOAO M.G. CARACA
Calouste Gulbenkian Foundation, Lisbon

1. Foundations: A Brief View From Europe

Foundations and associations share the principle that both incorporate the dedication of resources that have (or assume) the private nature of furthering the public good. However, associations draw their resources from the activity of individual persons, whereas foundations have their source in capital or other types of property. Both also share the principle of "non-profit" or no financial gain in their actions, the level of "self-interest" (of members) introducing a demarcation between classes of associations.

Foundations, then, follow in the liberal tradition of Europe (as opposed to the monarchic tradition) which conveys the conception that public good is not bestowed exclusively by the State. They are private entities serving public purposes. Foundations are neither entirely within private law, nor entirely within public law. But we must stress a point that is highly undesirable and creates confusion in the public opinion today: the proliferation of so many "beggar" foundations (i.e.) of foundations that despite their name have no capital fund of their own and rely on the public sector on other foundations) which may have adverse effects.

Modern foundations operate basically in two different ways or in a "composite" way, depending on their primary purposes:

1. as "operational" foundations, when they plan, finance and execute their own programmes; or
2. as "grant-giving" foundations, when their function is to support financially the activities of others.

According to the Hague Club (The Hague Club, 1988), the three foundations with a more voluminous annual expenditure in Europe are: the Volkswagenwerk Foundation in Germany, instituted in 1961 by an agreement between the governments of the Federal Republic of Germany and of the State of Lower Saxony; the Wellcome Trust in the United Kingdom, created in 1936 by the will of Sir Henry Solomon Wellcome; and the Calouste Gulbenkian Foundation in Portugal, established in 1956 by the will of Calouste Sarkis Gulbenkain. The Volkswagenwerk Foundation in Protugal, established in 1956 by the will of Calouste Gulbenkian Foundation functions both as a grant-giving and as an operational foundation in specific areas.

All these three major foundations have the promotion of science as their purpose: in fact, all S&T including humanities, by sponsoring research and university teaching in the case of the Volkswagenwerk Foundation; and the support of research in human and animal medicine and the history of medicine, by the Wellcome Trust.

Of the large foundation, only the Gulbenkian seems to encompass much wider purposes: the promotion of charitable, artistic, and educational as well as scientific goals—these representing some 12 per cent of its total activity.

2. The Promotion of Science: Roles of the National Authorities and of Foundations

In the 1960s, a universal model for S&T was accepted, that corresponded to an instrumental concept of S&T in relation to social and economic development. Nowadays, however, we know that it is not possible to isolate research activities from the social context in which they are conducted; this is reflected by the growing "scientification" of the cultures of contemporary societies as well as by the increasing social involvement of S&T,

of individual scientists and researchers, and of their organizations. A new need has been created: the need to make sure that public funds spent on S&T and R&D are used in a beneficial way for society—evaluation performing primarily the role of mediator in this process.

This is the reason why science policies at national level have been changing from a mission-oriented nature (from the launching of strategic sectors to the emphasis on the generation of technological innovations and the support of national "champions") to a more diffusion-oriented one, enhancing the mechanisms of technology transfer and valorization of research results. The role of the state in a modern economy is incompatible with the conduction of operations too close to the market (i.e. a "precompetitive" character of state intervention has to be preserved).

What is left then to action by the state is the building-up of infrastructure (including the development of human resources—the notion of human capital); the support of networking activities (hence the notion of human mobility); the financing of research programmes (with an increasing precompetitive tendency) in basic "pervasive" technologies; and provision of S&T services at national level.

What about the action by foundations?

In the past, the role of foundations in the promotion of science was easier to play in two aspects:

1. they were concerned, at most, with the national level
2. the national S&T systems were in a clear development phase.

Nowdays this situation has changed drastically. No foundation (unless specific clauses in their charter will prevent them) can claim to be concerned solely with the national level. This poses the problem of the specific character of the need of intervention by foundations and other private institutions dedicated to purposes of public good. Are these areas in which public good can be seen as endangered and in need of support?

The economy, as well as technology, is becoming global. Technological innovation and commercialization of new products and services are the result of increased co-operation networks between firms across sectors and countries, and between enterprises, universities, and public agencies. Global science, technology and economy are expanding rapidly.

What roles can foundations, thus, fulfil in a new world where networks designed for cooperation are seen as means for enhancing competitiveness and new organizational concepts are bursting in an aggressive mood?

The natural domain of action in science by foundations has always been vested in the time variable, i.e. in promoting or demonstrating excellence and top quality in the most fundamental and basic disciplines, or through projects of a highly innovative or pioneering nature.

Foundations have nowdays to resist the illusion of being able to compete with institutions emanating from national authorities and with economically-driven organizations that have been eager to adopt and reap prestige and benefits from foundation-type operations. Foundations will not succeed in this competition as the volume of their endowments will always be necessarily connected to their time of creation and will not expand at the rate of economic growth and complexity of modern nations.

The action by foundations will, thus, have to be strictly circumscribed to the time variable: to be ahead and look ahead; they must function as centres of reflection and rationality without any borders, promoting the understanding of issues of present societies and in their development; promoting and enforcing prospective attitudes and values; promoting systematically excellent science projects, thus contributing to the creation of a favourable climate to science, knowledge, and culture; and, finally enhancing the (sometimes unsuspected) capacity we all have, as human beings, to cooperate together, sharing visions and aspirations, in search of a better world.

20

The Role of the International Council of Scientific Unions (ICSU)

ANTHONY EPSTEIN

Chairman, ICSU Committee for Science in Central and Eastern Europe

The International Council of Scientific Unions (ICSU) was founded in 1931 to bring together scientists from all parts of the world in international scientific endeavour and to promote activity in the different branches of science and their applications for the benefit of humanity. It is the successor organization of the International Association of Academies (founded 1899) and the subsequent International Research Council (founded 1919).

Since its creation, ICSU has vigorously pursued a policy of non-discrimination by affirming the rights and freedom of scientists throughout the world to engage in every international scientific activity without regard to such factors as citizenship, religion, creed, political stance, ethnic origin, race colour, language, age or sex.

Structure

ICSU is a non-governmental organization made up of two categories members:

(1) 92 multidisciplinary National Members, Associates and Observers (scientific academies or research councils);

(2) 23 international single-discipline Scientific Unions and 29 International single discipline Scientific Associates.

General Policy is determined by a General Assembly of all Members which meets every three years. Policies are implemented by the Officers and an Executive Board assisted by a General Committee of Assembly representatives which meets annually. Specific tasks are assigned to appropriate Scientific, Standing, Special and *ad hoc* Committees or to Inter-Union Commissions.

The principle sources of ICSU's finances are contributions from National and Union Members, a subvention from UNESCO, and grants and contracts from other UN bodies, agencies and foundations.

Activities

ICSU seeks to overcome difficulties arising from specialization and accomplishes this role in a number of ways:

(1) *ICSU initiates, designs and co-ordinates major international interdisciplinary research programme.* Examples are the International Geophysical Year (1957-58), the International Biological Programme (1964-74), and the more recent and current International Geosphere-Biosphere Programme: a study of Global Change (IGBP) which aims to describe and understand the interactive physical, chemical and biological aspects of the total earth system. IGBP complements the joint World Meteorological Organization/ICSU World Climate Research Programme.

(2) *ICSU creates interdisciplinary bodies for research of interest to several members.* Examples of such activities include antarctic, space and water research, problems of the environment, genetic experimentation, solar-terrestrial physics and biotechnology.

(3) *ICSU sets up bodies to address matters of common concern to all scientists.* Such concerns include the teaching of science, scientific ethics, freedom in the conduct of science and for the free circulation of scientists, assistance for science in developing countries by capacity building, assistance for science in Central and Eastern Europe and the Former Soviet Union.

(4) *ICSU acts as a focus for the exchange of scientific ideas and information.* Scientific congresses, conferences, symposia and other scientific meetings are organized around the world—the total in excess of 600 a year—and a wide range of newsletters, handbooks, journals, and proceedings is published within ICSU and its "family" of memebers.

(5) *ICSU maintains regional networks of scientists with similar interests.* Regional Secretariats operate in Africa, the Arab Region, Asia and Latin America to foster networks and assist scientists in their regions.

In all these undertakings ICSU sustains close working relations with a number of intergovernmental and non-governmental organizations and, in particular, with UNESCO with which it co-operates in the launching and running of various international programmes.

Because ICSU is in contact, through its membership, with hundreds of thousands of scientists world-wide, it is increasingly being called upon to act as the spokesman for the world scientific community and as an adviser on scientific matters ranging from ethics to the environment.

21

The Role of the European Union in Science

MANFREDO MACIOTI
International Consultant, Brussels

The origins of the European Union (EU) can be traced back to the signature (Paris, April 1951) of the Treaty establishing the first European Community: the European Coal and Steel Community (ECSC).

At that time, Europe had decided to create the basis for a broad and deep Community—now the Union—among peoples for long divided by bloody conflicts. The two classical ingredients of war—coal and steel—of six European countries (France, F.R. Germany, Italy, Belgium, Netherlands and Luxembourg) were pooled under a supranational Institution (the High Authority). Common Institutions were created: the High Authority (now the Commission), the Assembly, the Council of Ministers and the Court of Justice. An article of the Treaty—art 55—mentioned research ("the High Authority shall promote technical and economic research relating to the production and increased use of coal and steel and to the occupational safety in the coal and steel industry").

Six years later, two more Treaties were signed (Rome, March 1957) providing for the establishment of the European Economic Community (EEC) and the European Atomic Energy Community (Euratom). The EEC Treaty mentions research in art. 41

("an effective coordination of efforts in the sphere of vocational training, of research and of dissemination of agricultural knowledge"). The Euratom Treaty has a whole chapter (Chapter 1) devoted to the promotion of research (articles 4 to 11).

Next to the two new Treaties, a Convention was also signed in March 1957 creating a single Assembly (now the European Parliament) and a single Court of Justice for the three Communities.

The first major revision of these three Treaties was the subject of the Treaty establishing a Single Council and a Single Commission of the European Communities (Brussels, April 1965). Soon after, the fundamental role which scientific research plays in the economic growth of Europe was explicitly recognized by the Council, the Governments of the EC Member States and by the Commission (1967). The main reason behind this high-level recognition was the technical gap which Europe had to close, in relation to other highly industrialized countries—particularly the United States—in several sectors which are essential to the development of a modern industrial economy.

At that time, the impact of the EC—level programmes in the R&D sector was rather limited. For the year 1967, the ECSC had a research budget of about 10 m u.a., the EEC about 5 m and Euratom circa 50 m.

In 1970, the EC launched the COST initiative (Cooperation in scientific and technical research), nativity a number of European non-member countries to join the EC Member States in cooperative research (the first two projects were initiated the year after). At present, 23 European countries and the EU take part in COST.

The year 1973 witnessed the accession of three new Members to the EC (United Kingdom, Denmark and Ireland) and the creation of the first EC Programme for scientific and technological policy. Under the new programme, the EC budget for R and D reached more substantial level: 230 m EUA under the three Treaties in 1978 and 300 m in 1980.

In 1975, at the time of the introduction of a budget financed entirely from the Communities' own resources, another revision of the Treaties established a new common Institution: the Court of Auditors.

With the adhesion of Greece in 1981, the EC reached a membership of ten. In 1983, the EC approved the first Framework Programme (FP) for Community scientific and technical activities , covering the years 1984 to 1987. The financial means available under the F.P. were 3,750m. ECU, or about 2.4 per cent of the EC budget. The two first priorities were energy (47 per cent) and industrial competitiveness (28 per cent). The first F.P. sanctioned the birth of the large EC research programs such as ESPRIT, RACE and BRITE. In that same year 1983, the EC ther-monuclear fusion experimental machine (JET, the Joint European Torus) became operational in the UK. JET is the largest "tokomak" machine in the world; Sweden and Switzerland and fully associated to the programme.

The year 1983 also saw the launching of the first EC programme for science and technology cooperation with the Third World.

In 1985, 18 European countries and the Commission adopted the EUREKA Charter to advance European cooperation in high-tech industrial sectors. At present EUREKA has a membership of 23 (including the EU). EUREKA'S military counterpart—EUCLID—was launched in 1988.

In 1986, two more countries, Spain and Portugal, joined the EC, bringing total membership to twelve. The year sono the signature in Luxembourg/The Hague of the Single European Act (SEA). For the first time, there is talk of a European Union (EU). Title VI of the SEA is devoted to research and technological development and defines the EC aims in the sector ("to strengthen the scientific and technological basis of European industry and to encourage it to become more competitive at international level").

The second FP of the EC in the field of research and technological development (1987-1991) was approved in 1987, with a budget of 5,396 m ECU. The priorities shifted to information and communications (42 per cent), energy (22 per cent) and the modernization of the manufacturing sector (16 per cent). The budget for R&D was 3.1 per cent of the EC overall budget.

In 1989, the third FP (1990-1994) was approved; it had a budget of 5,700m. ECU (plus 900 m. ECU voted in early 1993).

The science budget reached 3.9 per cent of the EC budget. Next to information and telecommunications (38 per cent), energy (16 per cent) and industrial and materials technologies (15 per cent) a new priority was born: life sciences (13 per cent).

In February 1992, the Treaty on European Union was signed in Maastricht. Title XV of the new Treaty deals with research and technological development. The objective of "strengthening the scientific and technological bases of Community industry and encouraging it to become more competitive at international level" is tempered by the intention of promoting the research necessary to underpin the other Chapters of the Treaty (such as Social Policy and Education, Culture, Public Health, Trans-European Networks and the Environment). A wide-ranging debate on the meaning of the European Union concluded with the entry into force of Maastricht in November 1993.

Meanwhile, in 1992, the EC launched its first initiative for scientific and technological cooperation (Copernicus) with the countries of Central Europe (including the Baltic States).

A separate scheme for R & D Cooperation with the Southern Mediterranean (Avicenne) was launched that same year.

In January 1993, the EC completed the establishment of a large integrated internal market. With German Unification in October 1990, EU population exceeded 345 m. This is now the largest market in the world (on a par with NAFTA). With some exceptions, the four freedoms of movement—people, goods, services and capital - are implemented in the market.

In 1993, the EU and its Member States launch the International Association for the Promotion of Cooperation with Scientists from the Independent States of the former Soviet Union (INTAS). INTAS has today 18 Members in W. Europe (including the EU) and 12 Partners in the CIS.

In April 1994, the EU adopted the fourth FP (1994-1998), with a total budget of 12,300 m ECU (plus 700 m ECU to be unfrozen later). The share of the R&D budget settled at about 3.7 per cent of the total EU budget. The Programme is structured on 18 different lines of action, grouped under the following headings: Information and Communications technology,

Industrial technologies, Environment, Life sciences and technologies, Non-nuclear energies, Transport, targeted Socio-Economic research, Nuclear Safety Thermonuclear research, International cooperation, Dissemination and Optimization of results, Mobility and Training of researchers. In financial terms, the priorities are information and communications (28 per cent), energy (18 per cent), industry (16 per cent), life sciences (13 per cent) and the environment (9 per cent).

This same year 1994, the EU finacial means devoted to R&D amounted to 2,620 m ECU, which is about 3.7 per cent of the total budget of the EU and a similar small percentage of the overall R&D investment (public and private) by the twelve. Two observations on this last point: (1) the EU moneys invested in a research project are, on average, matched by equal amounts contributed by other sources; (2) the EU financial means are targeted to priority areas.

It is, therefore, not surprising that in some areas of advanced technologies, the impact of EU support is significantly higher than is suggested by the above percentage. Taking the electronics and electrical machinery sector as an example, the business enterprise research and development (BERD) expenditure in the EU in 1990 was estimated at some 9b ECU. The direct EU support for R&D in information technology and telecommunications in 1990 can be estimated at some 530 m ECU or 5.8 per cent of BERD. Doubling the percentage (to take into account the matching funds provided by the industrial contractor), would give the EU a "research penetration" well in excess of 10 per cent. Note that this calculation only concerns EU funding and does not take into account the considerable amounts invested in R&D by other inter-European organizations (CERN, ILL, ESRF, ESA, ESO, EUREKA, EMBL, ESF, etc).

Thus, e.g. the 1993 ESA budget included some 445 m ECU for telecommunications, while EUREKA has underway over 125 projects—worth over 8 b ECU - in the areas of information and communication technologies.

The financial impact of EU support is not surprisingly—greater in some countries (e.g. Ireland and Portugal) and, overall, has a higher relevance for small and medium enterprises.

Beyond the sheer numbers, and perhaps more important than finacial support, are the immaterial benefits a partner can derive from collaboration sponsored by European programmes. Among these, should be mentioned a degree of internationalization and networking familiarization with European markets and standards, the acquisition of new scientific information and technological known—how, the improvement of skills, an orientation toward the long term, the enrichment and moderization of project management and working methods, a degree of costs and risks sharing, an improvement of name and image and an incentive to do more research.

In conclusion, since its inception some ten years ago, the EU Framework Programme has had a growing positive response from academic, public research centers and firms. The Programme is playing a positive, possibly a major role in the enhancement of the innovative potential of Western Europe as a whole. As the public R&D budgets of most European countries decline or stagnate, the impact of EU R&D funding on the European science scene is bound to increase.

22

Romanian Cooperation with International Scientific Institutions

MARINA RANGA

Director, International Agreements and Programmes Division, Romanian Ministry of Science and Tecnology

A factor of an essential importance for the promotion of the reform process of the Romanian scientific research and technological development is the enrolment of our country's research activities in the international scientific circuit.

It would be an error to consider the scientific research within an exclusive national framework, in a world speaking more and more often about globalization or even about "territorial states' instead of "national states".

International research can only be done through active collaboration between specialists, scientific groups institutes or laboratories, which have the capability, that "critical mass" that could allow them to form the excellence poles.

In a synthetic view, Europe could be considered as reunion of interconnected areas: the European Union, the European Free Trade Association (EFTA), the Central and Eastern Europe, then the new independent states of the former Soviet Union. In this geographical area, one cannot ignore the basic principle of the strong bilateral relations organization between scientific research institutions.

A further enlargement of these interconnected areas would include the industrialized countries outside Europe, mainly the United States of America and Japan, as well as several countries of Latin America or Asia.

In all her international activities, Romania tried to do the best possible to join the family of traditionally democratic countries, to share more of the spirit and experience of the European Union countries.

After a long isolation period from the important changes that took place in Western Europe, Romania's wish to strengthen her distinct position within the European culture, science and civilization, to re-integrate in the spirit of European traditions, appears as fully justified.

All these efforts are parallelly backed—up by the global effort to revigorate the national economy, in order to keep the transformation rhythm of today's society.

These efforts cannot be considered only at a national level, but within the framework of the general efforts that Eastern Europe makes to recover after more than 50 years of different conceptions, and only with a significant contribution of Western countries.

Is the West doing enough for Eastern Europe?

The question has become increasingly emotive and politically sensitive as the time passed since 1989, that year of momentous change. Then, there were high expectations on both sides, at a time when anything seemed possible. Five years later, the amount of commercial, economic, political and cultural interchange has grown, but also has suspicion and a sense of dashed expectations.

In the West, increasingly the image is painted of the Wild East, a source of poverty and illegal immigration and a sinkhole for money. In the East itself, cynicism has welled up over rich businessmen, pursuing their self-interest to the disregard of others.

The countries of Central and Eastern Europe want to know that they can be members of the Western institutions, want to be treated as equal partners and want an end to the restrictions they believe are holding back their economies. In Western capitals, there is the assumption that change must be gradual and evolutinary and a fear that more rapid moves risk splintering NATO and the European Union, the twin bulwarks of the Western European solidarity.

A great deal has happened and much more is planned. NATO has created its Partnership for Peace programme, and Alliance politicians talk openly of admitting some Central European states—but without setting dates or criteria for membership.

The European Union has its Association Agreements and is drawing up a pre-accession strategy to prepare for new entrants. There is a general acceptance that policy has to change, and radically, but the idea of new faces at the table raises huge questions in both organizations.

The East no longer wants a lifeline, it wants to be brought on board. The task of creating a European Union of 20 or more Member States will be vastly complicated and it raises some fundamental questions, not only about the Eastern Europe countries and their relationship to the European Union, but about the European Union itself.

Economic adaptation will play a crucial role in determining how the European Union expands, but questions of a more political nature are going to come to the fore in the next few years.

If the EU has to adapt before it admits new members, what impact will that change have on the existing members? And if the new EU states bring different conceptions of the continent and its fortunes, can these be accommodated?

Finally, this is a question of how the two sides see their history and their divided recent past, but also their visions of a common future.

The most important European Union initiative to support the economic transformations of the Central and Eastern Europe countries was the PHARE Programme, which stasrted to expand in Romania in 1991.

The PHARE Programme started initially as a programme of economic assistance for Poland and Hungary and became afterwards an initiative to integrate the Central and Eastern Europe countries in the European Union.

During the five years of its existence, through the PHARE Programme, about 4,3 billion ECU have been allocated to the 11 involved countries.

During 1990-93, about 360 million ECU have been allocated to the programmes initiated by Romania, which was, as a beneficiary, on the third place after Poland (882 million ECU) and Hungary (416 trillion ECU).

For the research and development field, a Romanian project was accepted. "The reform and restructuring of the Science & Technology System in Romania", which was provided with PHARE funds of 3 million ECU.

For the period 1993-95, it is expected that the PHARE funds provided for science and technology restructuring in our country will be much more significant, following the inclusion of Research & Development field among the national priorities.

Furthermore, the EU Commission recommended that up to 10 per cent of the PHARE funds, distributed at the national level, should be dedicated to support the participation of the Romanian scientists to the 20 specific research programmes included in the Fourth Framework Programme for research, technology and development.

The Fourth Framework Programme, approved by the European Parliament and the European Union Council on 26th April, 1994, sets forth the European Union policy in the Science & Technology field, including the specific research programmes, their objectives and ways of achievement, the general selection criteria of the proposed projects, the valuation of results, etc. following the conclusion of an Additional Protocol to the Association Agreement between the European Union and Romania on 17th October, 1994.

With reference to the COPERNICUS '94 Programme, the Romanian participation was represented by 26 projects, involving 45 research teams of institutes, universities, companies.

These 26 projects cover a broad spectrum of research fields, such as: information technology, communications, telematics and linguistic engineering technologies, biotechnologies, new materials, food industry etc.

Another innovation instrument, dedicated to support international cooperation in science and technology, is the EUREKA Programme, launched in 1985, in order to help Europe to posses and to exploit decisive technologies for its future in the competitiveness race.

The Romanian participation to EUREKA is included within the EUROTRAC project and it is expected that a new impetus will be given by the Brokerage Events, which are planned to be organized in EUREKA member and non-member countries, with the aim to enlarge information dissemination concerning the specific objectives of this programme.

Within the framework of the COST Programme, dedicated to European Cooperation in Scientific and Technological Research, the Romanian participation was represented by 10 projects, in different fields, such as: telecommunications, food industry, social sciences, chemistry.

In order to keep an updated situation of the information services market of the European Union and to provide technical assistance to end-users, the European Community Host Organization (ECHO) was created, within the framework of the IMPACT Programme, in 1980.

At present moment, ECHO gives free access to 18 data-bases among which UNESCO data-bases, economy, business and linguistic data-bases.

By means of the national information network, the academic network connected to Europal NET or directly through INTERNET, Romania has the possibility to access these international data-base of specific interest of scientific or economic projects.

Within the framework of the Romanian cooperation with international scientific institutions, a special attention has to be given to the cooperation with the North Atlantic Treaty Organization, which, besides the political and military dimensions, has also a third dimension, the scientific and technological cooperation, as a major condition for the human progress.

NATO Scientific Programme is a major component of Third Dimension of the organization, and, since its inception, in 1957, it involved over 250,000 researchers.

The collaboration within the two major bodies—NATO Scientific Committee and the Committee for Challenging the Modern Society—emphasizes the development of projects in different fields, as environment protection, advanced technologies, human resources, associated with several fellowships for the ongoing projects, together with pilot studies in areas of priority interest.

Reviewing the Romanian cooperation with major international scientific institutions, an important position has to be given to the scientific links with UNESCO, as an organization having a global reach and a multidisciplinary mandate and, also, a long and rich experience in building institutional capacity and in developing networks to link individuals and institutions across the five continents.

It can mobilize governments, agencies and centres of learning on behalf of development goals. And it can marshal the talents of outstanding individuals to serve humanity.

UNESCO's science activities emphasize international and regional cooperation, as ways to help developing countries become full partners in the world of tomorrow. The long term goals of eradicating poverty, instituting policies that respect the environment, while also promoting sustainable development, can only be achieved if nations agree on the value of a shared cultural and natural heritage.

Science provides some of the information needed in order to assess options and to make wise decisions. Scientific cooperation offers the model and the means for achieving a common objective.

As 1995 means also the UNESCO's 50th Anniversary, a special series of manifestations is organized in Romania, jointly with the 10th Anniversary of Youth International Year, under the title: First International Open University "Youth in Evolution". The main coordinators are: the Youth and Sport Division of UNESCO, UNESCO National Commissions and Clubs, the Ministry of Youth and Sport of Romania and the Romanian National Commission for UNESCO.

To these institutions the Ministry of Education, the Ministry of Research and Technology and the Ministry of Culture are associated.

Among the most important events to be held within the framework of the First International Open University "Youth in Evolution", one has to mention:

- The 4th World Congress of the World Federation of UNESCO Associations, Centers and Clubs (June 1-5, 1995).
- Youth International Colloquium (June 3-6, 1995)—International Workshops on data processing (May 1-26 1995).
- International painting and photography workshops (May 1995).
- International piano festival "Dinu Lipatti" (May 1995).
- International science competitions and exhibition of young inventors (May 1995).
- International archaeological camps (July 1995).

Several prominent personalities of the international community will be invited in Romania to attend these manifestations, starting with Mr. Federico Mayor, Director General of UNESCO, Mr. Adnan Badran—Deputy Director General of UNESCO, together with numerous officials of UNESCO divisions.

Invitations will also be addressed to: Mr. Jaques-Yves Cousteau, as the Chairman of the Intergovernmental Committee of UNESCO for the MAB Programme, Mr. Javer Perez de Cuellar—Chairman of UNESCO World Commission for Culture, Mr. Carlo Rubia and Mr. George Emil Palade—Noble Prize winners, Mr. Anatoli Karpov and Mr. Yehudi Menuhin and many others.

The participation list to this series of events is opened to all youth associations, higher education institutes, cultural associations, UNESCO Clubs, association and centers, NGOs whose activities correspond to the mentioned fields of manifestations, together with national, regional and international institutions, either public or private, having ties or cooperation agreements with UNESCO in the fields covered by the manifestations. Registration deadine is February 1st, 1995.

Within the United Nations system of scientific institutions, Romania is a member of the UN Commision on Science and Technology for Development, recently founded and coordinated by ECOSOC, with Secretariat assistance of UNCTAD.

At present, Romania is a member of one of the three Working Groups, namely "Gender Working Group" and activiely participates in the elaboration of the Group's conclusions and reports.

Special attention has to be given to the Romanian participation to Senior Advisers on Science and Technology meetings, subsidiary body of the UN Economic Commission for Europe.

Our country's concern for the reform and restructuring of R&D activities, the institutional and legislative changes that are planned to take place are widely reflected by a comprehensive programme of reform, based on a thoroughful knowledge of other countries' experience.

The Romanian assessments of the necessary measures to be taken in order to accomplish the reform were often confronted to other foreign evaluations, as for instance the World Bank's conclusions, which proved to be very similar.

The proof was the World Bank's involvement by financing studies dedicated to the reform and restructuring of higher education and research systems in Romania.

Another proof of Romania's launching in the international scientific circuit is the affiliation to international institutions and organisms.

In this respect, only one example: formalities are now proceeded to achieve Romania's membership to the International

Centre for Genetic, Engineering and Biotechnologies of Trieste (Itlay), as a proof of the actual recognition of the importance this field has for the general progress of science, with its multiple implications.

A complete picture of the Romanian cooperation with international scientific institutions is hard to define in few words, and even harder is to properly assess all its effects and consequences.

But, from this point of view, one question comes up, instead of "Is the West doing enough for Eastern Europe?" and that question is "Are we all doing enough for Europe?"

Maybe the right answer or one possible way to approach this problem is to avoid these sensitive and emotionally charged questions, taking into account that the "enough" approach would mean an attempt to quantify the unquantifiable.

How could "enough" be expressed? Is absolute monetary terms, as an amount of US dollars or ECU, or as a percentage of GNP of donor countries? Neither is likely to come close to answering the main question.

In strictly economic terms, "enough" would be the point at which the supply of funds meets real demand in terms of the absorptive capacities of societies in transition.

But the question of "enough" is not a strictly economic one and it is certainly not an easy one to define. May be a more adequate way to approach this question would be to consider "enough" in a qualitative rather than a quantitative manner. And for this qualitative approach, maybe better than anything else, links between national or regional communities, can fill the gaps and remove illusions.

23

Participation of Ukraine in International Multilateral Cooperation

SERGEI BOROVIK
Councillor, Ukraine Ministry of Foreign Affairs

Sovereignty of Ukraine, its establishment as an independent state have opened new and wide opportunities for its participation in the international scientific cooperation.

It should also be emphasized that the National Academy of Sciences of Ukraine which is a major state scientific establishment, has obtained absolute independence as a subject of international relations. Already in 1992 the National Academy of Sciences of Ukraine became a national member of the International Council of the Scientific Unions. Its contacts with such respectable regional scientific associations as the Academy of Europe, Standing Conference of European Academies of Sciences, the Third World Academy of Sciences—have been intensified. Moreover, the National Academy of Sciences of Ukraine initiated the establishment of the International Association of the Academies of Sciences which includes National Academies of Sciences of 15 countries and plays an important role in maintaining single scientific space in the Commonwealth of Independent States.

One should also mention scaled up cooperation and a great number of direct contacts the Ukrainian scientists have established with their colleagues from other countries under multilateral scientific cooperation programmes in the UNESCO context. Out of these programmes of particular importance for Ukraine are the following: International programme on the World Ocean Research, Programme on Man and the Bioshpere (MAB), the Renewable Energy Programme, Intergovernmental programme on the Universal System of Scientific Information. By the way, in 1992, the Scientific and Research Centre at the Institute of Cybernetics of the National Academy of Sciences of Ukraine obtained a status of UNESCO International Scientific Centre.

The UNESCO European Science and Technology Regional Office (ROSTE) plays an important role in enhancing Ukraine's participation in the international multilateral cooperation.

In April 1991, negotiations on scientific cooperation between the National Academy of Sciences of Ukraine and ROSTE were held in Kiev. As the result of the negotiations a respective Agreement was signed.

Two international scientific fora partially financed by ROSTE were held in Kiev as pertaining to this Agreement implementation: a Symposium in the field of virology and immunology as well as a Seminar on the problems of energy saving technologies. The Centre of research on scientific-technical potential and history of science named after G.M. Dobrov on the National Academy of Sciences of Ukraine was involved in the implementation of the international research project "Problems of brain drain in Europe". Under the contract with ROSTE this centre conducted research on the problem of intellectual migration in Ukraine.

The matter of participation of the National Academy of Sciences of Ukraine in the development of project proposals pertaining to the study of the problems related to environmental releases in fishing zones of the Black Sea was also agreed with ROSTE. A contract on holding in Kiev an international conference "System monitoring of natural environment" was signed. The Academy of Sciences expressed also its interest in financing initiatives related to the "Blue Danube" project etc. The cooperation of National Academy of Sciences of Ukraine with ROSTE is comprehensive and involves a rather wide spectrum of research fields.

At present the Academy has prepared proposals on cooperation with ROSTE up to the end of 1995. The basic agreement has been achieved with ROSTE leadership on holding the negotiations.

24
Closing Session

TULLIA CARETTONI
President, Italian Commission for UNESCO

Director General, colleagues at UNESCO, friends from Genoa, I believe the meeting on science and power has been highly fruitful, as witnessed by the depth, enthusiasm and variation of the various contributions, at times even provocative, sure indication that we are dealing with issues close to people's hearts.

This meeting has been the first step down a long road: our Commission for some time now has elected to encourage longer-term programmes and projects in preference to one-off events, in order to probe deeper at each stage into each issue under debate, thus, making international contribution to culture in general, and also having repercussion within UNESCO.

Such a rich and lively meeting confirms that the issue of science and power is one of great concern to the cultural and political world—we shall now take the issue further, with a series of seminars and workshops—in Genoa, and perhaps Rome and Venice. We will be nominating a scientific committee to evaluate our views and conclusions, organize meetings, both formal and informal, some between top-level personalities from the worlds of culture and politics, and to bring the issue to international level, to your next general conference of UNESCO, Director-General, to other general organizations in particular the

UN family, thereby exposing it to the scientific community, society, and to the communities of our major cities which are after all political factors with the great advantage of having direct contact with our men and women.

This meeting calls on us to take responsibility, to find a positive solution to what is our duty, notwithstanding the various pessimistic aspects we have necessarily come across. This positive attitude is more important for the man-in-the-street than for the scientist, and is certainly vital for humanity as a whole. It is a path we must take, in order to safeguard those billions of monuments under our protection, monuments that are human lives.

I believe that our past makes up our present, and we, especially our young people, are monuments to be preserved, not least because this means respect for the human person, for life, for peace. And also in this way we can move on from empty slogans, on to what Professor Bisogno has said, that we need to ensure that science and research in the modern world become increasingly a means through which to raise the stature of the human person.

We have debated democracy, and whether or not science has an intrinsic decision-making value, difficulty in being democratic. But one view underlined at the meeting is that science has the role of reducing ignorance and of increasing knowledge, elements of democracy. We know this by looking at statistics from the Third World: even a small increase in the cultural base has a wide effect on development.

Our Director-General frequently calls on intellectuals to leave their ivory towers and to move among ordinary people: I am convinced that this meeting too has served to mobilize those intellectuals who can promote peace.

It is very fitting that the city of Genoa, city of Columbus, city with a great intellectual past and also civil history, should act as the centre for this cultural operation: and we are asking the Mayor of the City just that. It is essential that the age-old issue of science and power be relaunched at a very profound level, and this City is ideal as a headquarters of such reflection, which can eventually become a part of our civilization as a whole.

I would like to thank everyone again for their support, and remind you that this meeting is not an end in itself, but the beginning of a series for reflection. Some have talked of Utopia here: may this meeting be a positive contribution at the deepest level to all.

I would like to thank you, Director-General of UNESCO, for coming to Genoa and for your magnificent presentation which has undoubtedly fallen on extremely fertile ground. At a time like this, the United Nationals Organization is undergoing certain difficulties, but even so I am convinced that on this, the eve of its 50th anniversary, if the Organization did not exist, it would be necessary to invent it. I am also convinced of the extremely significant contribution being made by someone of such culture as yourself, in directing this Organization, on which the future of humanity, in its highest expression—that concerned with truth and reason and that distinguishes mankind within this Universe—depends intimately.

Departing from normal practice, I would now give the final word to the Mayor of Genoa, major actor not only in today's work but in the future of our project. May I thank the Municipality of Genoa, the Director-General of UNESCO, the University of Genoa; I would also like to thank my colleagues at the National Commission. With this meeting, the Italian celebration of the 50th anniversary of UNESCO begins, in the presence of the Director-General and of the Mayor of one the most highly regarded and international cities in our country.

ADRIANO SANSA

Mayor, City of Genoa, Italy

While I have been pursuing my work as administrator in our city, it has been reassuring to know that you were here setting out on the road we must take together. We are bringing the meeting to a close now, but I remember the words of Professor Salvini at the opening session, when he remarked that the most intelligent form of altruism is utilitarianism; in other words, today utilitarianism is one of the major forms of wisdom and the highest expression of altruism. This too in the essence of the words of the Director-General of UNESCO, when he reminded us that we are all in the same boat, where everyone must pull together if it is not to sink. I believe that Salvini's words also hold a deep moral inspiration, and that rather than thinking altruism to be of value insofar as it is a good form of utilitarianism, he was referring to the paradox in which we find that besides the heart, feelings, spiritual choice and so on, intelligence is essential—today altruism is to be our saviour.

So, this has been one general theme I have noticed. Another is that there has to be someone to prick our consciences; we may already be preoccupied with various problems, but we need a further push in order to get going to resolve these new issues.

And today the answers have begun to appear. I have already talked of the need to become involved and for consensus, for surely the relationship between science and power, probably in both directions, probably hangs in the reality of democracy.

What other channel than democracy allows goals to be set? And science within modern society has to operate through the painstaking filter of consensus, through participation.

And I ask: for what reasons, beyond formality, has the Director-General of UNESCO called us here? I believe there is a single topic—a design for the world, and we are here to discuss the century's main themes, misbalance between contingents, causes of migration, the environment technical solutions to find new ways forward, and thus, the role of science, of the politics of power, of administration, all the way down eventually to the city. And this then brings us to the responsibility of the citizen himself, and of the scientists, the administrator, the politician, all contributing to a grand design. Prof. Mayor spoke of the Education, Science and Culture of UNESCO, and I too would underline the importance of education, literally a "leading", leading towards culture.

I am not a scientist, but from what I have heard and seen, I recognize the immense value of this seminar and of the follow-up planned, meetings that recognize the need to look forward to the future, with all the psychological, moral, political, civil and professional power it takes.

One of the most original concepts reiterated here with conviction has been the need to turn our attention towards the cities. We talk of civilization which has the same root, *civitas*—and it is the cities that have to hold up the future, with their links to the past, the cities which have the breakthrough ideas, the universities, cultural programmes, so often created from these aggregations of man, not from the bureaucratic structures but from the natural communities in which we live.

To look towards the city is, thus, modern, useful, but evokes high responsibility. Certainly I for one accept this responsibility. Recalling Federico Mayor's words, I acknowledge that we must take up the cause of those who have been left aside in today's world. It is fitting that this initiative has set sail form Genoa, city of Christopher Columbus, and one open to the world and to exploration of new ideas. Genoa will do what it can, with its culture, its fine university, its will. But we cannot rest, knowing that our future is one of a minority; we must be aware of what is happening elsewhere.

Look at Rwanda this year, the African continent as a whole, terrible evidence of the misbalance which must be set right—the problem of our century. As I say, I take on the responsibility, aware of the long road to be trodden: UNESCO can be assured that it has in Genoa a full partner in its initiative.

The ways, timing, the means with which these issues are confronted should also take justice into account, and also the problem of poverty. In all these issues, the city has to take a real part.

The director-general of UNESCO, as a poet, has spoken with great incision and energy in laying before us his design. We all accept the challenge; this city is partner too, and in this sprit of participation I thank you all deeply, and hope for the very best outcome of your efforts.

EDOARDO BENVENUTO

Dean, Faculty of Architecture of Genoa, Italy

In our examination of science and power, science and politics, we see them in a relationship that can imply conflict, collaboration, integration, between two separate entities. In other words, an extrinsic relationship inside which the structure of science and the structure of power are not involved. Dr. Mieli has talked of science as a place of freedom, whilst power is a place where limits are imposed. But other meanings of the relationship between science and power can be brought into this image.

For example, in the 18th century, state power was measured by the might of the army, in the 19th by the richness of state reserves, but then later on, perhaps at the end of the 19th century—or even between the Wars—it came to be measured by the power of scientific and technological organization.

This is certainly an issue that needs examining. But I would like to put forward a number of questions that intrigue me as a scientist, regarding the nature of science and power. Specifically, are not "knowing" and "being able" intrinsic science and to power?

I refer to the magnificent writings of Antonio Genovesi, Neapolitan sage writing at the end of the 18th century his student text (*Elements of Experimental Physics*). Given the background in science at the time, his conclusion was that science had been dominated by the tyranny of Aristotle, until the revolution of Galileo and Newton. Immediately, the then followed the major national schools—Des Cartes in France, Newton in England, Leibitz in Germany—which aimed at counterbalancing that tyranny through the creation of three metaphysical rivals. However, none of these managed to displace Aristotle, and an oligarchy took root. But in the 18th century, the oligarchy was replaced by a republic, a democratic republic, since from the golden century of science, only dominions in which the precision of experiment meeting calculation were admitted. I do wish to overemphasize the work of Genovesi, but considering that it was written at a time when the social set-up was dominated by all other powers and hierachies, I think it important to note that science as a democratic republic was also of major political interests.

So, we have science as a revolutionary alternative policy in conflict with power; but I would also like to remember science as freedom—not because science is a place where freedom operates, but because science has freedom as a goal, and freedom makes it free. But what concepts of truth have determined the path of science in its interaction with politics and power? I believe that science has led to a change in the power of power, and also that power has intervened, and that there is probably a force behind us or within the scientist's mind today that is stopping us from getting to that purest truth which should be the focus of science.

In ancient, or in mediaeval science, there was the search for the principle, to find the principle in order to explain the law and thence to generalize. There is an analogy within society. Within an ordered hierarchic society, power was understood as a change in the ruling Prince—the Prince himself counted, not just what he could do and for what he was responsible. There are parallels in science, research, philosophy, for example the search not for the conservation of energy, but for what conserved energy, the prime mover, and all its equivalents.

This was the case at the beginning of modern science too, but at that time, there also existed the division "for" and "against" nature—for example the idea that nature "abhors a vacuum". So what can it means—to modern politics too - to have eliminated the category of "against nature", bringing all nature into line, within the confines of the possible? Science has removed dimensions of power and social hierarchy, and installed relationships, science's deduction method, and led to the creation of a pluralist reality.

There is clearly need for a deeper study of the intrinsic relationship between science and power, partly to get to the bottom of some of the major questions. For example, the question of technique in Heidegger's writing, and the concept of scientific research. Heidegger maintains that scientific research is a project aimed at reducing the world to images, thereby eliminating the subject-object relationship. Also, Heidegger's analysis renders science and power one single entity, although perhaps to an exaggerated extent. Some points from today's science require distinction.

But the technical of today is no longer that of Heidegger, the science of means and issue of reason. Heidegger thought of the plough, how the food it procures comes and goes whilst the plough remains. Nor is it the technique of production that Heidegger examined and condemned, containing as it does the major threat to man who produces in a mad rush but then finds nothing more than a source from which to produce the next thing.

No, today the technical is essentially information, which has changed the world of understanding and interpreting physical phenomena; once psychoanalysis interpreted the psyche through references to pulses, reactions, etc., whilst today all biological sciences read the physical reality in terms of information, DNA, RNA, and similar. But the greater this information becomes, the more it becomes divisive. Take applied mechanies, field in which even only 60 years ago just one new magazine was something that united, enriched. Today there are already over 800, and the next one will only be the creation at a niche, with its own language. I think this is an interesting question, both political and scientific.

This second working session, addressing the social aspects of science its influence on society, involved direct comparison with the results of the first session on science and power.

The first point to come out of the discussions is that of the neutrality of science—weakness and strength at the same time - that gives power to scientists' decisions and is thus also the prison that holds science and its freedom, its humanity and pride. Bisogno denies the right of science to consider itself neutral.

Nevertheless, the neutrality of science is based on its appeal to higher reason, to truth, to reasoning above power. And so we see science in the modern era has a role similar to that of other forms of human activity—religion and philosophy. What is different about science today is that it is located within specific limits, and does not pretend to have a global overall hold of the truth but has only a partial view.

This modern outlook is one in which man leaves aside problems he cannot resolve. But John Lock, as every philosopher, is aware of the reality of the past; here and in the later development of scientific thought, this self-limit gives way to reductionism, where truth can only be accessed within one's experience. And today, this reductionism is urgent, the era one of technology, which has altered the way we deal with science.

From certain issues raised here—the technologies of information and of genetic engineering, or the role of science in economic development—we see that the distinction between science and technique has collapsed. In earlier times, technique was preparatory to science, then it became the offspring for science, and today science is technique. And technique needs organization, so closely linked to power, which lies behind Bisogno's conviction that science cannot be neutral. And for this reason we need to remain watchful, since there can be political aspects within science of which we are unaware.

Education is one major element here, and certainly schooling needs more attention. It is valid to propose an educational project in which the themes of science and technique are developed: only thus, may the student take up a critical sense and learn to judge from an impartial distance, stance which today represents that appeal to higher reason that has always been the counter-balance to the rationality of scientific form.

25
Closing Remarks

FEDERICO MAYOR
Director-General of UNESCO

Dr. Sansa, Lord Mayor of the City of Genoa, Senator Carettoni, President of the Italian National Commission for UNESCO, Mr Sayyad, President of the UNESCO General Conference, Your Excellencies, my dear Colleagues, Drs. Forti, Caraca, Kouzminov and Proctor, Ladies and Gentlemen.

May I first express pleasure at being here in the City of Genoa for this meeting on Science and Power. We are here to launch an initiative which examines science—the "S" in UNESCO—in its relationship to power. It is very opportune that this meeting is being held in Genoa, a city renowned for its openness. The City of Genoa is a symbol of exploration, and exploration is precisely our task. There is a need to reverse many existing trends in order to find new ways to contribute to the dignity of human life, particularly for those who find themselves excluded from the social mainstream.

This first meeting has been an excellent starting point for the Genoa Forum. I strongly believe that this series will have a profound impact on many people at many levels - national, regional, international—as well as on the relationship between science and government. The Genoa Forum should also be helpful in guiding scientific communities which need to adapt themselves to the socio-economic and political transformations taking place in many parts of the world, particularly in Central and Eastern Europe, Cooperation will be essential to the success of the Genoa initiative, and I would like to express my appreciation of the cooperation that has led to this undertaking, particularly that involving the Italian National Commission for UNESCO, the UNESCO Venice Office (ROSTE), the Italian National Research Council, the University of Genoa and the City of Genoa.

This international symposium on Science and Power has been a forum for elaborating new visions of humanity's mission. One of our immediate goals is the drawing up a draft document, using input from these two days of discussion, and after consultation with the universities and research centres, detailing what can be done, and by whom. This document will be submitted to a number of scientific institution heads around the world, in order that we may present the Genoa Declaration to the next UNESCO General Conference.

But for an appeal to be effective, its content must be crystal clear. And for that, we must be sure from the outset on certain issues—the terms it is to be drafted in, to whom it is to be addressed, by whom it will be implemented, where and to what extent. For such clarification, your efforts in contributing to a better understanding of the role of science in human society and the relationship between science and power in general and the governmental structures in particular will be of the greatest value.

Each group or individual, the academic, the scientific community, the teacher, the writer, the architect, can make a contribution to the reshaping of priorities.

The city will be a key element in this process. It is the city where the citizen lives, and where education can work to unlock the potential of all humans and forge attitudes of peacefulness, of ethical responsibility, of constructive dissent—perseverance but never violent. This outlook is the responsibility of all our families, of teachers, of mayors, because it is at the level of individual citizens than the possibility of democracy exists. And thus "*cogito ergo sum*" from the viewpoint of the citizen becomes "I participate, therefore, I exist". If I do not participate I do not exist as a citizen. And if I can participate, it is because I know, since I have access to knowledge. I can share this most important element of life, to know, in order to be able to make my own decisions, my own choices. It is this capacity for decision-making by every individual man and woman that lies at the basis of the culture of peace. This initiative, here in Genoa has the task of giving people the means to allow them to decide, at national, regional, international level, and so to plan their own destiny.

It is the process of deciding and choosing that allows us to shape the future as distinct from merely adapting to external events. It is up to us to anticipate, to see what is the best option for the future. We can not allow ourselves to be led by external forces, by society, by the law of the market. I as a scientist and human being react strongly when this is suggested. No, events must not be the driving force, and the universities, the intellectual organizations, UNESCO, are there to lead, not to be driven. Leonardo da Vinci would have leapt from his grave, horrified at the idea of us accepting such an impoverished vision. It was Leonardo, the person, the intellectual, the artist, who gave us metaphors to show there is no colour of the skin, no age, no wealth. We are all one in a storm-tossed boat, and must work together to keep it from sinking.

It is our task to discover the best option for the future that is our unique untouched heritage, one that UNESCO must protect. The past has been inequitably divided, resources have been unevenly appropriated. As with other heritages, UNESCO intends to protect the human cultural heritage of the future from conflict, from lack of security, from the unjust distribution of wealth. To do so, we must innovate, invent, and find new methods, different from those of the past. We can no longer be content, like spectators, with passing the responsibility for the ills of this world onto the superpowers. We must all be actors and help the decision-makers, the governments, the mayors, at all levels. To discover just how and where to act has been our task here in Genoa, debating the ways we can intervene, in this case in the world of science, in its interaction with prevailing power structures, providing the decision-makers with the necessary scientific knowledge and scientific rigour.

In debating the future of science, we need to reflect on its nature. Science is first and foremost basic knowledge, research, discovery, reflection, innovation, invention—leading to new knowledge and applications of this knowledge. There is also science in its popularized form, used to create global awareness at citizen level in order that this awareness shall influence decision-makers through the media. Then there is the science that is taught, which must also be given very careful attention. But there is another science so vital today—science employed for the purposes of persuasion. It is sometimes necessary to deploy very concise and precise scientific arguments to persuade decision-makers who, with the best will in the world, are made short-sighted by the pressures under which they operate. Scientific persuasion of this kind—which requires the best possible messengers, high-level personalities—should focus in particular on the phenomenon of irreversibility. In scientific decision-making, time can be of the essence—my experience as a biochemist has taught me that. A decision made too late can even kill. The ethics of time thus, represents, in my view, a key element for science. This must be reflected in the way science is presented at the popular level, in teaching, to the decision-makers. Another important point is that we must always present positive alternatives if we are to persuade. The point is well illustrated by a visit I made to China, where we were discussing energy. The Prime Minister shared his concern with me. They had been advised that coal power was out for pollution reasons; hydroelectric power was no alternative because of possible ecological damage; nuclear power was not possible. So China finds itself up against a real problem, and the world responds with one "no" after another. Rather than adopt such a negative approach, we must provide solutions—for example, by suggesting and devising ways in which China's energy projects can operate cleanly, or ecologically, or safely.

Of course, in order to make decisions democratically and altruistically, our decision-makers must be informed, and this immediately raises the question of the need to be viewed clearly by the power-brokers is the role of basic science, at risk in today's climate of rapid commercialization of science. And this risk to basic sciences is heightened by the attitude of modern society, with its not infrequent mistrust of science. Here, we need to be absolutely clear: knowledge is always positive; it is its application which can have negative or even perverse consequences. So it is at the point of application that major social impacts must be considered. Meanwhile, there will be no applied research if there is no science to apply, a logic that must lead decision-makers to promote basic research. This is particularly important in view of the constant involvement of the private sectors of national economies in the R&D process. In fact, the rapid commercialization of science could lead to a diminishing of the role of basic research as a principle component of R&D: this needs to be understood by our governments, parliaments, as well as by society.

One of our major problems is how to get our voice to be heard by those holding power. Power has a large variety of representatives, one of the major being political. Fortunately, political power in a democracy invested in the parliament. It is here that we can lobby for basic research, for sustainability provisions to be included in national and international agreements, for example. Then there is economic power, particularly the transnational economic power, so great that we may sometimes believe it to be impenetrable, a giant machine with laws of its own. And then there are the powers of education which are very influential, and of culture. Cultures themselves are used at times to block change, used as a pretext for dissuading efforts to change the world. We are confronted with cultural identities, religious feeling, that make change impossible. But I am nevertheless optimistic. First, because I consider that education and the sharing of knowledge in a broad, open-minded and tolerant way will allow people to make their own decisions, and in the common good. In this way, we can come to realize that the problems of—say—religion (so significant right now in many parts of the world, including Europe) are problems of interpretation, of institutions, but not of the essence of religion itself.

We must take advantage of all these powers, and as Senator Carettoni was saying, we must beware of remaining in our ivory towers. Now, more than ever it is essential that intellectual power goes out into the street, to realize what people want and need. This done, they can then report to other powers—this latter might be ICSU for example. Powers like ICSU or the academies that represent international science and power are critical, in my view, for establishing new priorities and strategies. I also believe that on the eve of the new century, UNESCO must take a leading role and speak out so that the voice of science, science as solution to man's problems is heard by power. If we disagree with some of the present trends, or present solutions to the world's problem, then we must raise our voice. UNESCO is ready to take on this leadership role: it is essential that it is assumed by an institution at international level. We must act in accordance with the elements supplied to us by those in the forefront of science and research. The institutions themselves need a new image. They may be prestigious in top-level international journals, but they need a top-level image in the media too. For herein lies a further giant power, the press and media in general. The media today is a major actor in the building of a new society, in the establishment of a culture of peace—which is the ultimate role of UNESCO.

UNESCO, as I have said, is ready to assume this leadership role. We are working closely with many funds and institutions related to science, particularly with the regional banks, the Inter-American development bank, on various projects like the utilization of the global environment facilities for environmental issues. One challenge is how to establish closer working relations with, for example, the regional economical and political associations, with the European Union, the organization of African Unity, the South-East Asia Association. We must reach the intergovernmental organizations that are part of the diffuse power structure.

But, Mr Mayor of Genoa, as I have already said, where we need to begin to sow the seeds is in the cities, at local level, downstream. Because we can not hope to exercise influence upstream if we do not create this kind of mobilization of consciences at the city level. Today, the future of democracy and better sharing must begin in the cities, because it is there that the citizen, each man and woman, lives out each day. And it is at downstream level, in the context of the municipalities, that we have the all important productive sector, which forms part of wider networks at regional and global level. There are vastly important areas, in both public and private sectors, where we must establish links—such as in the field of energy, pathology, genetics, biotechnology, superconductors—area of science and technology that are critical for the quality of life and where there are important ethical issues to be considered. In all these areas, it is essential that we make connection between the upstream and downstream levels, in order to influence the various power to adopt new strategies and priorities.

I recall that the British Minister—Butler—who thought that an organization relating to education and culture would be very important in the aftermath of the War, initially excluded science because he considered the results of science to have been so destructive. But science was eventually include, in the hope that its applications would in future be more humane and would always take the social dimension into account. Yes, we must face up to the issue of the misuse of science, just as we must harness science to the need for preventive action in a wide range of areas. We are too often unprepared for rapid intervention, for humanitarian assistance, for averting civil conflicts, even in the heart of Europe. We are prepared for war but not for the task of peace. There is, thus, a vast change to be made here in mentalities, in our attitudes to knowledge and to the ways in which it is applied.

In this area, the research centres and universities have a major responsibility. We also need to ensure that there are very competent bodies able to provide the soundest ethical advice regarding the use and misuse of science. Bioethics is an important area because too much scientifically incorrect and potentially dangerous information emerges from the field of genetics. This is one of the reasons why UNESCO has set up an international bioethics committee to inform and advise in this crucial field.

Despite the difficulties, I am optimistic. I believe that ethical issues can be resolved, that international policies will be developed, that the sharing of knowledge can be achieved. We have the means, the methods, the equipment, even the funds. But at the same time, we must make it clear that governmental or non-governmental institutions are able to help countries provided they have the will to help themselves. For example, in February this year, at the opening of the Symposium on Science and Technology in Africa, held in Nairobi, I presented the World Science Report, together with a UNESCO contribution of a million dollars to establish the International Fund for Technological Development in Africa. I chose Africa to plant a seed which could grow, through other projects involving the African Development Bank, or the GEF. What we expect in return is that Africa should play its own part in this process, mobilizing its existing centres of excellence and making its own contribution to its scientific development. One of the most gratifying moments of my life in UNESCO was when I was in New Delhi last year, and India decided to double its investment in education. We need to see improvements in China, Nigeria, Egypt, Brazil, and this means billions of dollars, But it is vital, and our duty now is to draft appeals that emphasize the importance of science in relation to teaching, persuading, setting one's own priorities.

UNESCO is prepared to encourage any initiative that aims to bring about a new dialogue at the highest level, with governments or within societies, on issues relating to science, technology and society. Let me conclude, then, Madame Carettoni, by saying that UNESCO could not function properly if what you represent, the National Commissions, did not play their mobilizing role, that of being the permanent ear, listening in to what people in different countries want and need. I think the founders of UNESCO were very wise to establish the National Commissions, which serve as a platform for the media, journalists, scientists, poets, all those who represent our intellectual strength. They are key partners in the pursuit of our goals—in particular the one that matters most in the long run—promoting the transition from an age-old culture of war to a culture of peace.

We want a new vision of science in its relationship with society, with people educated in such a way as to take their own responsibilities, to be the sole designers of their future. I believe that this momentous transition, from the logic of force to the force of reason, can be facilitated by this appeal that will bear the name of Genoa.

26

Aims and Outcome of the Meeting

Introduction

Science is strongly associated with the powers of politics and economy in a series of conflicted areas like ethics and financial interest. Other powers, too, like the military establishment, the media, culture and religion, have far-reaching influence. One has to look no further than bioethics, in current hot debate round Europe. These areas of conflict, if left to drift, can work against man's own good.

The Genoa Forum on Science and Society took root in 1994, called by UNESCO in response to recognition and concern that a worldwide crisis of civilization is taking place, a crisis influenced by the relationship between science and power: wars, famine, fire, flood, poverty, energy emergencies, ecological disasters. The role of science, its potential, in improving man's quality of life and contributing to the dignity of human life, is given far too little merit or attention. The time has come when economic powers and governments can no longer decide without science what the future should be. Now is the time for it to take responsibility and not give in carelessly. The future our planet is to inherit is at risk.

Scientific research, as it becomes increasingly a phenomenon of political and economic relevance—for its vote-winning potential, the funding costs, the technological spin-offs it generates, its value in the war context—has begun to influence power, and is increasingly influenced by it. Not just influenced, but manipulated, since global science is heavily dependent on the financial power and strategic will of governments, the gaint institutions, the transnational corporations. Science has no power of its own. Science and power need to work in symbiosis or they will both sink together. The science and power meeting comes in the context of other UNESCO initiatives—the Culture of Peace and the Transforming of Scientific Communities in Europe. It can be seen as just one strand in the spectrum of a fresh examination of science and society.

New peace-building structures and new state policies are needed to find a new global ordering of priorities—financial, educational, scientific, cultural, social, human—to tackle global and local problems that threaten man's security and well-being, ranging from social injustice to the environment.

History

Until the end of last century, science lay in a domain of its own, in a world where power was measured by military power and richness of human resources. It was national and non-conflictual. But now, our nations are losing individual political power, with the newly opening up globalization. Instead, it is science that has become international and conflictual, the measure of power of a state. And as a super-power, science must accept responsibility.

In the centuries since Galileo's time, there has been the need to liberate science from the external constraints that distorted it. Today, there is a different risk. Science is being profaned, exploited to win votes, to wage war, to make huge personal profit—ethics to the wind.

Following the atomic and other tragedies of the past war, many pressure groups were established to guard against the misuse of science—for example the Club of Rome, founded in 1968. It was recognized that science needs directing, guiding, since it is patently creating as many problems as it is solving. Or worse—it is not even solving the issues it could. In fact, most catastrophes are the result of short-sighted politics and dishonesty.

The development of the computer sprang from the need to calculate ballistic paths for use in the last world war: the race to the moon had a strong political component; abortion and other bioethical issues are under the influence of the Catholic church in Italy; the media brought the radioactive lettuce scare to Italy; the human gunmen project walks a fine line between laboratory and stock exchange.

Instead, science can be of enormous benefit to mankind, used as a tool for progress. Not only for man but for economy and industry, to build up a nation's strength internationally.

Science and Power—Definitions

In order to examine the issues on the agenda, to identify where the real power lies, how it interacts with science, the meeting sought definitions of science and power, science that represents a realm of freedom, as such confronting power which by its very nature tends to constrain, particularly state power.

So what does science represent? The pursuit of science is universally regarded as one of the most fulfilling activities for both the individual and for society. The discoveries of the scientist are an immediate addition to humanity's heritage of knowledge and become a symbol of universality, though at the same time, it should be remembered that science has always more to learn, is subject to error that is corrected with time. The humility of science, however, is not a barrier to ambition for progress. From the point of view of ethics, science as it becomes increasingly applied is in danger of being used as an instrument of domination, an instrument of power over things and, more importantly, over people, even as an instrument of people's death. Then, from a geopolitial point of view, science is becoming increasingly sophisticated and expensive, and ever more out of reach of those without resources. The knowledge gap is widening between the major scientific centres mainly in the North, and the less developed countries.

In the context of cultures and society, science is synonymous with modernity and is a source of material and symbolic power. It certainly opens up prospects for development. But at the same time, it must tread carefully to preserve a balance between the cultural past and the unpredictable future. As an "imported" commodity, it risks rejection. Instead, the perception of the role of science and scientists is decisive for the establishment and development of a scientific culture and for the teaching of science.

Science as a discipline can be considered under two headings—basic and applied. Basic science is based on the need to understand, a pursuit that cannot be programmed. Its duty is to spread knowledge and eradicate ignorance, in order to set the stage for democracy. Knowledge, on the other hand, is a commodity that gives power to those who possess it, though in itself it is neutral, at one and the same time its strength and its weakness. Applied science, on the other hand, depends on economic, political and military policy decisions.

Power largely lies in the political or economic domains, though mainly in the latter—industry and banking, today's undisputed driving forces, since it is an uncontested fact that political power depends on economic power. The media also comes as a subset of economic power, and military subordinate to political power. Other major powers are culture, ethics and religion.

At present, science has a subservient position in all nation states, for which reason the direction of science is not under the control of scientists, but of their political and economic masters, who have no clear understanding of the political and economic limits of science. This situation can not be allowed to continue, if science is to deliver what will serve mankind's good.

To set the balance right, there are the counter—powers of justice, of the lobby, of the non-governmental organizations, and the UN, whose roles are examined. It is the Un's task to make appeal to the altruism between nations, to set a straying scientific agenda on track for the next millennium.

The Symposium

The First Reflection Meeting: International Symposium on Science and Power, as the first step of the Genoa Forum of UNESCO on Science and Society, was held in Genoa on 1-3 December 1994, and organized by the UNESCO Regional Office for Science and Technology for Europe (UNESCO-ROSTE) and the Italian National Commission for UNESCO, in collaboration with Italian national research institutions and with the City of Genoa. The meeting brought together top-level scientists, experts, and policy-makers from Central, East and West Europe, and the United States of America, including representatives of national commissions for UNESCO, international governmental and non-governmental organizations, and other prominent institutions.

Objectives

Worldwide, public, press, commerce and politicians appear deeply concerned about the state of global governance. Deep cracks are appearing in social structures, no part of the globe immune. The scientific community is being solicited to provide a vision to save the situation. The aims of the symposium were to give a first airing to the different facets associated with science and power, to discuss the relationship of science and scientists with the prevent power structures—how science is used by these power brokers. As part of this process, the meeting considered how the scientific community perceives itself vis-a-vis power. The goal was to reshape priorities and present trends. With a clear vision, appeals can be made for support and demands made regarding the direction of the future of science, with specifically identified targets—what to do, when to do it, whom to approach, what sort of science can be passed to the various powers, how power can be made to interact with science, to influence organizations of scientific research and transfer of knowledge, how the nation state can define and implement national science policies, which fall outside the interests of the giant corporations that hold the giant purse strings.

Opening of the Symposium

The meeting was hosted at Palazzo Tursi, the City Hall of Genoa, and sponsored by the Italian National Commission for UNESCO, the Municipality of Genoa and the University of Genoa. Welcome addresses and opening remarks were made by Senator T. Carettoni, President of the Italian National Commission for UNESCO; A. Sansa, Mayor of Genoa; S. Pontremoli, Rector of the University of Genoa; G. Mori, President of the Region of Liguria; Ambassador A. S. Sayyad, President of the UNESCO General Conference; P. Roseta, President of the

Committee of Science and Technology of the Parliamentary Assembly, Council of Europe, Strasbourg, G. Salvini, Vice-President of the Accademia dei Lincei, Rome, P. Mieli, Editor of the *Corriere della Sera*, Milan and V. Kouzminov, Chief, UNESCO Venice Office.

Working Sessions

The programme of the symposium was arranged in three major working sessions:

- *First working session.* Science and power/antagonism between these two human phenomena: historical and epistemological perspectives.
- *Second working session.* Social consequences of science and its influence on society.
- *Third working session.* Role of international scientific institutions in present science.

The participants' presentations during working sessions were followed by intense discussions: summaries of the debates were presented by moderators at the closing session.

The contributions of the moderators are strongly acknowledged: first working session A. Forti and E. Benvenuti; second working session P. Bisogno and L. Capogrossi-Colognesi; and third working session V. Kouzminov and J. Caraca.

Some 50 people attended, of whom 20 made formal presentations. Annex I contains a list of participants, whilst their presentations are collected in Annnex II.

The Next Step

Areas of interactions of science and power—science and parliament, science and local authorities, science and the mass media, for example—will be identified. Working groups will discuss these issues and bring their findings and recommendations at the various levels addressed to the Second Meeting of the Genoa Forum on Science and Society, scheduled for September 1995 in Genoa.

It is expected that the basic document reporting the outcome of this meeting, *"The Genoa Declaration of Science and Society"*, will be presented at the 28th session of the General Conference of UNESCO, which will take place in Paris in October-November 1995. It is also anticipated that UNESCO will continue worldwide discussions of the relationship between science and society in order to identify clearly the role of science in the third millennium.

Discussion

The meeting discussion took two overlapping forms—questions and comments arising directly from the presentations, and more protracted exploration during dedicated sessions. In the following, the main issues raised have been assembled under the various categories addressed: the types of powers being considered, problems associated with misdirected science, global catastrophes today, scientific literacy in modern government, the power of science itself, persuasion of the powers towards altruism, the real role of science and technology in Europe, priorities and reforms in science in countries in transition, science and responsibility, freedom of science, the influence of science on society, science education, military conversion, the culture of peace as a factor of transformation of science, the face of democracy, the costs of research, the role of international organizations, UNESCO programmes, international foundations, academies, science in the European Union.

Science and Power—Definitions

Basic and applied science were distinguished, the various forms of power that influence science and the areas where science influences power examined, and the crisis of science today highlighted.

Finding: Powers considered include economic, political, military, science, culture, ethics, religion, media, justice.

Finding: Basic and applied science are separate, the former a need to understand, pursued to spread knowledge, the latter closely linked in a two-way relationship to economic, political and military policy decisions.

Finding: Science represents a realm of freedom, and as such confronts power which by its very nature tends to constrain, particularly state power.

Finding: Science and knowledge are neutral. But they can be used to serve the ends of their manipulators.

Finding: Science is at the mercy of power, and can no longer be left in the hands of unscrupulous or universes decision-makers.

Finding: Science is fragile: there is a vital need to maintain the traditions and schools of science.

Recommendation: Governments need to be made aware of the crisis science is living. The findings and recommendations of this and related meetings must be communicated to governments, parliaments, scientific institutions, transnational corporations, etc., which are in a position to influence the direction of science.

The Responsibility of Science

The word's industrialized nation states are now living in a post-industrial, information-processing, post coldwar, reconstruction phase and as such are increasingly dependent on science. Science and its spin-off technologies shape the societies that sustain them. Their résponsibility could not be higher.

Finding: Science has the capacity and is the right medium for solving problems deriving from within science itself, as well as those external.

Finding: Science and scientists can and must take responsibility for solving these problems. In fact there is a worldwide call upon science to resolve them, through greater responsibility in education, culture, the environment, demography, thereby reaching an appropriate and desirable level of socio-economic development of society whilst respecting individual cultures.

Finding: Science represents a major facet of human development, and is one of the most fulfilling activities of an individual or a society.

Finding: Science has a subservient position in all nation states. It is directed by politics and economics. This situation must change if science is to serve the future of the planet.

Finding: New ethical rules are needed to halt abuse and limit the threats to mankind that are being created.

Finding: Some science is intentionally kept under rein, and results held secret, even in democracies. Overseas development aid can suffer from the financial interests of the supporting nations. For example, governments are reluctant to fund third-world co-operation in strategic and money-spinning areas like biotechnology.

Recommendation: Effort must be made so that science can learn to contribute to peace, to popularize, educate, persuade. Science must become altruistic, in an effort to solve the poverty, hunger, ecological problems it has in part created. Appeal to the political powers to this end must be made through the non-governmental organizations, UNESCO, etc.

Recommendation: Scientists must learn how to request funding.

Recommendation: The UN organs need to be instructed as to how to adapt their operations in the field of science and international co-operation, in order to meet human needs more efficiently.

Recommendation: The academies and research councils need to be restructured. They are heavily bureaucratic and fail to respond to today's requirements.

Democracy

The democratic value of science was examined.

Finding: Democracy implies a balance of power, and is strongly linked to equality.

Finding: Only a democracy can set the goals or limits science needs to have. It is important to go through a tiresome consensus that is democracy, in reaching decisions.

Finding: Science is a democratic republic, it induces democracy.

Finding: All those skilled in some area or field should have the same opportunity. This is democracy.

Recommendation: All modern democratic institutions and structures existing at national, regional and international level should be kept informed of science problems and be involved in an identification of the major orientations of the scientific development of society.

Recommendation: Democratic methods should be introduced and put into practice in all scientific communities.

Level of Interaction—Science and Culture

Science and culture progress together. Science policy must take culture into consideration at all levels.

Finding: Science is part of human culture; their interaction must ensure the progression on the cultural development of mankind, at all levels, starting from the citizen in his local community.

Finding: Science does not have a monopoly on culture.

Recommendation: Science policies should be elaborated at national level to ensure that the cultural identity of local communities is respected.

Level of Interaction—Science and the Media

The mass media hold vast power to influence thinking, from individual opinion through to that at political level. It thus has a responsibility not only to present undistorted facts, but also to guide the way science is perceived, so that it can be exploited to man's good.

Finding: The mass media is a major power capable of influencing public opinion, governments, and so on. It can therefore take on various tasks, including the elimination of scientific illiteracy.

Finding: Science can use the world of information to achieve its own counter-power.

Recommendation: Science needs to build and maintain a close link with the media in order to remain in control of the way it is presented. The scientist must make every effort to furnish unbiased, objective information to the media.

Recommendation: The role and purposes of the media should be clarified: this could be the task of UNESCO.

Recommendation: The media should review its own purposes, and assume the responsibility of contributing to cultural development through carefully identified scientific approaches.

Level of Interaction—the Citizen

The value of the individual in contributing to his own future by becoming involved in the problem of guiding science and power was emphasized.

Finding: Science has the task at citizen level of removing the mystery and mistrust surrounding science.

Finding: Global problems often stem from local ones. Citizens are mainly interested in resolving local problems, related to their own socio-economic and natural environment. For this reason, science should take on a major role at local scale; moreover, a good relationship with local power is essential to its success at local level.

Recommendation: Action must be taken at city, local, regional, national, international and global levels. The role of the cities, the extent to which local authorities can contribute, can be considerable and needs careful consideration. Reform can and must begin with the citizen. Cities are called upon to use education to awaken the citizen and forge attitudes for peaceful behaviour.

Level of Interaction—Government

For their decision-making, governments need input and guidance from scientists, but at the same time should be scientific literate.

Finding: Scientific literacy is an essential part of modern government.

Recommendation: Science must be presented in a positive way to the relevant powers: science as an element for decision-makers to persuade the powers. Acceptable alternatives must be offered. Scientists must enter discussion directly with politicians.

Level of Interaction—Intergovernmental, International And Non-Governmental Organizations

UNESCO is the institution that at international level is ready to raise its voice and dictate to power the needs of science and the societies that support it. It is ready to assume more responsibility in science, and could have no stronger a promoter than Director-General Federico Mayor.

Finding: The international organizations—the UN, the European Union, the European Community, the World Bank, the major foundations—have become worldwide superpowers, and guide science to their own purposes.

Finding: Science has penetrated into almost all scientific organizations compared with 50 years ago, when only UNESCO of the UN family had a role in safeguarding and guiding science. Today, all members of the family have a strong influence on science policy.

Finding: Bodies such as ICSU exist to support and defend the scientist. For example, ICSU intervenes vigorously with regimes or governments that suppress scientists.

Recommendation: The role of the intergovernmental institutions, international foundations, international societies should be given close examination. UNESCO and other international organs should continue or set up programmes to identify areas for reform or lobby.

Recommendation: UNESCO should take on more responsibility in science. There should be a stronger coordination between members of the UN family.

Recommendation: Educational programmes such as those of UNESCO should be used to teach the distinction between science and technology.

Recommendation: UNESCO has been a long-term builder of a culture of peace, through its educational, scientific and cultural aspects. But there should be more emphasis on the culture of peace in pre- and post-conflict situations. A campaign teaching preparedness against disaster, conflict hot spots, etc. should be given stronger emphasis.

Recommendation: Cultural reform for tolerance should be promoted, through UNESCO, mobilising intellectuals and scientists. Attitudes favouring peaceful behaviour should be foreged.

New Directions

Science must change direction. New priorities need to identified. The role of science is being studied by UNESCO in the multidisciplinary context of its other programmes.

Finding: Military conversion, involving largely nations in transition, must be handled with care in order than its inherent science is not lost. Basic science is at risk of losing its funding as the military—industrial complexes are dismantled.

Finding: The process of military conversion has the by-product of unemployable or underfunded military personnel or sciences or technologies. Strategically-driven military conversion aims to minimize waste of intellectual resources and maximize the exploitation of existing technologies for civilian use.

Recommendation: New legislation coupled with normative economic measures are required for individual nations to meet their individual requirements for military conversion and science preservation.

Nations in Transition

Nations in transition are having to reorganize the way science is governed. They are under pressure to preserve their scientific inheritance, but at the same time can seize the opportunity to change for the better, to bring awareness of the issues of science and power to their governments and decision-makers.

Finding: The symposium was useful to countries of East and Central Europe, in identifying problems, conflicts, and modalities with which the West is more familiar.

Finding: The issue of military conversion is particularly pressing in these nations, since it is this sector that has employed most science and scientists.

Recommendation: Solidarity should be promoted through collaboration with less-favoured regions.

Recommendation: Careful attention must be given to define priorities and reforms in science in countries in transition, as part of the battle for the survival of science itself in these countries. Existing facilities should be united and supported.

Part II

MILITARY CONVERSION AND SCIENCE

Outcomes of the Round Table on Military Conversion and Science

VENICE, 27-29 NOVEMBER, 1994

Introduction

The dramatic and far-reaching socio-economic and political changes in Central and Eastern Europe that began in the late 80's have prepared the ground for the establishment of global peace. Mankind had already been expecting the arrival of a widespread peace for half a century, and many societies widely believed that many vital but still open issues that threatened the globe's natural harmony could at last be settled.

As a result, "peace building" and "peace keeping" have become key words in our vocabularies, not only through our expectations of peace, but most particularly because peace has become a reality of our days, on that our offspring should enjoy.

The end of the Cold War and the dissolution of the superpower blocs has changed the role of international institutions, first and foremost that of the United Nations and its specialized agencies in their peace-building structures are needed to facilitate the transition from a culture of war to a culture of peace. Enormous opportunities for the socio-economic development of mankind have opened up, on the basis of the "peace dividend" resulting from the recent decline in global military spending.

UNESCO has always undertaken long-term actions to build the foundations of peace through education, science and culture, and communication and social sciences. These activities lie within the framework of one of the basic provisions recorded in UNESCO's Constitution by the organization's founders, which in particular declares that: "peace based exclusively upon the political and economic arrangements of governments would not be a peace which could secure the unanimous, lasting and sincere support of the world, and that the peace must therefore be founded, if it is not to fail, upon the intellectual and moral solidarity of mankind."

In response to the challenge of peace-building contained in the UN Secretary-General's Agenda for Peace, UNESCO has assummed a new and dynamic role, aimed at encouraging and reinforcing culture of peace in post-conflict, and especially pre-conflict situations. This is why UNESCO has launched its culture of peace programme. A culture of peace is the process of building trust and co-operation between peoples. It means learning to use words instead of weapons to resolve conflicts. It means fighting hunger and social injustice rather than each other. It means governments spending their resources on social programmes, not armies.

Of course, this is not an easy task for people and for organizations involved in the culture of peace process, especially at this initial phase.

Within this process, science, a unique phenomenon of mankind and integral part of his culture, occupies a special, very delicate position since has been one of the major contributors to the creation of giant war arsenals worldwide. During the Cold War period, many countries made intense use of both fundamental and applied science for military research and development, for creating sophisticated arms for mass-killing. Enormous capital investment have been made to date in building research centres and production capacities for this purpose. Into this military-oriented R&D effort were poured the best brains of almost all industrially developed countries: in consequence, the military-industrial complex is a possession of high intellectual potential which can and should be used for resolving the world community's most urgent problems.

The process of military conversion or defence conversion was begun on the basis of historical agreements between superpowers to drastically reduce their military arsenals and consequently military-oriented research and arms production.

The first roots of military conversion were put down a few years ago in the USA and the Russian Federation, followed soon after by other nations. Unfortunately, it was discovered that this process needs at least initially considerable capital investment in order to convert military R&D to civilian needs.

Moreover, it was discovered that in some countries this process is accompanied by new phenomena capable of causing additional tensions and instability within and external to the countries concerned.

One such is the "brain drain": it has been studied and discussed in detail at a number of international meetings held by different international organizations including UNESCO-ROSTE.

The problems of military conversion and their interaction with science, probably one of the most fragile components of the military-industrial complex, constitute a uniting global issue for learned societies, academies and organizations supporting and advancing basic research and technological development.

Many questions then arise. Just who should support science in this transitional period, in what way, how should the transformation be managed to be most effective, to avoid loss of intellectual potential at national and international level; how can defence-research science be redirected towards basic and virtually important problems such as environmental protection, human health, food production, and so on, how should this branch of science contribute to the peace-building and peace-keeping process throughout the world? These and other issues need close analysis, not least in order to be prepared for some of the conquences that can flare up and are hard to predict, even at this current stage of socio-economic development.

The International Round Table on Military Conversion and Science was convened in an attempt to clarify just such issues.

Military Conversion

Military conversion, or defence conversion, is taken to mean the management of change in the military and its supporting industrial base that has resulted from the problems in the current global political and economic climate. Today's military systems are extremely complex and have become too expensive to maintain: as a response, governments worldwide envisage a conversion to simplified and cheaper systems. But in all systemic environments, the switching from one stable state to another will require the consumption of energy. With social systems, this means the expenditure of effort and funding. Piecemeal reduction of a stable out undesirable system always results in chaos, and not stability. In this context, in the absence of specific defence conversion, military capability disintegration will ensure. In fact, what we are seeing at the moment is military contraction and not military conversion. We must consider the long-term vulnerability that is consequence of such action.

There are three major inter-related aspects to be dealt with: (i) the maintaining of a "minimum" state-of-the-art capability (military readiness to deal with a politically chosen part of the threat spectrum which must be preserved); (ii) the doing away with redundant capabilities and capacities; and (iii) absorption of products and personnel into the general economy.

Issues to examine include science and technology, human resource dislocations, incentive strategies, socio-economiic phenomena such as brain drain, the transformation of educational and scientific institutions and of culture in general. The machinery of conversion is to driven in parallel with the new culture of peace being promoted by UNESCO.

The process of military conversion has the by-product of unemployable or unfounded and underfunded military personnel and of scientists and technologists. Strategically driven military conversion aims to minimise waste of intellectual resources and maximise the exploitation of existing technologies for civilian use.

While global war is now less likely, regional threat to security has increased and the probability of local, tactical wars remains unchanged or even increased by the need of ethnic and religious groups for self-protection. The UNESCO Culture of Peace Programme aims to use transdisciplinary education to teach tolerance, overcoming resistance to change, and encouraging openness to the idea of learning to learn. Increased worldwide employment of women in science and their greater role in peace-keeping policy generation, implementation and evaluation, could lead to a softening of masculine, aggressive decision-making. A great deal of thought must be given to the effects of the change on future generations. We are already experience a disillusionment with science among school children who perceive little reward for the years of effort needed to become qualified scientists. It is, nevertheless, clear that science is one of the most important aspects of society, and should be given stronger promotion and made more accessible to non-scientists.

Science

Within the military-industrial complex is a high proportion of the world's science and scientists. Conversion will, therefore, mean a new outlook for science itself as well as the absorption and redeployment of scientists. In this new science, there will be reduced R&D expenditure, which prompts the question of who is to pay for basic science.

Cost

High capital investment is required, at least in the short-term, to create an efficient and stable long-term solution. It will be at least as costly as maintaining the status quo.

A few governments may benefit from military conversion by investing in dual-use technologies. In addition, some cost benefits may arise from international agreements or exchanges of commodities or capabilities.

On the whole, though, there will be no profit from military conversion itself. The anticipated benefits of redirecting military budgets into welfare are as much a myth as the peace dividend.

Timing

Medium- to long-term planning is essential not only for decision-making processes but also bearing in mind the intertia of industry. It must be recognized that there are no "quick fixes" to military conversion—20 years of patient effort may be needed for conversion to the civilian sphere, and even then the likelihood of success is uncertain. Constant monitoring should be written into any proposals, for measuring the overall success of conversion and non-conversion. Through time, it must be remembered that defence conversion is strongly context-dependent.

Legislation

New legislation coupled with normative economic measures are required by individual nation states to enable them to meet their individual requirement for military conversion and science preservation, including safeguards for the protection of new technologies and attendant intellectual property rights.

Personnel and Brain Drain

Care must be taken to absorb discharged military and civilian personnel employed by government to minimise potential conflicts within the general employment market. Attention must be given to maintaining jobs for the employable and incentives for retaining should be established. The talented scientists should not be left adrift in the wrong environment or given cause to seek satisfaction or remuneration in undesirable situations, or to be lured away from science into more remunerative employment in the business world.

Types of Conversion

Military establishments should be involved. While some three-quarters of military structures can convert easily (buildings, some jobs, some equipment), the rest (laboratories and the brains of some types of science) will not convert either quickly or cheaply.

Care must be taken with the speed and degree of military conversion, achieving as nearly as possible as workable balance between the military-industrial complex and the rest of the civilian economy. Unrealistic expectations could destroy the military industrial base and produce very costly dislocation in civilian industries. This suggests that regional, continental and international joint ventures or consortia could produce less costly, more sustainable solutions.

1

"It was the Best of Times, It was the Worst of Times"

IAN ANGELL

Prologue

UNESCO-ROSTE has brought together a formidable panel of international experts to discuss the transformation of the military-industrial complexes around the world. I am delighted to be invited to this meeting, and as the first speaker, it is my role to put your discussions into a broader context. In my talk today I will give you my vision of tomorrow's history, and advance the notion that military conversion is but a small part of far larger socio-economic changes.

Introduction

"It was the best of times, it was the worst of times, it was the age of wisdom, it was the age of foolishness, it was the epoch of belief, it was the epoch of incredulity, it was the season of Light, it was the season of Darkness, it was the spring of hope, it was the winter of despair, we had everything before us, we had nothing before us, we were all going direct to Heaven, we were all going direct the other way".

The first words of *A Tale of Two Cities*, used by Charles Dickens to describe the French Revolution, ring hauntingly true today. For we are on the verge of another revolution, a new social and economic reality, perched on the "Edge of Chaos"—

an Information Revolution that is taking us out of the Machine Age, into . . . who knows what.

This "Information Age" (see Daniel Bell [1]) will be just as significant as those of the Industrial Revolution. The very natures of work, of society, and even of capitalism itself, are mutating. These mutations are confronting each other in the political power vacuum left by the fall of communism, and the increasing impotence of liberal democracy when facing both the mass unemployment of its citizens, and the likely mass migration of the exploding population of the Third World (95 per cent of the world's population increases is in developing countries: see Kennedy [2]).

The End of History?

Francis Fukuyama [3], in his book *The End of History and the Last Man,* claimed that liberal democracy had triumphed. Like Hegel and Marx before him, he saw the perfectibility of the political system, hence "the End of History". The Soviet "evil empire" had fallen with hardly a shot being fired; the Berlin Wall likewise. US President George Bush foresaw a democratic "New World Order" in the end of the Cold War—aimed to give the voters a nice warm glow? But it is a glow of wishful thinking, encapsulated in terms like the "peace dividend" and "human rights"; a glow that is merely an illusion that will be shattered before the global economic realities to come in "Information Age". The "peace dividend" already looks like a sick joke to the redundant of the world's defence industries; how long will it be before the notion of "human rights" is as outdated as the "Divine Right of Kings"?

These sumug claims of a complete victory for enlightened liberal democracy sound singularly hollow before various military adventures in the Third World, the rabid nationalism of "ethnic cleansing", and hypocrisy of national boundaries slamming shut against the mass movement of populations. Perhaps the optimists are deluding themselves? Perhaps it is raw capitalism and not democracy that has prevailed? Perhaps today's fashionable version of democracy is the next to fall?

The world's media is speculating on a growing sense of global foreboding, uncertainty and gloom, bemoaning a worldwide crisis of confidence in social, political and economic institutions. The very past success of these institutions has made them degenerate, and has spawned systems of such complexity, that the old certainties are beginning to fail: *"nothing fails like success"* (Kenneth Boulding).

The New Barbarians

So is it the End of History? No! *"History is the natural selection of accidents"* (Trotsky) and our world is now full of accidents waiting of happen. *"Those who can't remember the past are condemned to repeat it"* (Santayana). Without a sense of the historic context of the present uncertainty, we will be unable to comprehend the forces of disorder that are undermining today's certainties.

Our present situation sounds hauntingly familiar. The more things change, the more they stay the same. In 358 AD Rome, a long-standing civilization based on organizational skills, commerce and technology, confident in its superiority, fell to the barbarian, hordes that were once its servants. Rome didn't just disappear, choice fragments were looted and reformed into new orders. Today the socio-political order of our civilization is on the verge of collapse. What will happen to us, now it is our turn? The coming millennium will be a time of amazing opportunities, emerging through the heroic actions of individuals and organizations; heroic, that is, in the classical sense. These opportunists, who will loot our civilization, I have come to call "the new barbarians".

"Now there are coming new barbarians cynics experimenters conquerors union of spiritual superiority with well-being and an excess of strength.

I point to something new: certainly for such a democratic type there exists the danger of the barbarian, but one has looked for it only in the depths. There exists also another type of barbarian, who comes from the heights: a species of conquering and ruling natures in search of material to mould. Prometheus was this kind of barbarian."

(Friedrich Nietzsche [4])

But why now? Quite simply, today's new technologies have unleashed unstoppable economic forces which are empowering adolescent forms of new barbarians. The new barbarians are imaginative outsiders who know that there are enormous opportunities for those who have the vigour and vitality to break free of the limitations of boundaries drawn from the past, and who can create their own boundaries, their own future.

The "new barbarian" hypothesis is not in itself a specific predicator of things to come. It is an account of the societal mechanism that drives transition and that recurs throughout human history, but particularly during times of turmoil, complexity and uncertainty. A mechanism whereby opportunists sweep away old moribund institutions, not in anarchy and chaos, but with new ideas, new moralities and new power structures; subsequently laying the foundations for new institutions: the "New Order".

No Pride and No Shame

Democratic politicians are perpetually surprised by these amoral opportunities who profit from leading a different path. In vain, our "representatives" try to legislate against them, and they have often succeeded in the past (witness USA against Leona Helmsely of *"only the little people pay taxes"* fame). But these politicians are just whistling in the wind of change (or should that be pissing into the wind?). Soon only the little people will pay taxes, the new barbarians will have a choice.

All the while, Western politicians are pandering to the masses by affecting the poses of CNN anchor-men (characterless good looks and perfect teeth), and exposing the fascism of political correctness. All the while they fail to see in it the excesses of a popular *"ideological thuggery"*; the hell of a collectivist heaven. But while the politicians are posing for the peasants, the new barbarians are carving out the New Order, as when money markets manipulate national currencies, and pour scorn on the pathetic pleas of finance ministers.

Impotent politicians worldwide (even Karl Marx anticipated politicians becoming ineffective, but for other reasons!) want to appear moral in their power broking. They seek the justification law". Yet they are thoroughly bewildered when the consequences of their actions finesse, even reverse, their best intentions.

But they should care? Politics has become a profession, and in these cynical and degenerate times politicians display no sense of pride and no sense of shame. More and more they are seen as self-seekers, losing all respect of those they represent. Nowadays, no-one believes them any more, or even cares. The latest "sleaze" scandals in Britain are not unexpected:

> *"giving money and power to government is like giving whiskey and car keys to teenage boys"* (P.J. O'Rourke)
> *"when buying and selling are controlled by legislation, the first things to be bought and sold are legislators"*. (P.J.O'Rourke)
> *"Professional people have no cares*
> *Whatever happens they get theirs"* (Ogden Nash)

The Myth of Control

What is going on? How have the pathetic politicians lost control over the course of events? How is it that they stand before us with sham, bluster, superficiality and panic, while their old certainties are falling apart?

All around the globe there is a growing sense of unease, and undercurrent of uncertainty, a feeling that it is all running out of control. With louder and louder voices, politicians parade and preen, and dabble on the world stage. The press and media cynically report it; they themselves now precipitate much that is news. Many business leaders are no better, as they perform the ritual incantations of market forces and pontificate about "Management of Change" and "Business Process Re-engineering". But it doesn't fool anybody. Their frantic search for a tidy and scientifically (= democratically) correct scheme is just an admission that the "experts" don't know what to do. Their Myth of Control is laid bare. All around us the institutional procedures that have stood the test of decades, centuries even, are degenerating. The sight of world leaders in a frenzy of meddling, and Nero-like fiddling is most unedifying. The glue of the old order, hypocrisy, is now coming unstuck.

History in Reverse

As you have already gathered, I disagree totally with Fukuyama's claims that History is ending and that there are *"No barbarians at the gates"* (a chapter in his book). For fundamental in his updated historicism of Hegel and Mark, is a belief in the unhindered continuation of collectivism; the tribe, the state, the herd supreme. As you will also realize, I do not accept that the utopian ideology of modern-day liberal democracy has triumphed once and for all. Like Imperial Rome, all I see in the triumph of universal franchise is "bread and circuses" for the masses (entertainment/television, sport, pop music), the death-throws preceding decline and fall.

Fukuyama fails to see that democracy is itself barbarism, an old and now degenerate barbarism. The barbarism of the many against the few, barbarism become respectable through being the norm, but barbarism all the same, a barbarism whose time has come . . . and gone. *"A democracy can not exist as a permanent form of government. It can only exist until a majority of voters discover that they can vote themselves largesse out of the public treasury"* (Alexander Tytler reported in [5]).

Make way for the barbarians, the opportunists awaiting their chance to hijack the future, and form a new order. The seeds of this new order are already here, they have always been here, they have already germinated. But are they friend or foe? They are the individuals and transnational organizations and companies that hold on loyalties to the herd. They are the press barons, the market manipulators, international businessmen, international terrorists, drug barons, neo-colonialist non-governmental organizations, criminal organizations, rejuvenated forms of older religious and political fundamentalists, amoral individualists; they are the power brokers, now cut free from the constraints of national boundaries by the new communications technologies. They are the virile, vigorous and vital opportunists who will strike at the power base of impotent politicians, bewildered businessmen and all the other trivialisers of our Age—and their time is coming, for *"history is on their side"*.

The new barbarians are here, they have already breached the smug walls of liberal democracy. They are the very reason for the uncertainty of our time. But blinkered by a present obsessed with past certainties, their growth remains shrouded to all but the most protective. The coming millennium will finally bury the ideologies of the presents century, the "century of the collective". The two hundred years of "social progress", instigated by the then-new barbarians of the French Revolution, are slowly being rolled back. History isn't ending, it is going into reverse (Baudrillard [6]).

Transition to a New Order

The drowning media are frantically clutching at straws. Many, if not most of today's commentators are deeply pessimistic, they see only chaos ahead. They see chaos because they are interpreting events in terms of the very control structures and institutions and are failing. They are reflecting an increasingly uncertain tomorrow in the distorting mirror of yesterday's defunct certainties. They want the world to be the way it ought to be.

The prevalent hope is that a flow tide of chaos can be turned back by re-imposing the old order, by reasserting strong social, political and economic control. Even though the times are changing, King Canute is alive and well, and has entered politics. His stance is a complete misunderstanding of the human condition. Control doesn't create order, just the opposite; order must be there first, and this order tolerates control. The pundits are confusing order with structure and stability; they are confusing cause and effect. Only by the concession of order, does the consequent control impose structure and stability. All order is transitory; order allows controls to work, and then order fails; consequently the certainty of control and structure collapses.

A new order is transparent to old perspectives; a new order can only be understood through the development of different ideas. *"The difficulty lies not in creating new ideas but in escaping from old ones"* (John Maynard Keynes).

The old controls and institutions are failing; uncertainty, as always, precedes the transition to a new order—and new controls. We live in a state of continuous and unremitting transition, it never goes away, it is only a matter of scale—sometimes that scale merits the label revolution. Will the future brand our present age as a time of revolution?

A New Philosophy

The Industrial Revolution seemed like chaos to those living through it. To old perspectives, any major transition to a new order seems like chaos; for the trend to a new order can only be recognized through the development of new and different ideas. "*When we lose the comfortable formulas that have hitherto been our guides among the complexities of existence . . . we feel like drowning in the ocean of facts until we find a new foothold or learn to swim*" (Werner Sombart, reported [5]).

So who will help us swim? Who will be the true voice of the new generation? Who will give us a philosophy to explain the new age? Who will be the new Karl Marx for the coming millennium? We wont't have to wait. He was born one hundred and fifty years ago (15 October 1844); he died just before this present century, which the would have despised, had begun (25 August 1990). Friedrich Nietzsche has given us his Zarathustra [7] and his "*philosophy with a hammer*" in numerous books [4], [8].

To him the future is going to be brutal; a future born of conflict. A conflict that is mitigated to a certain extent by a predisposition towards human virtues. But virtues based on strength, not weakness. "*I have often laughed at the weaklings who thought themselves good because they had no claws*". There has to be a disposition to confrontation—that even welcomes it. "*One is punished for being weak, not for being cruel*" (Baudelaire). Through conflict the new barbarians will be tempered in the flames of competition, and succeed. Their "*paradise lies in the shadow of swords*". Now more than ever before, the state needs its military-industrial complex.

Nietzsche recognized that democracy is basically a single platform—that of the virtue of tribal moralities: back to "basic values", the "*morality of the herd*", the "common good", power fixed in the tribe. But the new barbarians ignore tribal boundaries, tribal loyalties. The new barbarians see no particular virtue in the common good. To them the common good is not necessarily good, it is merely . . . common! They see modern-day democracy for what it is, a once-proud individualistic label that has been hijacked by collectivism. They know democracy in its presents form will continue for the time being, but it will be of no consequence to them. Times of uncertainty call out for leadership; but not leadership that panders to the "greatest good" and to egalitarian ideals, for that is a formula for mediocrity. "*There is no justice in equality*". To succeed, leadership must be strong in its striving—ruthless. New barbarians assert that healthy systems expel all poisons from within. *"Nature is not immoral when it has no pity for the degenerated"*.

"It was the best of times, it was the worst of times". We will be holding our discussion against the background of today's global degeneracy that I have described. Will we find *"the spring of hope"* or *"the winter of despair"*? You can guess what I believe. I am looking forward to hearing your opinions over the next two days.

REFERENCES

1. BELL D. (1976), *The Coming of the Post-Industrial Society: A Venture in Social Forecasting*, Basic Books, New York.
2. KENNEDY P. (1993), *Preparing for the Twenty-First Century*, Fontana, London.
3. FUKUYAMA F. (1992), *The End of History and the Last Man*, Penguin, London.
4. NIETZSCHE F. (1968), *Will to Power*, Vintage, New York.
5. CARR E.H. (1990), *What is History*, Penguin, London.
6. BAUDRILLARD J. (1994), *The Illusion of the End*, Polity Press, Cambridge.
7. NIETZSCHE F. (1969), *Thus spoke Zarathustra*, Penguin, London.
8. NIETZSCHE F. (1990), *Beyond Good and Evil*, Penguin, London.

2

Trends in RD Expenditures in the Community: Diversification in the Civilian Field*

ROBERT MAGNAVAL

The changes that have occurred in central and eastern Europe have drastically altered the perception of a global and immediate threat that previously existed in the West. This change is often traced back to the fall of the Berlin wall. In fact it was the Soviet US summit in Reykjavik in 1985 that set this process in motion. Western countries took advantage of the summit to cut their military budgets at a time when government finances were beginning to show serious deficits. The period from '90 to '92 witnessed an accelerating downward trend in the budgets of member states of the European Union. This reduction stabilized at around 3 to 4 per cent and is set to continue until 1996. In the USA real defence expenditure is expected to drop by 45 to 50 per cent from 1990 to the year 2000 (OTA 1993) and, according to estimates made by the European Research Institute

* Review of the literature based on data published in the "European Report on Science and Technology Indicators" eds. U. Muldur & L. Soete, Office for Publications of the European Communities, Report EUR 15897, 1994, 338 p. and "*L 'industrie europeenne de l'Armement:* Recherche, Developpement Technologique et Reconversion", STOA/GRIP Report, Ed. P. de Vestel European Parliaent, 1993, 109 p.

on Peace and Security GRIP (1993), the ratio of military expenditure to GDP through the Community will fall from 3 per cent in 1986 to 1.8 per cent in 1996.

Since the end of confrontation between the two blocs, tensions have nevertheless not disappeared. There are plenty of examples of conflict due to fundamentalist pressures, fervent nationalism and economic tensions but military intervention alone is no longer regarded as a course of action capable of solving these crises (SRI, 1994).

1. Reductions in Budgets and Changes in Employment

It is estimated that direct employment in the armaments industry amounted to 660,000 jobs in the Community in 1992. The rate of reduction in these jobs since 1984 has been twice as fast as the reduction in the turnover of the defence industry. On the basis of this data, two scenarios where predicted and described during a symposium organised by Science & Technology Options Assessment (STOA) in the European Parliament in 1993:

- One sconario assumes that the defence budgets of member states will fall from 117 billion ECU in 1992 to 103 billion ECU in 1996 (an annual drop of 3.2 per cent) with exports stabilizing and the turnover of armaments firms dropping from 49 to 43 billion ECU with the loss of 145,000 jobs by 1996;
- The other scenario foresees these budgets falling twice as much accompanied by an annual reduction in exports of 5 per cent which is the average rate observed since 1984 (Table 1). Job losses in manufacturing will amount to 220,000 jobs by 1996.

Cutbacks in civilian and military manpower in associated subcontracting activities and cuts in defence ministry personnel must be added to these figures. It is estimated that the number of jobs that will be lost every year the next two years will be more than 100,000.

Two other factors help make diversification unavoidable:

- The opening up of defence markets with competitive tendering by several suppliers forces companies to alter their customs and practices to match those in the civilian field.

- As far as the drop in exports associated with reduced defence efforts in developing countries and its consequences on industrial activity are concerned, the reader should refer to the data published by the Stockholm International Peace Research Institute (SIPRI) in 1993. It must not be overlooked that, between 1984 and 1991, exports from the European Union fell by 40 per cent in volume and that the armaments industry in Europe is more heavily reliant on exports than is the US armaments industry.

2. Industrial Conversion and Diversification

The process of conversion due to the reduction in public funding mentioned earlier has been accompanied by restructuring of armed forces in Europe intended to enhance their mobility, speed of intervention, specialization and multinational character. The main thrusts of this approach involve, in particular, aerial or space intelligence, communication networks, logistics and interopertability.

Many obstacles have been encountered in attempting to free up the necessary resources for these redefined needs. One of these is the inherent inertia of the military whose mode of operation and traditional missions do not naturally lend themselves to cooperation and exchanging information. Other problems are created by economic and social resistance in response to cut-backs in public expenditure whether they involve job losses or reduced purchasing of equipment (Table 1). Nevertheless, Europe is not completely inexperienced in matters of industrial restructuring. One could cite the case of the iron and steel industry which reduced its manpower by 52 per cent from 1975 to 1990 at a rate comparable to that planned in defence industries over the ten years from 1986 to 1996. The defence industry has several trump cards in can play in order to cope with this sudden transformation. The geographical distribution of defence firms is more balanced than that of the iron and steel industry. Some firms are located in regions that have significant capacity to adapt. The widely varied qualifications of personnel create the option of transferring labour from the military to the civilian field, an option that more traditional sectors do not have.

Faced with this economic situation, companies have had to make choices. They have often increased the range of their multiple products. They have blended a specialization strategy in the military sector (expanding niche market, export effort, cooperation between firms) with a passive (production cutback) or active retrenchment strategy (policy of acquiring stakes in civilian activities closely related to military activities (aerospace, car electronics, shipyards). Other firms have gradually withdrawn. Here too there are similarities and echoes of the process of transforming the economy from a war footing at the end of World War II, a task completed successfully within a few years. However, many companies involved in that process already had experience in the civilian field at the time whereas this does not apply to companies that are currently having to be converted. It is also clear that caution prevails; conversion in the strict sense of the word is rarely applicable, diversification is more frequently encountered. Regardless of the strategy adopted it is always confronted by an unfavourable general economic climate.

Such necessary adjustments are accompanied by intervention by government bodies. In Europe intervention is patterned on the measures taken as part of the restructuring of other sectors the iron and steel industry mentioned earlier is a good example. At the end of 1990 the Community launched the PER-IFRA initiative backed by 90 million ECU; 58 per cent of the funds supported projects linked to the reduction in military expenditure. In 1993 the KONVER programme was allocated 130 million ECU provided by the European Regional Development Fund (100 million) and the European Social Fund (30 million). In the future the KONVER II Community initiative will last several years and be allocated 500 million over the period 1994-97 (EC, 1994). In this regard, one should point out the weaknesses in statistical data making it possible to access the local impact of reduced activity in employment areas, something that makes it difficult to target intervention and concentrate Community action. KONVER differs in many respects from the programme implemented in the USA. It involves a regional rather than an engineering conversion campaign. As far as the support provided is concerned, the pluriannual KONVER plan is equivalent to half the aid provided by the American Technology Reinvestment Project programme.

3. Technology Research and Development

Member states invested 11.3 billion ECU in research and development in 1990; these amounts are calculated on the basis of the expenditure earmarked in the national budgets. These data differ from those of the OECD by roughly 4 per cent (Table 2). There are no precise details on R&D investment specific to companies which is estimated at approximately 2 billion ECU and mainly originates from French and British companies (GRIP, 1993). The distribution of research budgets between the various states revealed a wide variety of situations (Table 2). France and Great Britain are the European Economic Area (EEA) states most committed to military research effort, Germany, Spain, Italy and Sweden account for most of the remainder. Most military research is carried out within companies: 60 per cent in the case of Great Britain and 52 per cent in France (CREDIT, 1993). Table 3 summarises the data in Table 2 for the Big Three (Europe, USA, Japan) and shows that the American effort remains the biggest. Military research budgets in Japan and, to a lesser extent, in France are increasing and differ from the generally observed trend and, as is the case in the USA, this is explainable as stabilization after a sharp fall. Several reasons have been put forward to explain this development that has had little impact on research credits and sharp cuts in defence budgets (Table 1).

It is alleged that research capability is being preserved in order to multiply dual-use research and development lines with public support for research making it possible to accomplish the pilot phase (design of prototypes) without nevertheless financing subsequent production stages with a view to making savings. Major states are said to be carrying out an "upstream" technology watching brief.

One must nevertheless be cautious when interpreting the figures quoted for the defence industry because they do not necessarily correspond to research activities as defined by international bodies for civilian activities (CREDIT, 1993). One must also not overlook the fact that military research is generally scheduled over several years and, consequently, planned budgets and actual annual expenditure may differ significantly.

France and Great Britain, countries that are close to the American model, have an important share of DIRD that must be subtracted from normal mechanisms for directing and assessing research policy. The markets for which the results of such research are intended are often predetermined and have been protected for a long time.

The scheduling of this part of research corresponds to a linear representation of its role. Fundamental research, development and production are activities that are linked in a sequential and unambiguous manner. Comparative analysis of national systems for innovation shows that the weight of military research has also influenced, in these countries, the arrangements for defining the overall national research policy. Policies for missions with "targeted" or "enabling" programmes have been given preference rather than more horizontal actions (Nat. Inn. Systems, 1993).

In these countries, the relationship between science, political power and military research that had become clearly established before the Second World War has persisted during subsequent year. For a long time it was taken for granted that military technology, which benefited from unstinting finance, was ahead of civilian research. A number of examples to the contrary slightly altered this view in the 80's but nowadays the crumbling of defence budgets only highlights such doubts. Statistics that record the economic spin-offs from military research are nevertheless rare. British consultants ACOST (1989) estimated the proportion of the military R&D budget that could have civilian applications at 20 per cent. The demand for leading-edge technologies that meet the needs of a financially solvent civilian economy has now overtaken military demand. The process is being reversed to the extent that military application may depend on technology innovations of civilian origin or developments for civilian or military use (dual technologies). The Industrial R&D Advisory Committee (IRDAC) emphasized the importance of efforts to adapt defence-linked research in the report that it submitted to the fourth Outline Programme (1994-98) of the Community for technology research and development campaigns.

4. Coordination of Research and Development Efforts

Cooperation in matters of military research always involves tricky negotiations but it is necessary in Europe for at least two reasons. One reason is associated with the desire to avoid pointless duplication and the other reason is the interdependence of civilian and military R&D activities.

In the first matter, the European Independent Programme Group (EIPG) launched the European Cooperative Long Term Initiative in Defence (EUCLID) programme in 1988. This cooperation has now been entrusted to the Western European Armaments Group that reports to the UEO in 1993. Planned total financial backing for the EUCLID programme is 120 million ECU and roughly 50 per cent of this budget has already been committed since the programme was launched. Italy is one of the most active partners (12 per cent of resources). Despite this, cooperation is difficult to set up and contracts worth only 30 million ECU were awarded in 1993.

In the second matter, it was already been stated that the quality of technology performance in the civilian field rivals that in the defence sector. The boundary between military research and civilian research is tending to become blurred as the markets themselves open up and penetrate each other. Collaboration in defining research policies is inadequate. As the "Growth, Competitively, Employment" White Paper (1993) states: "this weakness is apparent in each member state between military research and civilian research carried out within fairly impermeable institutional frameworks". One might add that the organization of research departments in firms that have "dual" production also reflects this dichotomy.

Interdependence between civilian and military research raises the problem of coordinating the policies that sustain them. It is, therefore, not surprising that public intervention has been compelled to support the setting up of scientific and engineering networks that unite all those involved.

5. Cooperative Research, an Instrument for Diversification and Collaboration

Europe is in a good position to use all the resources offered by cooperative research in order to redirect and diversify the allocation of public funds in line with the needs of industry. Europe can draw on many national experiences in order to achieve this: Fraunhofer Gesellschaft, LINK programmes, community programmes: ESPRIT, RACE, BRITE-EURAM or European programmes: European Space Agency. Europe has also perceived the full benefit that it can obtain from such a mechanism. Note that the EUREKA civilian programme was launched in Europe in response to the American Strategic Defence Initiative in 1985.

Ten years of experience in matters of cooperative research demonstrate the richness of interaction between university and industrial research. This cooperation multiplies the economic effects anticipated by industry taken individually by a factor or 2 (EC, 1994).

DIRECT AND INDIRECT ECONOMIC EFFECTS OF COMMUNITY SUPPORT TO INDUSTRIAL TECHNOLOGY AND MATERIAL RESEARCH

CONSORTIA WITH ACADEMIC PARTNERS (1)
29 ECU

COMMUNITY RTD SUPPORT
1 ECU

CONSORTIA WITHOUT (1)
14 ECU

(1) *Based on an Assessment of the Brite Euram EC Programme Conducted by BETA, UNIV. Strasbourg (1993).*

In the current phase of bringing together military and civilian research, this interactive mechanism will, by its very nature, have an incentivising role in avoiding pointless duplication by encouraging flexibility and collaboration, if necessary, in a difficult budgetary context. The new US administration also has a global approach to national security questions that integrates technological development, economic performance and defence questions.

The benefits of the link between the Pentagon and US micro-electronics firms in the SEMATECH consortium have encouraged those in charge to promote more interventionist policies. The ARPA agency coordinates the development of dual-use technologies as part of the Technology Reinvestment Project mentioned under heading 2. The US administration is now keen to free federal laboratories from their dependence on the Department of Energy (DOE) and the Department of Defence (DOD). This implies a modification of US legislation: the Federal Technology Transfer Act of 1986 and National Competitiveness Technology Transfer Act of 1989 (NSF, 1993). The USA has used the mechanisms provided by cooperative research in order to facilitate the transfer of results of research as well as that of the know-how of researchers. One of the instruments used by all US Federal agencies consists of Cooperative Research and Development Agreements (CRADAs). The number of these agreements grew from 33 in 1987 to 1175 in 1992, all federal agencies included. The extension of CRADA agreements to national laboratories dependent on the DOE defence programme required long negotiations that lasted from 9 to 24 months before they could be implemented. There were only 15 agreements in 1991 as opposed to 382 in early 1993 (OTA, 1993) but the financial limits remain modest: less than 300 million ECU. Questions of confidentiality, copyright, national preference and legal responsibility linked to commercial exploitation have been systematized, but not without some difficulty. 40 years of close links between major armament companies and the DOD are not easy to reorganise. Many observers still have reservations regarding the outcome of this policy (B.Berkowitz, 1994).

At the Community level, the French General Delegation for Armaments (DGA) has recently analysed the capacity of the Community's fourth framework programme (1994-98) to facilitate the diversification strategy of industry. DGA estimates that one-third of the activities of the different research and technological development activities proposed for the period (1994-98) might be of interest for concerned industries or agencies. It corresponds to 3.6 million ECU out of the overall amount of 12.3 billion for that period.

Fourth Framework Programme (1994-98)	*Total amount Millions ECU*	*Dual use/ diversified. (1)%*	*Partial amount diversified*
Telematics	843	20%	168
Communication technologies	630	57%	360
Information technologies	1932	84%	1622
Industrial technologies and materials technologies	1707	30%	512
Standardization, measurement and testing	288	10%	28
Environment and climate	852	11%	93
Marine sciences and technologies	228		
Biotechnology	552		
Biomedicine and health	336	50%	168
Agriculture and fisheries (including agro-industry, food technologies, forestry, agriculture and rural development)	684	0%	0
Non-nuclear energy	1002	20%	200
Nuclear safety and safeguards	414	50%	207
Controlled thermonuclear fusion	840	0%	0
Transport	240	10%	24
Targeted socio-economic research (incl. Perspective Technological Institute JRC)			
Cooperation on research with third countries and international organizations	540	20%	108
Dissemination and exploitation of results	330	20%	66
Stimulation of training & mobility of researchers	744	10%	74
Total	**12300**	**30%**	**3652**

(1) An assessment of partnerships between public and private research shows that co-operative networking favours the emergence of innovation. Adapting and widening these intervention arrangements of a national and community scale are decisive means of making the transition towards diversification.

Table 1. Budget cuts and employment evolution within the defence sector.

Defence budgets for industrialised countries (1)			*Internal market* (1) *equipment*	
Country	**1984**	**1992**	**1984**	**1992**
Germany	25,617	23,771	9,980	8,121
Belgium	2,645	2,206	0,881	0,428
Denmark	2,020	2,016	0,717	0,622
Spain	6,359	5,440	2,412	1,973
France	25,379	26,857	10,752	12,660
Greece	3,264	3,027	1,218	0,858
Ireland	0,414	0,383		
Italy	12,422	15,566	3,727	3,849
Luxemburg				
Netherlands	5,891	5,668	1,607	1,417
Portugal	1,041	1,481	0,209	0,205
United Kingdom	33,722	31,035	15,518	11,782
Total E.C.	118,774	117,467	47,020	41,916
Austria	1,238	1,178	0,276	0,283
Finland	1,847	1,599	0,697	0,734
Norway	2,326	2,677	0,850	0,930
Sweden	4,283	4,148	1,536	1,659
Switzerland	2,940	2,773	1,473	1,375
Total EFTA	12,634	12,376	4,831	4,980
United States (3)	219,186	222,534	109,207	110,035
Canada	7,621	7,746	2,756	2,644
Japan	17,434	23,942	7,187	10,051
General Total	375,648	384,065	171,002	169,626

Table 1 *contd.*

	Turnover of Industry[1]		*Export Trade*[1]		*Direct employment in the armament production*	
Country	*1984*	*1992*	*1984*	*1992*[2]	*1984*	*1992*[2]
Germany	11,101	9,034	1,868	1,506	147.00	93.000
Belgium	1,366	0,527	0,672	0,165	28.000	8.000
Denmark	0,617	0,587	0,050	0,024	10.000	8.000
Spain	3,565	2,499	1,256	0,588	77.000	41.000
France	16,360	15,467	6,626	3,578	290.000	195.000
Greece	0,966	0,472	0,163	0,011	24.000	15.000
Ireland						
Italy	5,168	4,224	1,772	0,805	95.000	67.000
Luxemburg						
Netherlands	1,437	1,432	0,568	0,328	24.000	20.000
Portugal	0,269	0,190	0,182	0,027	16.000	11.000
United Kingdom	19,244	14,390	4,227	3,390	360.000	204.000
Total E.C.	60,091	48,822	17,384	10,423	1,071.00	662.000
Austria	0,579	0,270	0,350	0,0032	12.000	5.000
Finland	0,634	0,762	0,054	0,038	10.000	8.000
Norway	0,527	0,726	0,044	0,040	10.000	12.000
Sweden	1,800	2,019	0,425	0,480	24.000	23.000
Switzerland	0,835	1,389	0,261	0,170	12.000	14.000
Total EFTA	4,373	5,174	1,135	0,760	68.000	62.000
United States [3]	119,068	123,952	10,313	14,497	1,323.000	1,178.000
Canada	3,150	2,894	0,723	0,374	76.000	78.000
Japan	6,635	8,968	0,232	0,074	42.000	34.000
General Total	193,317	189,809	29,796	26,128	2,580.000	2,014.000

Source: G Defence. VE1— [1] expressed in billion constant ECUS 1990— [2] evaluation—[3] actual expenses (budget outlays)

Table 2. Government outlays for military R&D expenditures

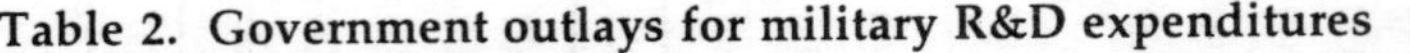

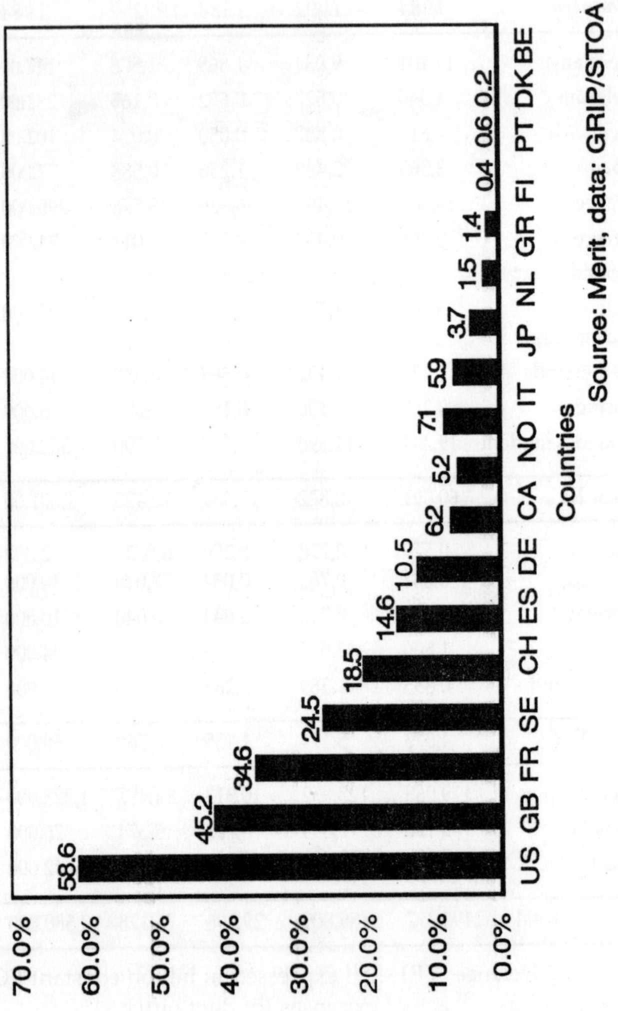

Table 3. Trends in military R&D expenditures government outlays

(in BECU, in constant 1990 prices)

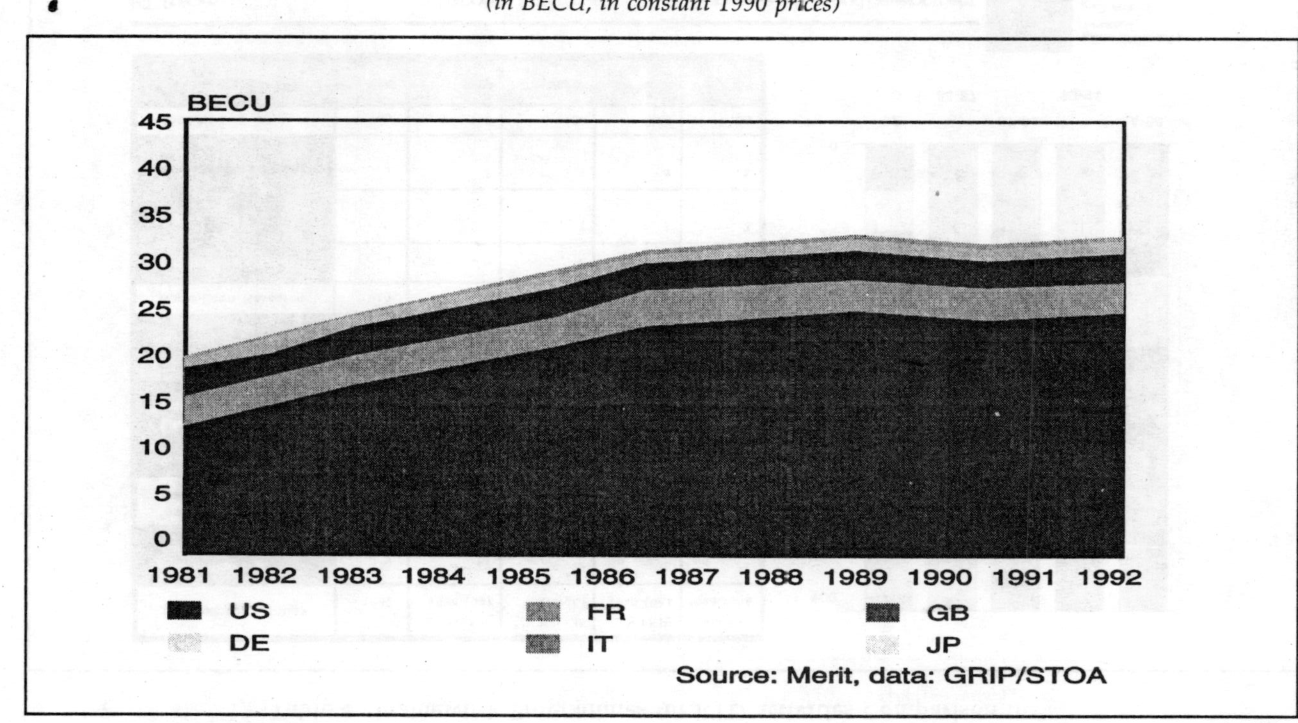

Source: Merit, data: GRIP/STOA

Table 4. Framework Programmes for RTD activities Comparison in %

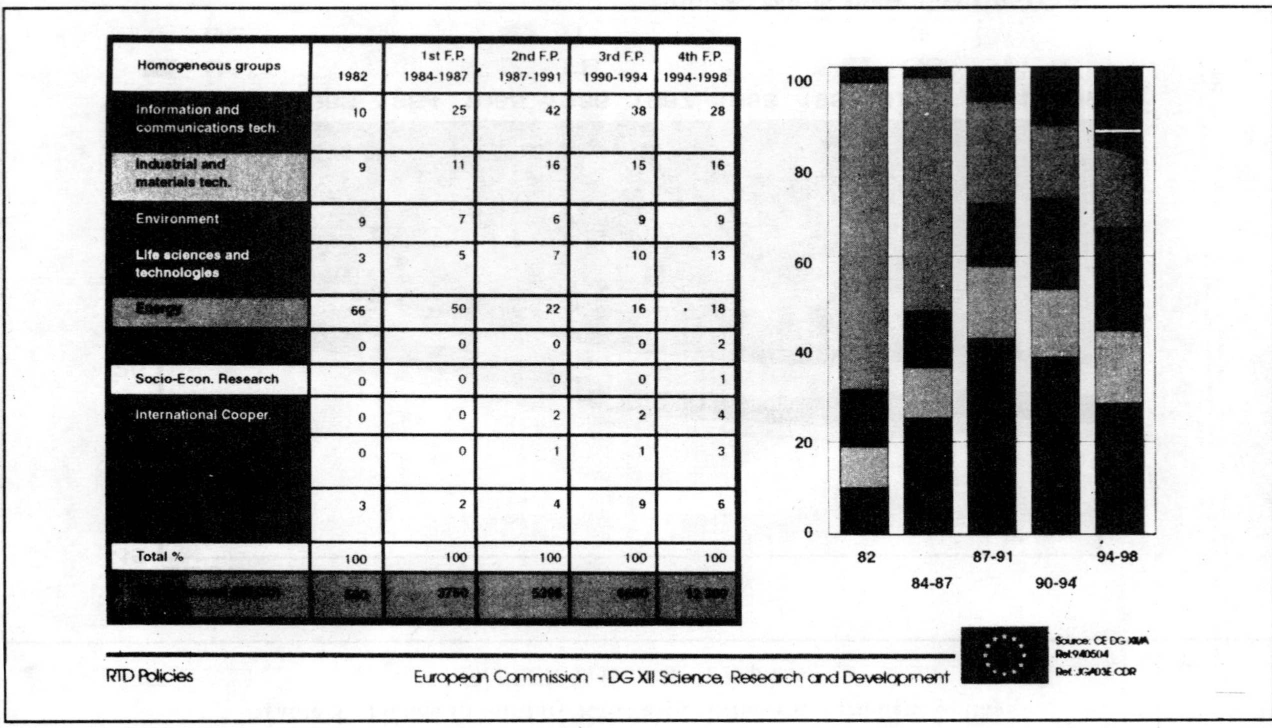

Homogeneous groups	1982	1st F.P. 1984-1987	2nd F.P. 1987-1991	3rd F.P. 1990-1994	4th F.P. 1994-1998
Information and communications tech.	10	25	42	38	28
Industrial and materials tech.	9	11	16	15	16
Environment	9	7	6	9	9
Life sciences and technologies	3	5	7	10	13
Energy	66	50	22	16	18
	0	0	0	0	2
Socio-Econ. Research	0	0	0	0	1
International Cooper.	0	0	2	2	4
	0	0	1	1	3
	3	2	4	9	6
Total %	100	100	100	100	100
[illegible]	[illegible]	3750	5396	6600	12 300

Table 5. Fourth Framework Programmes (1994-1998) Distribution in %

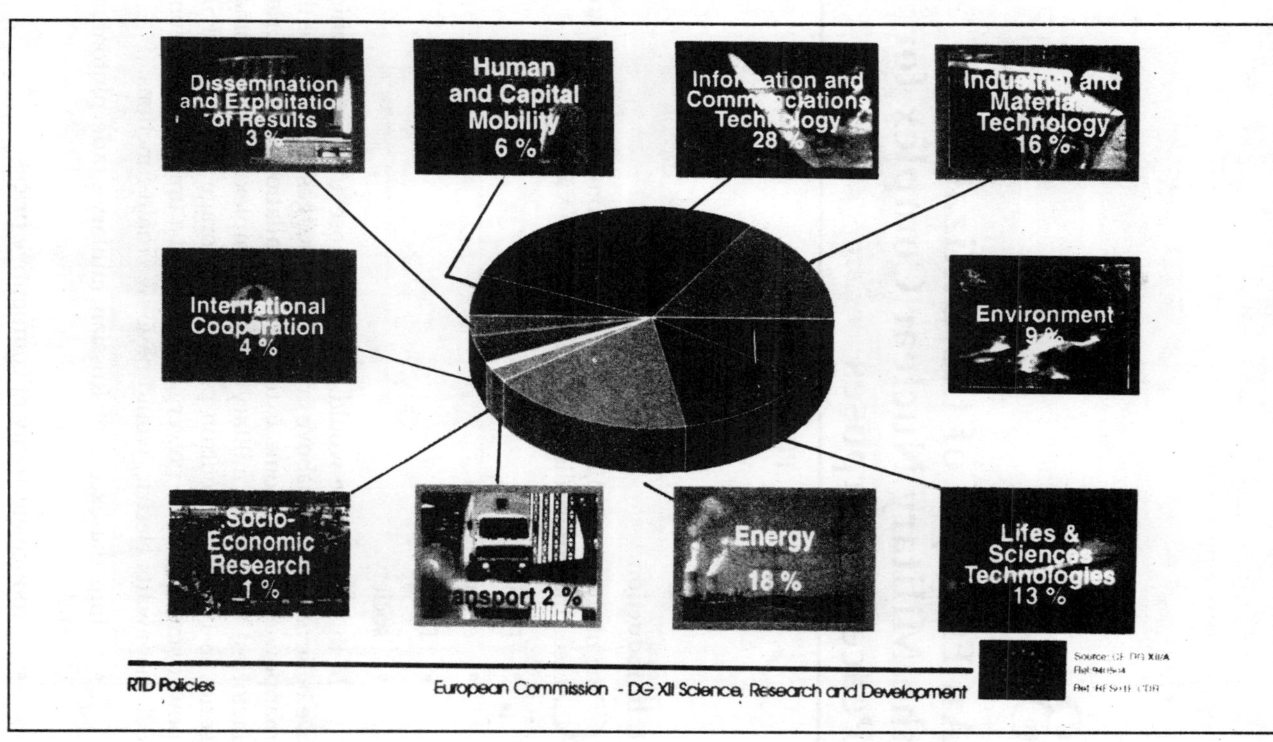

3

An Example of the Utilization of the Military Nuclear Complex for Peaceful Purposes

PIERRE ZALESKI

1. Introduction

One of the major difficulties in military conversion is to find cases that are realistic from the point of view of:

- politics
- economics
- financing
- society.

In this report, we would like to propose an example which we believe meets the above criteria. The suggestion is to use the manpower, and to some extent the installations (laboratories, factories) of Russia's military nuclear complex to build a small series (8-10) of fast neutron plutonium storage reactor (FNPSR) power stations. These power stations, with a unit output of some 800 megawatts electric, would have two main functions:

- store the excess of Russian military-grade plutonium, and
- produce electricity at competitive prices.

2. Political Aspects

As a result of the agreement on nuclear arms limitation between the US and Russia, there will be available a large quantity of fissile materials. The utilization of highly enriched uranium poses no major problems; the solutions exist and are in the process of implementation.

On the other hand, there is no clear and well-accepted solution for weapons-grade plutonium.

Indeed, there are two opposite attitudes:

- The first is represented by Russia and also by many OECD countries like France, Japan, and the UK. It can be summarized as follows:

Civilian nuclear energy is an important and very acceptable (from the economic and environmental aspects) source of energy for the long term. It is absolutely necessary to develop nuclear power during the next century if one wishes to satisfy the world needs for energy and especially the developing countries' needs. The other sources of energy—fossil, renewable...— alone, even combined with a substantial effort of energy saving and efficient energy use, will not be sufficient (Refs. 1 and 2).

To achieve this sustained development for the long term, it will be necessary sooner or later, but certainly during the next century, to use more efficiently uranium through the use of plutonium in fast breeder reactors. Therefore, in view of those countries, plutonium is a precious material which sooner or later will be indispensable and, even if for the moment its use for energy production in fast breeder reactors is not economic, it should be preserved for the future. We can observe that plutonium already contributes a very substantial part of the energy produced in light water reactors, where it is formed and burned in situ. It is also used in some countries, notably France, after extraction during reprocessing of standard fuels, and incorporation in mixed-oxide (MOX) fuel and utilized in light water reactors. This last technique is presently only marginally economic.

- The second attitude is represented notably by the US government, and can be summarized as follows.

There is no explicit statement that nuclear energy contribution to world needs will be limited, in fact, very limited. But the indirect statements, and most of the actions, of the administration of President Clinton indicate that nothing is done to ensure the long-term contribution of nuclear energy to world energy needs.

The opposition of the reprocessing of spent nuclear fuel, and endorsement of direct and irretrievable disposal of this fuel, as well as abandonment of all development of fast breeder reactors, clearly indicate that the US administration tends to consider that nuclear energy will play only a very limited role in the future. Indeed, by using present technology light water reactors and without recycling, the world's reasonably assured uranium resources, plus those expected to be recoverable at $130 per kilogram, would produce an energy equivalent of 350 billion barrels of oil. This represents only one-third of the proven resources of oil and gas, and one-thirtieth of the resources of coal (Ref. 3). From this point of view, plutonium is a nuisance, and its only quality—use for nuclear weapons—applied to excess weapons-grade plutonium becomes a major problem and concern. The only preoccupation of the US is how to destroy this plutonium, if possible, and if not, how to safely dispose of it.

The US National Academy of Sciences report on this subject considers two main ways to dispose of this plutonium. One is to incorporate it in MOX fuel and denature it by irradiation in light water reactors, and then dispose of it irretrievably in deep geological storage; the second is to mix it with fission products, and then dispose of the mixture in deep geological, irretrievable storage.

If one considers these two views and tries to apply them to the excess of weapons-grade plutonium in Russia, which may be estimated at some 80-100 tonnes, one has no really good solution:

- contamination by fission products and final disposal is not acceptable for Russia;
- burning it in Russian light water reactors is possible, but far from an optimal solution. It would have the following problems:

(a) It would take quite a long time. It would, therefore require long temporary storage, which costs money, and is not foolproof from the proliferation viewpoint. For example, with a change of government in Russia, it would be possible to re-use this plutonium a short notice for making weapons.

(b) the economics of recycling this plutonium as MOX under Russian conditions must still be demonstrated.

(c) It does not completely preserve the plutonium for future uses in breeder reactors, which according to View No.1, would be the preferable solution for the future.

A third solution has been suggested by the Japanese, namely burning the plutonium in a newly developed fuel (plutonium incorporated in a neutral matrix) in Russian light water reactors. This technique has not been demonstrated, and its economics are far from clear; it is also contrary to the idea that the plutonium shall be preserved for future uses.

Our proposal consists in building FNPSR reactors with an internal breeding ratio close to 1, no blanket, and with rather low specific power—some 10 to 15 kg of Pu per MWe—using large-diameter fuel rods.

These reactors, fueled with weapons-grade plutonium, shall be designed to obtain a very long residence time for fuel, up to 10-20 years. This solution may satisfy the US point of view, because plutonium in an operating fast reactor core is safe and more difficult for re-fuse in warheads than is plutonium stored in retrievable safeguarded storage.

It may also satisfy Russia, since with a breeding ratio near 1, after full burnup, the quantity of plutonium recovered and available for future use will be substantially similar to the original quality. It may also satisfy countries like France, Japan, and the UK, since this solution gives on the one hand the safest storage for Russian weapons-grade plutonium while producing electricity at a competitive price (see following paragraph) and maintaining know-how and increasing operating experience with fast neutron power station, useful for future FBR development.

After the maximum burnup is achieved (10-20 years), the following options would be possible:

- exchange Russian plutonium "denatured" in spent fuel for US weapons-grade plutonium, and use the latter for the second load of the FNPSR stations.
- reprocess the spent fuel and re-fuse the plutonium in the same reactors.
- store the denatured plutonium in safeguarded, retrievable storage for future use, and use civilian plutonium for the second fuel load.

After two or three fuel cycles are done in the FNPSR and the reactors have reached the end of their useful life, one will have to choose one of the following solutions:

1. If the American view prevails, definitively dispose of Pu in underground storage, or if American views still prevail but environmental concerns dictate it, burn the Pu in fast burner reactors (See Ref. 4, Capra programme).

2. If the first attitude prevails and nuclear energy is developed, use this Pu in fast neutron breeder reactors.

3. If the conditions are still not clear 40-50 years from now, store the plutonium in a new series of FNPSR power stations. This would preserve all options open and the decision would be made in a clearer context.

One of the important aspects of this kind of project is timing. For our idea, we could imagine the following schedule: 10 years for development and validation of the concept, notably fuel irradiation; however, the start of construction of the first reactors could be envisaged before all experimental results are in hand, for example, seven years after the start of the project.

Duration of construction could be estimated at 5-6 years, and one could conceive construction starts every year on three reactor units. With these rather optimistic assumptions, the total project would take some 15 years. Considering that this dismantlement of plutonium warheads will likely come after dismantlement of uranium 235 warheads and that one will need the plutonium for fabrication of first fuel loads for FNPSR some

8 years after the beginning of the project, the above schedule is rather consistent with safe disposal of military plutonium.

3. Technical Aspects

With plutonium value of zero or negative—indeed, the owner of plutonium may pay some fee for storage which otherwise is not free (safeguards)—one has to reoptimize fast neutron breeder cores. The natural idea is to tend in the fast neutron plutonium storage cores to use as much plutonium per MWe as possible, in view to store more Pu per MWe and also to increase the diameter of fuel rods, decreasing the relative contribution of fuel fabrication of the total cost of a kilowatt-hour. It is also natural to increase the residence time of fuel in-reactor, in view to simplify fuel handling equipment without penalizing the availability factor.

In achieving these objectives, one will get a higher Doppler coefficient, which plays a positive role in controlling power excursions, but one will also get a more positive sodium void coefficient, which has an adverse effect on safety. One will also get a higher internal breeding ratio necessary to allow longer residence time by minimizing the reactivity changes.

One will, therefore, have to optimize the core to ensure an overall safe behaviour. To do this, one can, for example, design a relatively flat core and ensure power design of the upper plenum so that any sodium voiding of a section of core will inevitably lead to sodium voiding of the corresponding section of the upper plenum, where the reactivity effect can be designed to be negative.

In addition, it seems reasonable to limit the size of the core by limiting the total output of each power unit. A reasonable value would be between 600 and 800 MWe. We may note that these values correspond to well-developed technology in Russia. The BN-600 fast breeder reactor has been operating very successfully for over 10 years, with an availability that is among the best in Russia, but also among the best in the world, all types of nuclear plants considered. Its average availability over 10 years was 97.5 per cent, with a capacity factor of 71 per cent.

In addition, Russia has developed detailed projects for the BN-800 fast breeder reactor type, directly inspired from BN-600 technology (Ref. 5). Therefore, with some cooperation from western Europe (Phenix, Superphenix, EFR projects) and Japan (Monju), Russian scientists and technicians should be able to design and build without too much development a safe 800-MW fast neutron power station.

The optimization of core mentioned above, the development and fabrication of Pu-bearing fuel with large diameter rods, will require close collaboration with western countries, notably with France, which has more experience in Pu-bearing fuel than Russia.

The last domain—core and fuel—is the most innovative for the FNPSR design, and will probably require the most R&D.

The typical goals for the design may be:

- fuel rod diameter about twice that used in present breeder designs;
- specific power in the range of 10-15 kg Pu per MWe;
- internal breeding ratio in the range of 0.9 to 1.0;
- residence time of fuel in the reactor, 10-20 years.

4. Economics Aspects

Even if the project shall for pragmatic reasons be closely related to the Russian BN-800 project, we will base our discussion of economic aspects first on the very recent (1993) EFR study carried out by utilities and manufacturers from France, Germany and the UK, since as far as we know this is the most recent, serious and pertinent study.

This study (Ref. 6) shows that in a western European context, a series of 1,500-MW FBRS, taking a plutonium value of zero, can be in the range of economic competitively with LWRs, as least with some uncertainty margin.

This series of FBRs was not optimized for plutonium storage; therefore, one can hope that some gains could be obtained due to:

1. simplified fuel handling equipment design (fuel handling every 10 to 20 years);

2. much lower cost of fuel cycle. The large fuel rod diameter makes it possible to produce more energy per rod (for example 4 times as much), and the cost of fuel rod fabrication should not be very sensitive to the diameter;

3. potential fees to be paid by plutonium owners (for the storage function).

Thus, these gains should lead in the EFR context to a situation very competitive with LWRs.

This result should be transposable to the Russian context, provided a well-planned construction of a series of identical plants is considered (8-10 800-MW units).

There may, however, be one penalizing point, namely, the 800-MW size, which was originally selected for core design and local pragmatic reasons (the existence of BN-600 and of a detailed project for BN-800).

This size is much smaller than the 1,450-MW contemplated in the EFR studies, and slightly smaller than the typical modern Russian LWR of 1,000 MW. The economic penalty for size effect should probably not exceed the advantage due to the re-optimization of the EFR core (see above).

One can, therefore, expect that this project has a good potential for competitively with LWR projects in Russia, that is, that it could produce electricity at the same price.

5. Financial Aspects

The need for new electric power plants in Russia is quite evident. Even if the domestic demand is not growing, because of the development of energy saving and efficient energy use, the possibility of exports to neighbouring countries and the need to replace older power plants, nuclear or not, justifies new construction.

However, because of the difficult economic situation in Russia, international financing seems necessary, at least for the major part of a plant, and at the same time appears to be possible. Indeed, the international community, and especially OECD countries, should be interested in resolving the problems of the safe storage of weapons-grade plutonium, and some of the OECD countries should be interested in maintaining world expertise and increasing operational experience in fast neutron reactor power plants, and the entire international community in helping the Russian economy in its effort of reconstruction.

A potential additional motivation may exist if Russian authorities accept to link the building of these new plants with decommissioning of older and less-safe nuclear power plants.

All this being said, the important question is how Russia can reimburse the money borrowed for these projects?

What will certainly reassure potential lenders is a contract expressing the reimbursement in a commodity exported normally by Russia, which has well-established international value and which is in demand in the lending countries, for example, natural gas.

The other advantage to link the reimbursement to gas is that Russia can consider that is saves gas when producing electricity with new plant, and reimburses only part of the saved gas.

Let us make some very simplified back-of-envelope calculations, which have no other intention than to indicate some trends.

In a French Ministry of Industry study (Ref. 7), the costs of a kilowatt-hour produced on the one hand by a combined-cycle natural gas plant and on the other hand by a nuclear plant are analyzed. The plants are assumed to be in operation in the year 2003, and the discount rate is 8 per cent for zero inflation. The capital cost (amortization and interest charges) of a 1,400-MW LWR plant expressed per Kwh produced by the plant operated in baseload mode represents some 64 per cent of the cost of natural gas in France necessary to produce one Kwh in a combined-cycle gas plant operating in the baseload mode, assuming a low (conservative) hypothesis for gas prices at the beginning of the next century.

If one assumes that a FNPSR power plant of 800 MW will have an overall capital cost of 1.3 times that of a 1,400-MW LWR plant in France (the 30 per cent extra cost being compensated by cheaper fuel cycle cost), the amortization and interest charge for this plant will represent 83 per cent of the cost of natural gas needed to generate the same under of Kwh.

In fact, as some eminent Russian scientists (Ref. 8) have indicated, in the present situation and for a given amount of dollars or other hard currency, the Russian nuclear industry may perform much more work than western industry. For some specific examples related to the upgrading of old Russian reactors, they indicate a factor of 16 for the cost-efficiency of Russian versus western industry.

Even if we may consider this factor as applicable only to some specific situations, it would not be extraordinary to consider a factor of two to four—let us say three—to characterize the relative cost-efficiencies of the two industries (Russian and western). This may be due to the relative low cost of labour in Russia expressed in hard currency, as well as the high contribution of labour costs in the total cost of nuclear construction.

If we assume that at least 75 per cent of work for construction of ENPSR stations could and would be done by Russian industry, we would then have a cost expressed in hard currency and in percentage of typical western costs for the same work equal to: 75%/3 + 25% = 50%.

In this context, it would suffice to devote 41.5 per cent of the gas saved to the payment of interest at 8 per cent and amortization of the capital cost.

We have taken 8% for the interest rate from the French study (Ref. 7). This is a rather high rate, but can be rationalized by considering that it includes some risk factor for political and economic uncertainties in Russia.

This back-of-envelope calculation indicates that construction of such reactors with western financing secured by Russian gas sales may be quite advantageous financially for Russia as well as acceptable for western lenders, such as some OECD countries and/or the EBRD and the European Union.

The total amount of financing—which should be less than $10 billion if our hypotheses are correct, notably about the cost of construction in Russia—should not be out of line with the possibilities of the potential lenders.

6. Social Aspects

Any major conversion of industry poses social problems, especially when it includes large training programmes and/or major relocation of workforce.

In the case we have proposed, there is no necessity of major retraining—perhaps some connected with transformation of plutonium warheads into plutonium-bearing fuel elements, but this task has only limited impact on the total project.

Relocation of workforce should be quite minor. The idea is to use existing laboratories, development institutes, and factories, necessitating little or no relocation of staff.

The actual construction of power plants would not impose site constraints different from those for other kinds of nuclear plants; it could take place on the sites already considered in Russian government plans for FBR plants. Therefore, it would not introduce specific problems of relocation of construction personnel as compared with regular practices of the industry.

There remains the problem of public opinion, which should be treated with appropriate attention. However, provided the safety standards are impeccable and proper information efforts are deployed to explain the advantages of a non-polluting electric power plant, and provided that the local population receives tangible benefits from this development, this problem should be solvable.

Indeed, a project transforming weapons material into useful energy should have some attraction for people.

In conclusion, we believe that this idea deserves a thorough study.

REFERENCES

1. STARR, CHAUNCEY, MILTON F. SEARL, and S.Y. ALPERT, 1992, "Energy Sources: A Realistic Outlook." Science 356, 981-87.
2. *Energy for Tommorrow's World.* World Energy Council, 34 St. James' Street, London SW1A 1HD, U.K., December 1993.

3. DAVIS, W. KENNETH, "The Future of Nuclear Power: The Fast Breeder Reactor." Paper presented at the Dixie Lee Ray Memorial Symposium on Science-Based Environmental Management, Seattle, Wash., August 31, 1994.

4. *"Le Project Capra: Enjeux et Objectifs."* Note de présentation du Commissariat a l'Energie Atomique, 29-33, Rue de la Federation, 75015 Paris, Frace. 6 June 1994.

5. SLESAREV, I "Strategie des Reacteurs Rapides: Russie." in *Les Centrales a Neutrons Rapides: Quel Avenir?* Centre de Geopolitique de 1'Energie et des Matiéres Premieres, Université de Paris Dauphine, Place de Lattre de Tassigny, 75776 Paris France. 1994.

6. *EFR—European Fast Reactor.* EFR Associates, 10 rue Juliette Recamier, B.P. 3087 F, 69398 Lyon Cedex 03, France.

7. *Les Couts de Reference—Production d'Electricite d'Origine Thermique.* Ministere de l'Industrie, des Postes et des Telecommunications, et du Commerce Exterieur, DGEMP-DIGEC, Service de l'Electricite, Paris, 1993.

8. PONOMAREV-STEPNOY, N. and E. ADAMOV, in *Proceedings of the MIEC-CGEMP seminar: La sécurité de l'approvisionnement en énergie de l'Europe—Role de la Russie.* Paris, France, March 1994. Centre de Geopolitique de l'Energie et des Matiéres Premiéres, Université Paris-Dauphine (see Ref. 5).

4

Military Conversion and Science from a Global Perspective

JOHN PROCTOR

We are still in the midst of momentous changes begun in the late 1980s which are continuing principally in Europe and the former Soviet Union, as well as in the rest of the world. These changes will have great impact upon political, economic and social conditions of most of the people of earth. For many of us, the impact upon the present state and future development of science is the issue.

Background

In Russian and Eastern European science, most of the state support of science has disappeared. Newspapers tell us it is because of a great economic crisis. But my visits there strengthen my belief that profound reconsiderations are underway of the place science is to have in the former Soviet states and countries of Eastern Europe. Civilian and military leaders of massive military oriented programmes were lavish in their support of basic hard science, key technologies and supporting disciplines. After the political and economic collapse of the Soviet state, hard science lost support; "Big Science" projects stopped, and as for the soft sciences, they appear to be struggling and gasping for credibility and support. [1 UNESCO-ROSTE Seminar, 1990].

In the United States as in Europe and the former Soviet Union, the "Peace Dividend" has not materialized for science and technology funding. Basic science is financially supported by nation states and that support has been weakened in the face of competing demands upon political decision makers.

The Russian Federation's funding of the Russian Academy of Sciences with its over 300,000 employees, dozens of institutes, libraries, test sites, observatories, publishing houses, research ships and planes has been cut from 3 to 5 times in comparable terms according to Kaptiza. [2. S.P. Kapitza, 1994.] Coupled with inflation of over 4000% in the last two years, the compensation of scientists, technicians, architects and medical doctors is ridiculously low. Youngsters are not entering science and technical careers; scientists are leaving science. Some say. "Fine. Science in the USSR was top heavy and overstuffed. Let the dismantling continue." Others say the pillaging of the former USSR and Eastern Block science is ridiculous, sadistic, or downright stupid in the face of possible nuclear proliferation, not to mention chemical and biological threats. Ignoring the promises of their science in bio-technology, advances in rocketry, mathematics, optics, and lasers is simply irrational.

The United States Department of Defence budget for Research and Development in 1991 was $30 billion in 1995 dollars. In 1995, it is $26 billion and by 1999, it is budgeted at $21 billion in 1995 dollars, a minus 30% change from 1991! [3. US Congress, Congressional Budget Office, 1994.] The private sector will have to increase its financial support of science and technology and that in turn, depends upon controlled economic growth. Having to depend upon open market forces to provide financial support for science and technology is risky indeed.

Military Conversion

The problems of defence conversion and brain drain provides a uniting global issue for learned societies, academies of art and science, and organizations advancing technology around the world to maintain pressure on decision makers to raise science and technology in their scheme of priorities.

While government at any level generally seeks to control and constrain organizations, science, engineering and technology organizations strive to open, share, and recognize the contributions of genius, innovation and hard work. For example, the Washington Academy of Sciences is focusing on its role as science advocate, communicator, and supporter of our Junior Academy of Science. We are clearly awed by the magnitude of scientist migration and the realization that while this is occurring in our increasingly complex world, the numbers of scientists and technologists coping with problems of humankind appear not to be increasing. A new form of apartheid may be developing in terms of the capacity to do brain work—a form of imposed segregation undermining humankind's security, health and quality of life.

Defence or military conversion, in my view, is a subset of the larger brain drain problems. It is not a scientific question *per se* but rather a matter for scientists to explore. Thus, the first question, always the most important, is what paradigm or concept formulation promises the most utility?

The problem of defence conversion and, to a certain extent brain drain, it seems to me, is a matter of business. That is taking joint venture risks in bringing technologies to market while governments continue support of basic science and education.

The paradigm I have been suggesting for the past three years is one that emphasizes incentives to encourage the reallocation of resources and would be essentially a cooperative effort between government and private business. The use of incentives in a defence conversion paradigm encourages the retention of critical military skills and facilitates the separation of those who need to be converted through training or direct absorption into the civilian occupation pool. Obvious incentives are pay, allowances, interesting work, relocation assistance, housing and living subsidies and educational opportunities.

Similarly, incentives are need to maintain civilian skills, encourage individuals in surplus jobs to seek training and to help workers shift to jobs with other employers. Finally, incentives [4. G. W. Miller, 1992] are needed for employers to stabilize the civilian occupation pool in critical areas such as science, technology and medical practice.

Priorities based upon a census by scientific and technical occupation in the states of former Soviet Union and the Eastern European countries would provide an important ingredient for conversion strategies which would involve sustainable contracts, the fostering of innovation, and focus on technical institutes, *inter alia*. [5. National Science Board, 1991.] Now, here is a particularly difficult problem . . . setting priorities. As Judge Brazelon of the US District Court has said: "The equal treatment of unequals is the greatest inequality of all". Whose fairness? . . . What objectives? These issues are discussed in my paper in a recent issue of the Journal of the Washington Academy of Sciences. [6. J.H. Proctor, 1992.]

The implementation in Russia of defence conversion strategies within a paradigm of incentives would require some new functions at the national, regional and local levels, such as "broker centres" for job posting, job application referral and hiring, employment agreements and negotiation assistance. Investment allocation decisions in terms of how much, to whom, for how long, would require decision support processes to be installed in Russia and Eastern Europe where there is no history of such investment/incentives; a most difficult aspect of any implementation. Programme evaluation and feedback to decision makers on the paradigm's implementation is the final step before repeating steps in different ways, at different speeds, in different socio-economic and geographical locations. I am pleased to observe that the partnership of the Russian Federation's Ministry of Science and Technology and the Russian Academy of Sciences is rapidly evolving.

Case 1: US Aerospace

In the United States, the US aerospace industry provides an example of an industry coping with defence cuts, a weak global economy and increased international competition. The US aerospace industry is a critical part of our country's domestic and export economies. It accounts for more than 25 per cent of all of the nation's research and development expenditures and is the country's leader in R&D spending on new technologies [7. Aerospace Industries Association of America, 1994]. Industry shipments are forecast to drop 11 per cent in real terms to $92.3 billion in 1994 and exports to decline 15 per cent to $34 billion. Employment in Aerospace companies will continue to be cut back as military programmes end, are reduced or delayed.

As part of the new spirit of cooperation between the Russian and American aerospace industries, an agreement was reached in September of 1993 to construct a space station blending elements of the US Freedom and Russian Mir projects. Another product of Russian aerospace collaboration is the four engine, long range aircraft, IL-96M. It will be powered by US built Pratt and Whitney engines and fitted with US advanced avionics. The Tupolev's TU-204, mid-range, 200 seat twin jet airliner will be powered by Rolls-Royce engines.

Case 2: Brain Drain in Russia

Military conversion in Russia could be a forcing function to accelerate or increase "Intellectual Emigration or Brain Drain."

The exodus on a massive scale of researchers, teachers and lecturers, engineers and technicians is producing actual damage to the national economies of the CIS and Eastern European countries. Estimates show that at the beginning of 1991 losses due to emigration of scientists and engineers from the CIS amounted to nearly 100bn rubles. If we add the calculations of UN experts that the emigration of one specialist of this category produces damage of about US $300,000 to his/her country. In terms of dollars, this means that emigration of scholars and engineers might bring an annual potential loss of US $60-75bn to the CIS countries. [8. S. J. Simanovsky, 1993]. From 1992 to the year 2000 the loss would be in excess of half a trillion dollars.

Steps to limit intellectual migration and promote successful defence conversion and the re-engineering of military industries depend upon job creation and innovative talent utilization programmes. Such steps as international conferences; three month to three year temporary visits or sabbaticals: cooperative forms of basic research; joint ventures in technology applications; scientific and teacher exchanges, and computer linkages are all positive. UNESCO has set up a "fund for basic science in Russia". Model cooperative agreements have been reached between the Russian Academy of Sciences and western organization such as AT&T, Corning, and the Soros Foundation. These steps to encourage positive mobility help avoid returning to a totalitarian state and the violation of basic human rights and freedoms as articulated by the United Nations. [9. Ministry of Science and Technology of the Russian Federation, 1994.] I personally am greatly encouraged by the current leadership of the Russian Academy of Sciences who support international cross fertilization of teams and institutions thereby reducing the likelihood of the re-emergence of the old fiefdoms and closed organizational structures that existed without accountability.

Personal Observations

What really breaks my heart when key memebrs of the academic community leave, is when books on science, technology, architecture, law, medicine and theology ceases to be published; when the continuty of research and teaching is lost and young minds lose mentors. [10. Scientific American, 1993.] We should also grieve for the unborn ideas and unrealized experimental plans.

I feel obliged also to stress the importance of moral factors in times of difficulty. In the face of adversity, the loss of courage and moral is a most significant feature. Anti-intellectual trends are now openly expressed in the United States. In Russian and Eastern European media, now freed of censorship and with a newly found responsibility of the press to society, "money makers" are the new heroes. Coupled with strident expressions of nationalism, anti-semitism, and anti-religion, it all combines to place fuel on the fires of frustration and despair, especially among the young. Fewer of the best and brightest enter math and science classes and careers, even more leave their jobs in research labs and university classrooms for business. The Russians call this "Internal brain drain" and it must be added to intellectual migration to estimate losses. Boris Vinogradov, Russian Federation Commission for UNESCO estimates that 27 per cent of scientific personnel in Russia (in some regions 50 per cent) transferred to commercial ventures in 1992. [11.B. Vinogradov, 1993.]

Conclusion

Learned societies and academies both non-governmental and government supported have clear roles in defence conversion and related issues of brain drain. [12. National Academy of Sciences, 1992.] These roles, as seen by the Washington Academy of Sciences and the World Academy of Art and Science, consist of (i) increasing public awareness of global issues facing science, (ii) encouraging young people to enter and stay in their chosen courses of higher eduaction, and (iii) developing strategies with our fellows in foreign Academies of Science and Technology. These three roles are compatible with or perhaps, in addition to, its Members and Fellows providing advice and council to decision makers. I can not overemphasize the need for us individually and collectively to combat anti-technological, anti-scientific, anti-intellectual trends which have been seen and heard in many places in North America, Europe and Asia. I would also encourage all of us to speak out of on these issues and breathe life into them with passion and indignation.

One exemplary effort many of you know about is the televised forum from Washington, DC on April 4, 1993 sponsored by the World Academy of Art and Science, the Russian Academy of Science, and the Washington Academy of Sciences. Fellows of the World Academy of Art and Science and from Russia and the US discussed global issues facing humankind to the year 2050. Of particular interest in this project was the willingness of imminent scientists to hold discussions before a large, live audience which included over 125 young students of the Metropolitan Area Washington Junior Academy of Science. We have now made video tapes in Russian and English of this discussion and prepared a book of selected papers by participants. These materials are available to our Follows for use with young students. The Russian Academy of Sciences is using the video tape and books with middle school students in Russia. We're proud of this programme and ask you to help it continue.

Our challenge is clear: to design and implement structures and processes for the modern world to deal with high technology, basic and applied science with the attendant great concentration of power and resources. People look to us to recommend revised procedures for funding transitional structures and processes for science. Nation states which prosper in the long run are those which earlier invested in research, particularly fundamental research. These procedures are needed now. I am personally concerned with the ethics and values of multi-national corporations and international art and science organizations in these matters. Again, whose values? Where will these values come from? Who is holding whom accountable? I urge all who would be helpers to facilitate positive defence conversion to proceed with caution and with respect to avoid worsening the very situation that the West is trying to improve.

REFERENCES

1. UNESCO-ROSTE (Regional Office for Science and Technology for Europe, 1261/A Dorsoduro, Venice, Italy 30123) 1990. Report of the Working Party on Brain Drain Issues in Europe, Lisbon, Portugal, 26-28 November 1990. I.O. Angell and V.A. Kouzminov (eds.), technical report no.3.
2. KAPITZA, S.P., The Future of Russian Science and Science in Eastern Europe, a paper under preparation, Spring, 1994.
3. US Congress, Congressional Budged Office, "Restructuring And Consolidating Defence Support Activities", Table 2. Department of Defence Funding by Major Programme. Page 8, July 1994.
4. MILLER, G.W. 1992, Interim report, Redeploying Assets of the Russian Defence Sector to the Civilian Economy. (Chair, National Academy of Sciences Committee on Enterprise Management in a Market Economy under Defence Conversion.) Washington, D.C. 20219, USA.
5. National Science Board. 1991. Science and Engineering Indicators. 10th edn. US Government Printing Office, Washington, DC 20219, USA.
6. PROCTOR, JOHN H.A. Theoretical Basis for International Organizational Change with Comments from a Thirty Year Perspective, Journal of the Washington Academy of Sciences, Volume 82, Number 1, Pages 1-18, March 1992.
7. Aerospace Industries Association of America, Inc., U.S. Industrial Outlook, "Aerospace Facts and Figures, 1993-1994", Chapter 20, Pages 20-1 to 20-5.
8. SIMANOVSKY, STANISLAV. Brain Drain from the Former Soviet Union and the Position of the International Community, Commission of the Russian Federation for UNESCO, Moscow, the Russian Federation presented at the UNESCO-ROSTE Seminar, 25-27 April 1993, Venice, Italy, pages 407-18.
9. Ministry of Science and Technical Policy of the Russian Federation, Committee on "Brain Drain" Problem Under the Commission of the Russian Federation For UNESCO 1994, "Brain Drain" From Russia: Problems, Perspectives and Ways of Regulation, A Seminar and Report, Moscow, 21-23 February, 1994.

10. Scientific American, 1993. Trends in Russian Science. February.
11. VINOGRADOV, BORIS, "Brain Drain in Russian in 1991-92", presented at the UNESCO-ROSTE Seminar, 25-27, Venice, Italy, pages 203-210.
12. National Academy of Sciences, 1992. "Reorientation of the Research Capability of the Former Soviety Union." A Report of the Assistant for Science and Technology to the President of the United States, 13 March.

5

The Finmeccanica Experience in Military Conversion

ANGELO AIRAGHI AND CARLO CORSI

FINMECCANICA

 Alenia | ANSALDO | Elsag Bailey

Aerospace, Defence, Energy, Transportation, Automation

FINMECCANICA: THE GROUP

OPERATING STRUCTURE

AERONAUTICS	RADARS AND SYSTEMS	MISSILES	DEFENCE	HELICOPTERS	SERVICE AUTOMATION
SPACE	ELECTRONIC EQUIPMENTS	ENERGY	TRANSPORT	INDUSTRIAL AUTOMATION	OTHERS

FINMECCANICA: THE GROUP

THE DEFENCE ACTIVITIES INVOLVES SEVEN AREAS

VEHICLES	RADARS AND SYSTEMS	MISSILES	WEAPON SYSTEMS	HELICOPTERS	SERVICE AUTOMATION
SPACE AND TELECOMMUNIC	ELECTRONIC EQUIPMENTS	ENERGY	TRANSPORT	INDUSTRIAL AUTOMATION	OTHERS

- PARTLY DEFFENCE
- FULLY DEFENCE
- FULLY COMMERCIAL

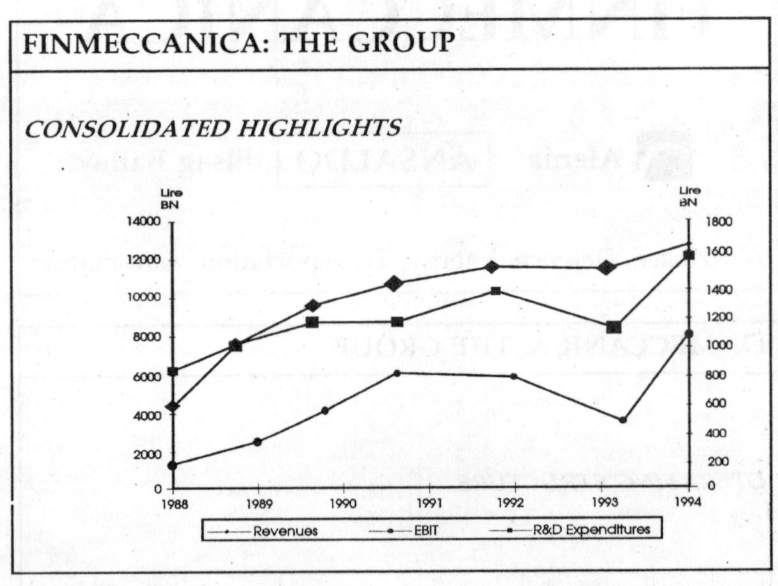

FINMECCANICA: THE GROUP

THE DEFENCE ACTIVITIES REPRESENT 30 PER CENT OF THE TOTAL TURNOVER

REVENUES BY BUSINESS AREA (1994)

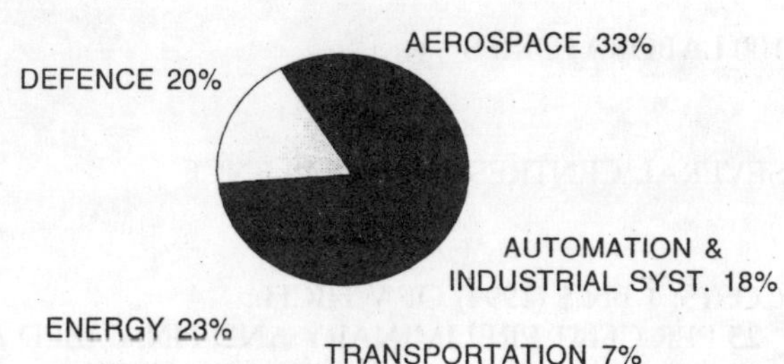

FINMECCANICA: THE GROUP

INTERNATIONALIZATION IS GROWING

FINMECCANICA REVENUES (1994)

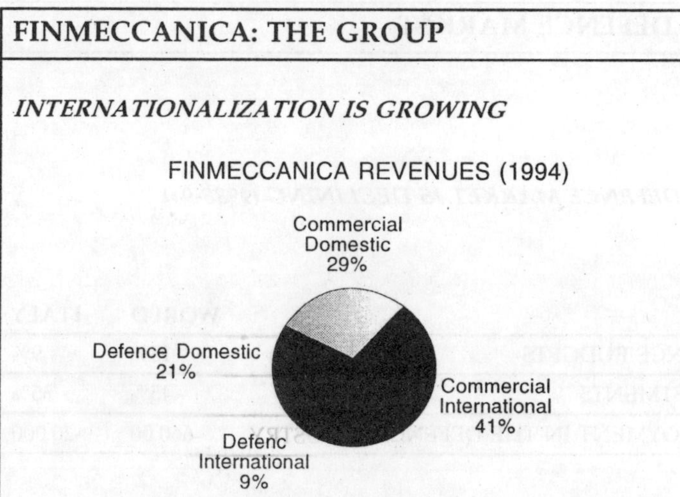

PUSHED BY THE COMMERCIAL ACTIVITIES

FINMECCANICA: THE GROUP

R&D—COSTS, STAFF & LABS (1993)

- 7000 FULLY DEDICATED PEOPLE
- 100 LABORATORIES
- SEVERAL CENTRES OF EXCELLENCE
- COSTS: 1 BN $ (1994) OF WHICH::
  * 25 PER CENT PRELIMINARY AND FINALIZED ACTIVITIES
  * 75 PER CENT DEVELOPMENT ACTIVITIES

THE DEFENCE MARKET

THE DEFENCE MARKET IS DECLINING (1988-94)

	WORLD	**ITALY**
DEFENCE BUDGETS	- 15%	- 9%
INVESTMENTS	- 45%	- 55%
EMPLOYMENT IN THE DEFENCE INDUSTRY	-660.00	-20.000

THE DEFENCE MARKET: IMPLICATIONS FOR INDUSTRY

1. SMALLER PRODUCTION VOLUMES

2. DECLINE IN R&D PUBLIC EXPENDITURES

3. LESS PROGRAMMES

THE DEFENCE MARKET: THE INDUSTRY'S CHALLENGE

HOW TO SURVIVE AND KEEP ALIVE THE HIGH TECH CONTENT

CONVERSION IS, IN PRINCIPLE, NOT VIABLE

DIVERSIFICATION DOES NOT, AGAIN IN PRINCIPLE, DEFEND THE HIGH TECH CONTENT

THE DEFENCE MARKET: THE INDUSTRY REPLY

1. **VS. SMALLER VOLUMES.............**

CONCENTRATION, THROUGH M&A

(a) THE NATIONAL CHAMPIONS

(b) THE INTERNATIONAL AGREEMENTS

THE DEFENCE MARKET: THE INDUSTRY REPLY

2. **VS. LESS R&D VOLUMES.............**

DEVELOPMENT OF A "COMMON" TECHNOLOGICAL BASE:

(a) PUSH THE DUAL USE

(b) COMMERCIAL UTILIZATION OF DEFENCE TECHNOLOGIES

THE DEFENCE MARKET: THE INDUSTRY REPLY

3. **VS. LESS PROGRAMMES.............**

RESTRUCTURING OF THE R&D DEPTS
(INTEGRATION DEF. AND COMM. ACTIVITIES)

CONVERGENCE BETWEEN COMMERCIAL AND MILITARY REQUIREMENTS

THE DEFENCE MARKET: THE CHALLENGE

SIMPLE STRATEGIES BUT DIFFICULT IMPLEMENTATIONS

LESSONS FROM THE PRACTICAL EXPERIENCE

FINMECCANICA: EXAMPLES

DUAL USE

- HELICOPTERS:
  EH 101: AGUSTA / WESTLAND
  A 129: AGUSTA

- AIRPLANES
  ATR 52C ALENIA / AEROSATIALE

FINMECCANICA: EXAMPLES

CONVERGENCE OF REQUIREMENTS

- AIR TRAFFIC CONTROL AND RADARS
- GPS

FINMECCANICA PRACT EXP

STRUCTURES RESHAPING

- ALENIA AERONAUTICS DIVISION
- ALENIA RADARS & SYSTEMS DIVISION

FINMECCANICA: EXAMPLES

TECHNOLOGIES MIGRATION

- ELECTROMAGNETIC COMPATIBILITY
- IMAGING
- HIGH PERFORMANCE COMPUTING
- CRYPTOGRAPHY
- ....
- ....

SOME CRITICAL ASPECT AND CONTRADICTIONS

6

Military Conversion and Its Impacts on Science and Technology: Elements of the Italian Case

FULVIA FARINELLI AND GIULIO PERANI

1. Introduction: The Italian System of Innovation

Italy represents one of the success stories of post-war economic growth. Over the past forty years, GNP growth has been higher in Italy than in most other industrialized countries. Similarly, productivity and income per capita have risen rapidly and manufacturing exports have increased considerably. In a relatively short period of time Italy has transformed from an agricultural and semi-industralized country to an advanced industrial economy. In addition, during the 1980's it experienced high growth rates in R&D (see Table 6.1), although Italian international specialization remains mainly in traditional products such as textile and shoes, as well as in mechanics and industrial equipment.

Why in Italy did the R&D growth of the 1980s not translate into successful performance in high technology products? According to a comprehensive analysis on the Italian system of innovation during the 1980s and the 1990s (Malerba, 1991), a full understanding of this matter has to start from the recognition that not one, but two innovation systems are present in Italy: a small firms network and a core R&D system. These two systems are quite different in terms of capabilities, organization and performance. The small firms network is composed a of large population of small and medium size firms (in some cases located in industrial districts), which interact intensively at the local level.

The core R&D system is composed of large firms with industrial laboratories, small high technology firms, universities, large public research institutes and the national government, linked through a complex organizational system at the national level.

The small firms network, grown up historically on a local, regional and vocational basis and characterized by capabilities accumulated through productive experience, has worked effective and performed successfully during the past decades up until now. Firms in the network are engaged in rapid adoption of technology generated externally and in the adaptation and continuous improvement of this technology. The success of the system is based on the close interaction of a large number of firms bound to each other by economic, local, cultural and social factors. Firms incrementally innovate through learning by doing, by using and by interacting with suppliers and users.

The core R&D system, instead, much more recent than the small firms network and developed at a much later stage than those of countries such as Germany, the United, Kingdom. France and the United States, is not characterized by advanced technological capabilities and does not perform satisfactorily in terms of innovation and international competitiveness. In Italy, in spite of a relevant quantitative growth of R&D during the 1980s, some of the qualitative elements needed for an effective and successful working of such a complex system are still missing or are not fully developed. In fact, first, several industries actors do not have advanced research and technological capabilities. Second, public policy for R&D support still exhibits major flaws. Third, an advanced national infrastructure of services for R&D and an overall coordination of public policies is still lacking. Fourth, advanced basic research performed in universities and public research centres is very unevenly distributed across institutions. Fifth, shortages of skilled scientists and engineers are present. Finally, there is no tradition of successful industry-university co-operation in research.

Table 6.1. Total R&D expenses as Percentage of GDP, 1971-92

	1971	1976	1981	1986	1991	1992
USA	2.46a	2.30	2.45	2.91	2.75	2.74
UK	2.10a	2.17b	2.41	2.34	2.08	2.00
France	1.88	1.75	1.97	2.23	2.42	2.36
Germany	2.20	2.16	2.43	2.73	2.66	2.58
Italy	*0.85*	*0.77*	*0.87*	*1.13*	*1.32*	*1.38*
Sweden	1.49	1.79b	2.30	2.89c	2.90	2.90
Japan	1.71	1.80	2.13	2.56	3.05	3.00
	a:1972	b:1975		c:1985		

Source: OCDE, 1994

2. Military R&D Activity

If we apply what is mentioned above to the military sector, we can see that adequate financial resources for R&D are available only within the major industrial military groups, which are often less efficient in performing innovative activities. As in the civilian sector, there is too little room (and funding) for small high-tech firms which are, on the contrary, more flexible than larger ones and able to implement innovations in a more efficient way.

In terms of GDP the level of R&D investments continues to remain low, and R&D funding is concentrated mainly in less advanced sectors without an effective coordination between research institutions and firms. Besides, the share of military R&D of total public R&D spending is high with respect to more dynamic countries like Germany or Japan, and low with respect to more similar industrial countries such as France or UK (see Table 6.2).

Table 6.2. Military R&D as a share of total public R&D

	1986	1987	1988	1989	1990	1991	1992
USA	69.4	68.6	67.8	65.4	62.6	59.7	58.6
UK	49.3	45.5	42.7	43.6	42.5	44.8	45.2
France	34.0	35.9	37.3	37.0	40.0	36.1	34.6
Germany	12.1	12.7	12.4	12.8	13.5	11:0	10.5
Italy	*8.5*	*7.0*	*10.2*	*10.3*	*6.1*	*7.9*	*7.1*
Japan	4.1	4.5	4.8	5.1	5.5	5.7	5.9

Source: OCDE, 1994

Finally, in the international context Italy seems to have competitive advantages only in traditional sectors, such as household appliances, or in sectors characterized by significant "learning by doing", such as industrial machines. In the military related sectors data provided by patents analysis stress a relevant weakness in areas such as missiles, aircraft, ships, communication equipments (see table 6.3).

3. Military R&D Funding

In Italy military R&D is financed by the Ministry of Defence budget; the National Applied Research Fund (law 46/1982); the National Fund for Technological Research (law 46/1982); the Ministry of Industry Fund for the Aerospace Sector (law 808/1985); the National Research Council (CNR), mainly through the so-called "Finalized Programs"; military firms (especially public owned ones).

In the Ministry of Defence budget there are at least four main items in which it is possible to find financial resources for R&D:

- item 7010 is specifically devoted to scientific research, but also items regarding weapon systems acquisition include a relevant share of R&D;
- items 4011, 4031 and 4051 refer to military procurement for Army, Navy and Air Force, but include also expenses for research, development, industrialization, acquisition and maintenance of weapon systems, which means a large amount of military R&D (see Table 6.4).

Table 6.3. Index of technological specialization of advanced countries in military-related SIC classes

		USA	UK	F	D	SW	I
Guided Missiles and	(1)	1.23	1.77	1.77	1.03	1.22	0.21
Space vehicles	(2)	1.21	1.41	1.82	1.00	1.64	0.19
Ship, boat building	(1)	1.05	1.10	1.32	0.66	2.30	0.70
	(2)	1.09	1.14	1.54	0.69	1.62	0.43
Ordnance	(1)	1.12	0.65	1.21	1.41	2.69	1.10
	(2)	1.14	0.58	1.22	1.41	3.19	0.70
Aircraft and parts	(1)	0.84	1.46	1.39	1.32	0.85	0.87
	(2)	0.74	1.39	1.54	1.70	0.79	0.12

(1) Patent granted by the US Patent Office
(2) Patent citations, 1975-88
Source: Pianta, Archibugi, 1991

As regards the public resources assigned to defence as national goal, the following table shows that the Italian government is spending about 10% of total R&D outlays for military R&D. Thus, Defence is the main goal pursued by the Italian government in the R&D sector outside universities. It is important to point out that the largest share of this amount is devoted to industrial R&D.

Finally, Table 6.6 shows a relevant interest of the Ministry of Defence in financing technological research, but also its commitment in sustaining research activities in mathematics, chemistry and nuclear energy. Additionally, it is worth nothing that the Ministry of Defence is the largest customer of manufacturing industry within the public sector.

4. Military R&D Organization

The Ministry of Defence is directly responsible for all military R&D activities in Italy. Within the Ministry of Defence, the Joint Chief of Staff defines, together with the Chiefs of Staff of the three Armed Forces, the guidelines of Defence R&D and military procurement.

Table 6.4. Ministry of Defence R&D expenditure 1987-93 (billion lire, current price)

Year	Item 7010 (Scientific Research)	*Scientific Research Expenditure in Other Items*				
		Item 4004	*Item 4011*	*Item 4031*	*Item 4051*	*Total*
1987	53.8	0.2	158.6	101.0	178.0	491.6
1988	94.3	2.1	329.3	242.3	207.0	875.0
1989	130.0	0	158.2	33.0	49.4	340.6
1990	303.2	0	1,610.0	1,208.2	1,918.2	5,039.6
1991	292.0	0	70.4	56.4	98.0	516.8
1992	336.2	0	87.0	121.1	607.4	1,151.7
1993	410.4	0	26.2	101.6	656.1	1,194.2

Source: Ministry of Defence Budget Appropriations, various years

Table 6.5. Government R&D outlays for social-economic goals

	1988	1991
Ground environment	1.8%	1.4%
Ground protection	0.9%	0.4%
Environmental pollution	2.1%	3.0%
Human health	6.4%	6.5%
Energy	9.3%	5.4%
Agriculture	2.9%	3.3%
Industry	5.6%	7.2%
Defence	12.0%	8.4%
Total research activities within universities	36.8%	33.4%

Source: Ministry of Defence Budget Appropriations, 1993

Table 6.6. Sectors of R&D spending of Italian government and Ministry of Defence (million lire, current price 1991)

Sectors	*Ministry of Defence*	*Total government spending*
Mathematics	2,203	2,203
Physics	267	7,592
Chemistry	1,749	2,229
Technological research	743,989	787,899
Nuclear research	2,270	2,270
Space research	84,000	786,923
Interdisciplinary research	17,700	1,109,002
Others		526,923
Total	852,178	3,225,041

Source: IEFE, 1991

The Defence Technical and Scientific Council (CTSD) is the advisory body of the Joint Chief of Staff in this field. A major role is played by the General Secretary of the Ministry of Defence (the highest technical and financial official of the Ministry), who represents the Italian Armed forces within the NATO-CNAD group as National Armaments Director. The General Secretary leads the technical branch of the Defence and is in charge of the definition of technical and commercial relations between the Ministry of Defence and industrial firms.

The Italian Ministry of Defence defines military R&D as those activities which, using state of the art technologies and the findings of technological research, can produce equipment to answer to specific operational needs. Thus, the process of developing a new equipment or system involves:

- the Minister of Defence (indirectly the Cabinet as a whole) at a political level;
- the Joint Chief of Staff, together with the three Chiefs of Staff, at a command level;
- the General Secretary-National Armaments Director, responsible for defining R&D programmes, reducing duplications, evaluating programmes, managing relations with industrial firms and foreign partners, at a coordination level;
- the Defence Technical and Scientific Council and the Defence-Industry Committee as advisory bodies at a consulting level;
- the Branch Offices, as operational bodies, at a management level;
- the Organizations which carry out research activities, at an executive level.

Military R&D is currently carried out by three main groups of organizations: research organizations of the Ministry of Defence, private and public military firms, universities and other research centres. However, Italian military research centres are very few. CRESAM (Centre for Research and Studies for Military Purposes), located in Pisa, is the most important research centre of the Italian Defence, and is dealing with four major research fields (nuclear energy, opto-electronics, electro-magnetic compatibility, and diagnostics materials). Besides, there are some technical centres which depend on the Army, the Air Force and the Navy, such as the Air Force Air Division for Studies, Research and Experiments (DASRS), particularly relevant for its collaboration with the aerospace industry. Some experimental centre and firing grounds, then, depend on the three Armed forces as well. The areas of *Salto di Quirra* (Sardinia) for naval experimental activities, and Nettuno for ground artillery are well known.

According to the Defence White Paper 1985 (last source available), in 1983 there were 1,227 employees involved in Defence R&D activities, of whom about 600 are classified as "researchers".

As already mentioned, in Italy the major performers of military R&D are military private and public owned firms. Anyway, a general survey of the National Statistic Institute on R&D activities in the Italian industry, carried out in 1989, points out that investments of industrial firms in R&D military related activities can be considered relatively small, and that there are very few industrial groups totally involved in military production. More frequently firms produced both civilian and military products using the same technology. In this case the major part of investments for the development of gas turbines, ground vehicles and aircraft must be considered as civilian investments, while only investments for the development of new technologies in the armaments sector are totally devoted to military aims (see Table 6.7). Unfortunately, as will be remarked in the concluding chapter, lacking a coherent R&D policy linked to the Ministry of Defence procuement policy, till now research activities carried out by individual firms have been driven only by medium term commercial tasks (such as to join an international programme), without defining priorities resulting from wider policy choices.

5. Italian and EU Research and Technology Policy

In Italy the Ministry of University and Research publishes, ever three years, a *Three Year Plan for Research* orienting national R&D activities towards some specific areas. In the 1994-96 Plan ("Research and Innovation for Development") a section is devoted to defining, in a very general way, a military research policy. In this document there are two main aims strongly emphasized:

1. orienting research towards dual-use activities;
2. coordinating the Ministry of Defence military programmes with other civilian research programmes, mainly related to the so-called "diffusive technologies" (i.e. information technologies, biotechnologies and new materials).

With reference to the general aims of national policies in this field, the Ministry of University and Research proposes to support five priority tasks of the Italian Armed forces: air defence; air deterrence, aeromobility, advanced training and C3I2 capabilities. To answer to such requirements it seems crucial, for the Italian Air forces, to acquire a national production capability in six weapon systems families:

- air defence systems (fighter aircraft, SAM missiles, ABM missiles, UAVs, etc.);
- air reconnaissance systems (satellites, aircraft, UAVs);
- transport aircraft;
- C3I2 systems;
- radar air defence systems (both airborne and ground-based);
- simulators for advanced training.

Table 6.7. Research Personnel and Research Investment in Industrial firms for selected Military Related Sectors, 1989

Sector	*Researchers*	*Technicians*	*Total personnel involved*	*Research investment (million lire)*
Gas turbines, reactors	108	–	108	19,608
Nuclear reactors	122	50	218	26,381
Telecommunications device	5,214	3,440	10,218	1,041,982
Aerospace vehicles	2,008	1,460	4,118	969,753
Ground vehicles	1,526	3,140	9,317	1,272,734
Naval vehicles	110	156	289	46,681
Arms and ammunitions	368	359	966	73,933
Optics, fine mechanics	428	281	769	183,723
Total industrial sector	30,520	21,301	64,944	8,698,468

Source: ISTAT, 1992

The main technological areas involved in these productions are: artificial intelligence, robotics, optoeletronics, composite materials, laser technology, radar technology.

As regards the Ministry of Defence technology policy, a forthcoming *Military Technology Plan* published by the Office of the Secretary General is expected to replace a 1989 document which listed 13 technological areas considered as a priority for the national defence. These technological areas were only practically related to technologies defined "critical" in both NATO and IEPG7 Euclid contexts. On the other hand, technologies which will be considered in the next Technology Plan (which are not available yet) are almost completely matched with technologies pursued within the WEAG/Euclid Programme.

Finally, it is worth making a few remarks on the EU research policy. Promoting scientific research at European level is currently one of the main tasks of the EU. In the framework of the EU research policy, a lot of European programmes are aimed at sustaining R&D projects dealing with new technologies carried out by small and medium firms. Considering only the programmes acting in fields related military activities (thus, potential conversion tools), we can list:

- Brite-Euram for promoting basic research on advanced materials, technologies for aeronautical safety, industrial innovation;
- Craft for funding external R&D activities (for small and medium firms without research facilities);
- Esprit for strengthening the European competition in micro-electronics, system engineering in electronics, multimedia technologies, sensors and robotics, artificial intelligence);
- Race for projects on communication system integration;
- Joule and Thermie for energy saving.

In this context, a particular role could be played by the Sprint programme, which is aimed at promoting technology transfer within the EU between research centres and other bodies. Even though conceived for technology transfer between civilian sectors, Sprint could be an important actor to promote a transfer of industrial and technological competence from military to civilian sectors.

6. Problems of Military R&D in Italy

Concluding this brief overview on the Italian military R&D, it must be emphasized that the R&D activity carried out within the Armed Forces and the Ministry of Defence research centres is very limited if compared to other European NATO countries. This implies two important consequences: (a) the military R&D activity is highly concentrated within military firms, and, consequently, activities related to product development or applied research, which have more immediate economic results, are preferred to base research; (b) a clear definition of the defence technological priorities is still missing.

On the one hand, the Italian Defence has systematically shown a strong dependence on US-NATO technological choices and on the industrial capacity of domestic defence industrial base; on the other hand, military firms have preferred to acquire foreign technology rather than to invest in research activity, thus remaining at a medium-low technological level.

Lacking a coordinated national industrial and technological policy—in the military sector as well as in the civilian one—military firms have been free to define their own strategic priorities, often supplying the Italian Defence with no "state of the art" equipment. In fact, the Italian military procurement can be defined as a "relief procurement", aimed at maintaining national industrial capacity in some military sectors without considering technological innovation and market competition. Actually, the fall of Italian arms exports, experienced in the last years, can be widely explained by the patterns of industry-Defence relationship.

A low level of activity in military R&D can not bring to relevant spin-offs in civilian sectors (neither within the Ministry of Defence, nor within military firms). Thus, in Italy there are no public or private programmes for spreading military technologies. In the military industry a key issue is currently the development of dual-use equipments (or, with less emphasis, of dual use technologies). As already explained, in Italy there are many military firms producing either for the civilian and the military sector, but they supply in both cases the same customer: the Italian State. Thus, a major issue in the Italian debate on conversion is "how to make military firms more efficient and competitive", no matter whether in military or civilian activities. Effectively, conversion is strictly linked to an increasing capacity of competing in open markets.

In this regard, it is maybe worth remembering that when the EU Commission decided in 1991 to establish European initiative to support national conversion activities, great expectations grew in Italy for this possibility to charge the Commission with the definition of national conversion policies (and of part of its financial burden). So, in the first phase of the Konver programme the Italian government asked the Regions to prepare some proposals for conversion initiatives to be selected by the Ministry of Industry. The final results was a collection of industrial projects with on coherent national or regional strategy, highly criticized by the Commission for being too focused on an industrial policy perspective rather than on a regional one. Actually, Konver is not an industrial recovery programme, but it is specifically oriented to support regional policies of conversion/diversification. Thus, the Ministry of Industry has substantially modified its approach to conversion policies, in order to put into action the 1993 phase of Konver and to regulate the future implementation of the mainstream 1994-99 Konver programme. Currently, EU co-financed activities to support conversion include: assistance to newly established companies employing workers dismissed by military firms, funds to military laboratories and research centres to shift their military activities towards civilian fields, financial support for military firms diversification, and retraining activities for workers dismissed by military firms.

7. Conclusions

From this brief overview of the structure and competitive ness of the Italian innovation system, it is possible to draft some suggestions, also in order to face the problem of how to absorb technological and industrial capabilities coming from eventual reductions in military programmes.

First, *the role of small/medium size firms should be emphasized.* It is really important, in areas affected by lagging of economic development or decline of traditional industries, to create a number of small companies acting in different sectors, with the aim of developing an "entrepreneural" culture and spreading technological know-how. A basic reason to support this type of approach is avoiding the economic waste often related to large recover initiatives, such as large public financed programmes carried out by military firms. On the contrary, it is important to sustain market oriented activities with *ad hoc* measures, that is to say providing industrial infrastructures, banking assistance, legal and tax consultancy, technical training and marketing services. In some countries, local governments created so-called "firms incubators" which have the task to support the creation of new companies. A network of these centers—Business Innovation Centres (BID)—is currently sponsored by the EU.

Small and medium size firms cannot only manage business in providing services or in producing handicraft: evidence show that in Italy small innovative firms can play a key role in spreading science-based knowledge (including military technologies) and carrying out an industrial, especially high-tech, activity. A national policy of technology transfer can support this process creating joint ventures between large high-tech public owned firms, universities, research centres and small innovative firms. Some Italian laws are currently financing these activities, and local governments are fostering the creation of "scientific and technological parks", partially financed by the national government and the EU, aimed at developing science-based industrial productions.

Second, *different public policies should be coordinated more efficiently*. A frequent obstacle to the implementation of economic development policies is the difficulty in matching a wide range of goals. As an example, the task of transferring workforce and technologies from military aerospace large firms to a number of locally spread small firms should be analysed not only considering the technical and economic feasibility of such a move, but also general concerns regarding national policies in fields such as defence, technology, national economy, industry, trade, labour, etc. Thus, an agreement aimed at transferring a military technology from military firms to the commercial sector could be jeopardized if the Ministry of Defence considers that technology as strategic. Or a national policy of support to some industries could crowd out local investments for exploiting regional potential in terms of resources and technologies. This means that an institutional framework within an industrial recovery plan should always be developed. In this context, EU general regulations must be considered as the general framework of all industrial policies.

Third, *industrial and technological policy should be matched together*. A characteristic of the Italian situation is the spreading of decision-making procedures related to military industrial activities over a lot of ministries. The Ministry of Industry is responsible for industrial policy decisions, the Ministries of Foreign Affairs and Foreign Trade control arms exports, the Ministry of Scientific Research coordinates research activities, and so on. It should be important, instead, to coordinate different national and EU policies, offering to military firms (which are often the only Italian firms in high-tech sectors) a clear perspective on: Armed Forces and social needs, export opportunities, scientific and technological national priorities, civilian and military procurement policies, industrial, economic and employment policies.

Fourth, *investments on dual use technologies should be increased*. Since the Italian military system cannot be present in all arms industry sectors, it is vital to concentrate industrial resources according to national defence priorities and to international collaborations, on those areas in which we have competitive advantages, such as ATC radars, trainer aircraft, AFVs, etc.

In these fields the Ministry of Defence could sustain R&D with special interest in developing dual use technologies. Obviously, if it was possible to produce a large share of civilian production using the same technologies (civilian ATC systems, airframes, tractors, etc.) the Ministry of Defence commitment to acquire large amounts of military equipment, in order to finance military industrial activity, would be reduced.

Finally, it is necessary for the Ministry of Defence, facing shrinking budgets, to identify its needs in a more accurate way. In fact, *a more selective procurement policy* would lead to a wide process of restructuring military R&D and production system. In this context, the number of military firms would probably diminish, and the remaining ones would have to increase their presence in competitive civilian markets.

REFERENCES

1. AAVV (1986), *Rapporto sulla situazione e sulle prospective della scienza in Italia,* 1st. Poligrafico e Zecca dello Stato, Rome.
2. AMENDOLA G., PERRUCCI A. (1990), *"La competitività dell'Italia nelle industrie high-tech: un approccio per prodotti"*, L'industria, XI, 2.
3. ANNUNZIATO P. (1992), *La capacità innovativa dell imprese,* XIV Rapporto CSC sull'Industria italiana, Roma.
4. ARCHIBUGI D., EVANGELISTA R., PIANTA M. (1992), *"Il sistema innovativo italiano:punti di forza e di debolezza"*, paper presented to the Conference "Ritardo tecnologico e integrazione europea". Cnr, Rome, 16 December 1992.
5. BISOGNO P. (1986), *"Politica della tecnologia e sicurezza"*, in JEAN C., *Sicurezza e difesa,* Angeli, Milan.
6. BOITANI A., CICIOTTI E. (1992), *Innovazione e competitivita nell'industria italiana,* II Mulino, Bologna.
7. CENTRO MILITARE DI STUDI STRATEGICI (1990), *L'organizzazione della ricerca e sviluppo nell'ambito difesa,* Rivista Militare, Rome.
8. CENTRO STUDI CONFINDUSTRIA (1992), XIV Rapporto CSC sull'industria italiana, May 1992.
9. COMMITTERI M., ROSSI S. (1992), "Tecnologia e competizione nel mercato unico europeo", paper presented to the Conference on "Ritardo tecnologico e integrazione europea, Cnr, Rome, 16 December 1992.
10. IEFE (1991), "Per una politica degli usi produttivi della tecnologica in Italia", *Economia e Politica Industriale,* 70.
11. ISTAT (1991), *Indagine statistica sull'innovazione technologica nell'industria italiana,* Rome.
12. MALERBA F. (1991), *Italy, the National System of Innovation,* CESPRI, Working Paper n.45, June.
13. MURST (1993), *Piano triennale della ricerca scientifica e tecnologica in Italia,* Istituto Poligrafico e Zecca dello Stato, Rome.
14. OECD (1991), *Choosing priorities in science and technology,* Paris.
15. OECD (1992), *Technology and the economy: the key relationships,* Paris.
16. OECD (1993), *Science and technology policy outlook,* Paris.
17. OECD (1994), *Main science and technology indicators,* Paris.
18. ONIDA F., MALERBA F. (1990), *La ricerca scientifica,* SIPI, Rome.

10. OFFICE OF TECHNOLOGY ASSESSMENT (1992), *Defence conversion. Redirecting R&D,* Congress of the United States, Washington.

20. PERANI G. (ed., 1992), *Ambienti per l'industria italiana,* ENEA, Rome.

21. PERANI G., PIANTA M. (1992), "The slow restructuring of the Italian arms industry", in BRZOSKA M., LOCK M., *Restructuring of arms production in Western Europe, SIPRI,* Oxford University Press.

22. PIANTA M. (1988), *"I programmi a tecnologia avanzata: ricerca militare o innovazione per l'economia?", Economia e politica industriale,* 57.

23. PIANTA M., ARCHIBUGI D. (1992), *The technological specialization in advanced countries,* Kluwer Academic Publishers, Dordrecht.

24. PIANTA M., ARCHIBUGI D. (1992), "Convergenza e specializzazione delle attività innovative", paper presented to the conference "Ritardo tecnologico e integrazione europea, Cnr, Rome, 16 December 1992.

25. SPINARDI G. (1992), "Defence technology enterprises: a case study in technology transfer", *Science and Public Policy,* 19.

26. STEVENS G. (1991), "Les industries stratégiques dans les années 90", *L'observateuer de l'Ocde,* 172.

7

Military Conversion: A View from Brussels

MANFREDO MACIOTI

The ending of the cold war and the beginning of a new paradigm in the relations between East and West may be taken to have begun five years ago, with the dismantling of the Berlin Wall. Cuts in defence spending and a process of economic adjustment have been in progress since that time. It has not been an easy transition, as the economies of the East have been severely retrenching over the past few years, while the West has gone through a phase of recession or, at best, sluggish growth. Unemployment has been and continues to be a great problem in both Regions.

Military Research and Defence Budgets

Government-funded R&D has an important part to play in a conversion strategy, as it is Government spending that has dominated defence research. There are seven countries in the OECD area whose Governments invest more than 10 per cent of total Government outlays for R&D (1992) in military research and development. These are the USA (58.6 %), the UK (45.2%), France (34.6%), Sweden (24.5%), Switzerland (18.5%), Spain (14.6%) and Germany (10.5%).

In the USA, defence-related R&D investment was in 1992 of the order of 44 b. $ (N.S.F. Science and Engineering Indicators, 1993). The Member States of the European Union (E.U.) invested about 11b. ECU in defence R&D in 1990 (EU European Report on Science and Technology Indicators, 1994).

Data for military R&D in the former Soviet Union (FSU) are moral difficult to obtain, but estimates put the figure at over 60 per cent of total R&D in the 1980s and it probably still is nearly 50 per cent of the total today. Russian R&D expenditure alone has been estimated at 140 b. Roubles in 1992 (perhaps equivalent to 1 b. $ at the time). However, there has been a dramatic reduction in funds for both civilian and defence research since 1991 virtually throughout the whole of the ESU.

Of the dozen or so other countries active in military science and technology in the world, it is probably China and India (with a reservoir of respectively 400,000 and 100,000 research scientists and engineers—RSE) which have the largest military-related research programmes. Japan—which has a larger research reservoir = 520,000 RSE—devotes a limited percentage of Government outlays (5.9%) to military expenditure. Thus, the Japanese budget for military R&D barely exceeds the Swedish one.

Government statistics from India indicate but about 20 per cent of national R&D expenditure is defence-related (S&T Data Book, 1991).

Direct employment in the EU armaments industry amounted to about 660,000 jobs in 1992. The peak level was reached in 1984, with a total of over 1 m. jobs (STOA, European Armaments Industry, Nov. 1993). Since then, employment has been steadily decreasing. Further cutbacks in defence budgets will further reduce this pool of specialized manpower by 150,000 to 200,000 individuals by the year 1996. In 1992, the military budget of the Twelve (EU) was 117 b. ECU, while the figure for the USA was 222 b. ECU. EU defence—related expenditure had decreased by 4.2 per cent between 1989 and 1992, while the US decrease over the same period was nearly 10 per cent. Not so Japan, whose military expenditure increased by 8.6 per cent (from 22 b. ECU in 1989 to 23.9 b. in 1992).

Conversion

Generally speaking, in the EU, the principle upheld by the Governments for many years that military research takes precedence over civilian research, is gradually giving way to the concept that there is a common denominator in military and civilian technologies, at the level of basic or generic research (*e.g.* in such fields as mathematics, aerodynamics, propulsion, semiconductors, etc.).

At the initiative of the European Parliament, the EU launched at the end of 1990 a special action, PERIFRA (Peripheral Regions and Fragile Activities), with a budget of 90 m. ECU, including some 56 m. ECU allocated to projects connected with the reduction of military expenditure. Another similar programme, KONVER, launched in 1993 with 130 m. ECU will assist the conversion of regions of the EU which are dependent on declining military activities. Over the years 1994-7, KONVER II should have a budget of 500 m. ECU.

As the monies available for defence-related expenditure continue to diminish in Europe, it is to be expected that the well established tradition in the field of military ventures at the European level (*e.g.* Jaguar, Alphajet, Tornado, E.F.A . . . .) will receive a new impetus.

European cooperation is also due to grow in military research, where the European Independent Programme Group launched the European Cooperative Long Term Initiative in Defence (EUCLID) in 1988. This cooperation has been since 1993 entrusted to the Western European Armaments Group of the WEU.

Note should be taken of the fact that some of the EU own research programmes—such as ESPRIT, RACE, BRITE—partly cover research in technological fields which are of potentially "dual use". The share of "dual use" increases as we move from "Industial Technologies and Materials" to "Information Technologies".

E.U./FSU Cooperation

The E.U. programme of technical assistance to the Commonwealth of independent States (TACIS), which launched in 1991 with the aim of spending up the processes of economic reform and transition to democracy underway in the FSU. The TACIS budget for 1994 is 510 m. ECU, the projects supported are mainly in the areas of human resources development, energy, nuclear safety, food production and distribution, transport, telecommunications and company services. Conversion projects were first included in 1993 and a total of 13 m. ECU has been invested so far by the EU in this area.

In 1992 the EU launched the International Association for the promotion of cooperation with scientists in the New Independent States of the FSU (INTAS). The emphasis of INTAS' action is on joint research programmes, involving laboratories in Western Europe and in the ESU. INTAS has 18 Members in the West (including the EU) and twelve partners in the East.

At about the same time, an initiative was launched at international level to help redirect the skills of highly qualified military researchers in the FSU toward civilian scientific projects. The International Science and Technology Centre (ISTC) opened its doors in Moscow earlier this year. It is found by the E.U., the US, Japan and Russia. Several countries have joined the ISTC since, among them Armenia, Georgia, Belarus and Kazakhstan. It is projected that 4,000 to 5,000 scientists will eventually be involved.

Another useful link between the E.U. and the FSU is the TEMPUS programme, devoted since 1993 to strengthening relations in higher education between Western Europe, Russia, Ukraine and Belarus. Since the current academic years 1994/5, four other Republics (Kazakhstan, Kyrghyzstan, Moldova and Uzbekistan) have been participating in the TEMPUS programme. It is foreseen that three more FSU States (Armenia, Azerbaijan and Georgia) as well as Mongolia will join in 1995/96.

The Examples of Belarus and Ukraine

Belarus. As part of the FSU, Belarus started a programme for the conversion of military production as early as 1989. The programme required each defence-related enterprise to embark upon the production of civil products. Most enterprises "converted" by simply producing what was easiest for them from an engineering and technical point of view, without preliminary investigations in the potential markets. As a consequence, effective progress in conversion has been limited (TACIS, Contract Information 1993, January 1994).

Belarus has about 5 per cent of the former Soviet defence-industrial base. The military industry of Belarus consists of some 120 major establishments employing about 400,000 workers (including research institutes with 20,000 staff). The current decline in demand has heavily affected the sector. It is estimated that military enterprises in Belarus are working at some 20 per cent of their nominal capacity. On the positive side, the defence industry has been employing highly qualified people at senior level, and well skilled staff for design, research and manufacturing activities. There are accordingly in Belarus valuable human and physical resources available for conversion. This is particularly true in such areas as radio and telecommunications, optical system, electronics and military transport technology.

The TACIS assistance for the conversion of Byelorussian defence industry for 1993 totals 1.7m. ECU and consists of actions in the areas of telecommunications equipment (Agat, Gomel, Lunch, Zenit, Lös, Cri . . .) and optical products (Belomo).

Ukraine. Ukraine has roughly between 15 and 30 per cent of the former Soviet defence plants and military R&D facilities. There are in particular some 700 plants with 500,000 employees directly active in defence industries, and perhaps another 1 m. people contributing to defence output. Within the FSU, Ukraine is the second largest producer of weapons and military equipment after Russia. Ukraine is capable of assembling all major categories of such equipment (ships, missiles, transport aircraft, land arms and radars). Some Ukraine facilities have unique capabilities: thus Ukraine has the only shipyard in the FSU currently capable of building aircraft carriers (CIA, The Defence Industries of the Newly Independent States of Eurasia, January 1993).

The defence sector is at present confronted with a sharp drop in demand for military equipment and components, but the great majority of the employees are still on the pay-roll. The Ukarinian Government has established an ambitious programme for the conversion of more than 500 military enterprises. Funds have been earmarked at the level of the new Ministry of Engineering, Military-Industrial Complex and Conversion, to foster the conversion programme. First priority is given to the production of medical and agricultural equipment, as well as to the production of equipment for the energy sector (TACIS Contract Information 1993, January 1994).

TACIS will, under the 1993 conversion programme, provide 2.58 m. ECU to assist the following three projects:

- development by Hartron in Kharkov of two high-tech control systems in the field of energy;
- conversion by two enterprises in Kiev (Realy & Automatic and the Electronic Instrumentation Research Institute) with a view to developing and manufacturing medical equipment;
- development of business relations with Western markets by the Donetsk Institute of Automation and two enterprises in Kiev (Elektroapparat and Monolit).

Furthermore, TACIS will assist the Ukrainian National Programme with 6.36 m. ECU for the retraining of military officers (and members of their families). This European effort complements the assistance that Germany has granted to Ukraine (DM 23 m. over the period 1991 to 1994) for the training and retraining of discharged military personnel and their families following their return from Germany to Ukraine.

Conclusion

If we define defence conversion as the process by which skills, research, technology and equipment in the defence area are shifted into alternative economic applications, then conversion is not an easy process to implement. Nevertheless dual-use approaches—technologies, processes and products with both military and commercial applications—can be developed in several areas of industry. This is particularly true at the lower levels of a vertical product hierarchy. Thus, research may conveniently cover fields common to both areas. Examples range from composite materials to sensors, information science, modelling and simulation, robotics and artificial intelligence, telemedicine, fibre optics and photonics, laser systems, to acoustics and mathematics.

In any case, the success of a conversion policy is highly dependent on the general economic context and a sound legislative framework. A poorly developed banking system, hyperinflation, reluctant privatization efforts or legal uncertainties in such critical areas as trade, investment and industrial property rights, will neither favour real conversion, nor attract an appropriate level of international cooperation and investment.

BIBLIOGRAPHY

Government of India (Department of Science and Technology)
Science and Technology, Pocket Data Book 1991
New Delhi, 1991

CIA (Directorate of Intelligence)
The Defence Industries of the Newly Independent States of Eurasia
Washington, January 1993

National Science Board (N.S.F.)
Science and Engineering Indicators
Washington, 1993

STOA (European Parliament)
European Armaments Industry: Research, Technological Development and Conversion
Luxembourg, November 1993

TACIS (European Commission)
Contract Information, Budget 1993
Brussels, January 1994

European Commission
The European Report on Science and Technology Indicators 1994
Luxembourg, 1994

8

Impact of Defense Conversion and US Response

NICHOLAS MONTANARELLI

In March 1993, President Clinton announced a conversion plan that would spend $20 billion over five years. Of that, $1.7 billion was spent in the remainder of fiscal year 1993. In fiscal year 1994, $3.3 billion would be obligated and by fiscal year 1997, funding would be increased to $5.3 billion per year. This money was to help people find new jobs, create technologies that have both civilian and military uses, and assist commercial technologies of national importance by using new methods such as information highways.[1]

Reacting to public concern over higher taxes, the US Congress has reduced the funds of half of what was called for in 1994 and the outlook for the next few years will likely reflect these current reductions.

As a result of the end of the Cold War many members of Congress campaigned in 1992 with a call for 50 per cent cuts in the defence budget. Ironically, they must now find ways to create jobs in states like California that will lose an estimated 650,000 defense related jobs. Many of us who are responsible for making defence conversion work are constantly remained how difficult it is for a company to take new products into new markets. It is even harder for a defence company to be competitive in many commercial markets with the kind of overhead structure that have geared toward defence.

Many times it takes as long as 20 years of very patient efforts to make the conversion from military to civilian products. It is a generally accepted rule that conversion efforts take a long time and the probability of success is uncertain.

It is also difficult to measure the success of overall conversion efforts. While all the evidence is anecdotal, it seems to indicate that federal programmes work slowly, at best. A number of small companies have successfully diversified already. But many of these firms have done so, thanks to strategic planning, a strong management commitment, and realism that it would be accomplished with little or no government funding. Many of the early conversion programmes were seeking an elusive panacea to magically create jobs and produce products on a scale similar to the defence production that preceded it.

The US defense industrial base faces a radical restructuring that will continue over the next several years. Concerns for deficit reduction by the general public will results in new domestic spending priorities. Not only is US defense policy undergoing a major review of roles and missions in the post-Cold.War era but within the armed forces, such basic concerns as force structure, US basing, and overseas deployments are in flux.

The long-term downward trajectory of US defence budgets has generated considerable uncertainty for both large and small companies doing business with the Department of Defence (DOD). The US defense budget declined 29 per cent between fiscal year 1985 and fiscal year 1993. Under the Clinton Administration proposed budget funding for national defence is projected to fall from $273 billion in fiscal year 1993 to $227 billion in 1997, a further 17 percent drop. Projections by the Electronics Industries Association (EIA) suggest that defence budgets could fall to around $215 billion by the turn of the century, while there have been calls in the US Congress and elsewhere to reduce military funding to $180 billion by fiscal year 1997.[2]

The effects of funding changes, and their impact on the both defense and industry will be described in brief scenario specific descriptions that we hope will effectively make the audience aware of the vast complexity of implementing the transition of what is referred to as defense conversion.

Meeting the Challenge with Federal Assistance

There are over 50 government programmes funded to assist in defence conversions. We have focused on the three programmes, we feel, will have the greatest impact on the US economy.

The largest programme is the Technology Reinvestment Project (TRP) whose mission is to stimulate the defence transitions to the high tech areas of the industrial complex. The TRP is managed for the DOD by the Advanced Research Project Agency (ARPA). It provides the most advanced, affordable military systems and the most competitive commercial products. The TRP's individual programmes are structured to expand on high technology employment opportunities in industry that will demonstrably enhance US competitiveness. This is being accomplished through the application of defense and commercial resources to develop dual-use technologies, manufacturing and technology assistance to large and small firms. Each enhance US manufacturing skills and target displaced defence industry workers.[3]

In order to meet future demands for advanced technical weapons capability while the defence budget declines, the DOD, by direction of the US Congress, budgeted $465 million in 1993 for the TRP. The funds were used to stimulate the transition of defence technology to a growing, integrated national industrial capability that provides the most advanced, affordable military systems and the most competitive commercial products. Over 212 projects were funded in the areas of technology development, technology development, and education and training in manufacturing.

Technology development programmes were funded to accelerate the commercialization of the dual-use technologies that foster integration of the defence and commercial industrial bases. At the same time, they provide for the national defence by promoting cutting edge commercial and defense capabilities. Programmes funded in the area of technology deployment assist new and established manufacturers in becoming globally competitive and achieving world class standards.

An added feature is the coordination of Federal, state, and local resources to improve and concentrate the flow of services to areas of opportunity. Education and training programmes are intended to build a highly skilled manufacturing work force for the future. Defence engineers and technicians will be retrained so they can contribute to the commercial and defence industries to today.

All of the TRP programmes mentioned have three common requirements. Each programme is made through a competitive award; it must emphasize partnership, when possible; and to reduce risk, each award is cost-shared at least 50 per cent.

The success of the first year of this programme is indicated by White House and Congressional direction to budget $670 million for the 1994 TRP.

The second largest programme is the Federal government to help offset the impact of defense conversion is the Advanced Technology Programme (ATP). Begun in 1990, the ATP, located at the National Institute of Standards and Technology (NIST), promotes the economic growth and competitiveness of US business and industry by accelerating the development and commercialization of promising, high-risk technologies with substantial potential for enhancing the US economy. The programme provides technology development funding on a cost-sharing basis through cooperative agreements to single businesses or industry-led joint ventures. In selecting broad programmatic areas, the ATP relies on its overall strategy of drawing on industry's ideas.

To date there have been four annual competitions with $515 million total funds committed ($247—government; $268—private). Eighty-nine awards have been made ranging from $500,000 to $20 million.

A good mixture of participants has resulted in 23 awards to joints ventures and 66 to single applicants. The nature of the ATP has allowed for the entry of industries that are vital to continuing economic growth. These industries include biotech, energy, chemicals, electronics, computing, communications, and, very important, manufacturing. The success of this programme so far has produced a strong market orientation that calls for an annual budget of $750 million by 1997.[4]

The current administration has put great faith in the role small business will play in helping the US adapt to the economic slow down resulting from military base closings, and cutbacks in defence and aerospace.

NIST has been given a broad-base task to build a nationwide system of technology services for the nation's small manufacturers. The Manufacturing Extension Partnership (MEP) is designed to be a comprehensive, yet locally responsive network to help firms upgrade their equipment, improve their processes, and strengthen their business performance. The MEP, which is made up of Manufacturing Technology Centres (MTCs), state, and partnering organizations, will be an entry point an integrated national system of technical resources, services, and expertise provided by the government.

The MEP builds on NIST's many years of experience in manufacturing extension and on productive partnerships forged with public and private organizations at the national, state, and local levels. Through the MEP, the Clinton Administration has set a goal of creating a nationwide network of 100 manufacturing centres by 1997.

Its mission can be simply stated; technology gaps will be resolved by using resources of improved manufacturing technology as required by small and midsize companies that need it. Centre staff activities work with companies through one-on-one assistance and in groups organized around common needs, industries, or technologies.

The goal of the MEP centres is not to create jobs but rather to protect existing jobs. Results are measured through reduced costs, increased sales, improved productivity and product quality, enhanced customer satisfaction, and greater profits. As of September 1993 an estimated Federal investment of $54 million has had a bottom-line result of over $320 million in savings. In addition, the corresponding changes that firms make with MEP centers' assistance improve manufacturers' abilities to compete, to grow, and to sustain high wage, high quality jobs that strengthen the US manufacturing base. By saving and improving current jobs in the manufacturing sector, we can sustain, to a certain degree, the impact of defense cuts.[5]

Issues and Needs of American Industry

The US Department of Commerce is working with US business to address issues resulting from defence conversion that will promote sustained economic growth, job creation, and a rising standard of living. To compensate for the continuing reduction in defence spending, changes in three major areas of technology policy are recommended. They are technology development, technology diffusion, and technology infrastructure.

To increase US technology development, many industrial organizations urge increased financial support by the Federal government for generic research and development (R&D). This could be accomplished through increased funding for large government programmes, such as the Advanced Technology Programme and the Technology Reinvestment Project, and more support for manufacturing and process technologies. Individual states that are greatly impacted by defence cutbacks would like to have a bigger say in setting Federal research priorities. There is a general feeling by industry that if low-priority government programmes that duplicate industry efforts to enter the market place are eliminated, there would be greater initiative to start new ventures. Government programmes should facilitate precompetitive research and test-bed development. Federal support is ideally directed to particular research subjects including manufacturing and process technologies, best manufacturing practices, high performance computing and communications, environmental technology, and service sector technology.

Two main tax policy recommendations that could help industry are that the research and experimentation (R&E) tax credit be made permanent, and the whatever tax there is on capital gains be lowered relative to the tax on ordinary income. Tax credits for all R&E expenditures should be considered. Other incentives to stimulate industry cooperation would be providing a 10 per cent credit for industry-sponsored university research; providing a special credit for companies engaged in collaborative R&D; and considering ways to improve the tax credits available to smaller firms.

In the area of technology diffusion, industry would like greater exposure to technology transfer.

In the 1980s, the US Congress passed a number of laws focused on helping industry and universities to work closer with Federal R&D to meet the challenge of foreign competition. These laws are playing a major role in meeting the goals of defence conversion through technology diffusion. As a result, many organizations want more and are having more private sector involvement in Federal technology transfer, commercialization, development, and development policies.[6]

The Defence Department is currently giving the private sector more responsibility for maintaining defense equipment. In turn, this frees up vital military resources while creating jobs in many industrial sectors.

New Federal programmes, discussed in a previous section, have been implemented to accelerate industrial modernization. Programmes such as Cooperative Research and Development Agreements between governments and industry are in the process of being streamlined, while government agencies with research laboratories are devoting more resources to marketing their technologies to the private sector. Several new national data bases are being formed to assist in this process.

What is needed is more attention to bridging the gap between the Federal laboratories and US industry. There are several investigative panels looking into ways the Federal government may involve itself directly in the commercialization process, such as providing loans and equity, without becoming competitive to the venture capital and investment banking sectors that are vital to our economy.

Many advocate a variety of tax proposals to foster technology commercialization. Some of these proposals urge re-examination of current. US international tax policies in light of the fact that US companies must increasingly compete in the global marketplace. Issues, such as ways to improve how foreign earned income is taxed and how royalties on intellectual property are realized, need to be readdressed.

Some organizations representing industry are pushing for new laws to support investment tax credit, more accelerated depreciation, and reforming our Alternative Minimum Tax which tends to reverse innovation incentives for certain taxpayers. Many groups are lobbying against any increase in the current corporate tax rate. They are asking for lower corporate tax rates in exchange for the elimination of generous write-offs.

There is a strong effort by this administration to increase the importance of manufacturing as an element of national policy. Many would like to see it as a main technological focus area such as those in defence, space, health, and energy.

If defence conversion is going to work, we need to make major improvements in government procurement. Some of the recommendations include letting industry use commercial practices; simplifying audits and oversight; and increasing the use of "best value" techniques to account for factors other than the lowest price. We should also create incentives for the use of advanced manufacturing technologies; removal of the bias against commercial products in defense procurement; and providing more multi-year procurement and budgeting.[7]

To meet the need to employ individuals affected by reductions in defence, major infrastructure changes, through an enhanced coordination of Federal education programmes, must be made. Upgrades in achievement standard, raising maths and science levels, curriculum changes, promoting team building, and more technical education are required. Better coordination of Federal education programmes, increased prestige of the teaching profession, and experimental programmes in different regions are helping to upgrade the work force. Additional programmes, in new vocational categories where the jobs exist, are being funded by the government in areas affected by military base closings. Extensive support, in the form of tax incentives, is given to companies having employee stock ownership programmes that let individuals deduct the cost of formal education and training for a new job.

Some industrial organizations (professional societies and trade associations) want the US to rely on voluntary industry standards allowing more private sector input on a National Information Infrastructure (NII).

There is considerable support for strengthening intellectual property rights at home and abroad, including increased protection for software, and the property rights resulting from Federally funded technology (e.g., technology produced by industry-governments cooperative agreements).

Recommendations on standards for US-produced products vary. Industry would like to strengthen the US system for getting US standards accepted internationally.

Industry is on record to help do whatever is required to increase savings and investments, lower the budget deficit, and make more long-term, low-cost capital available for business. Some specific measures are: create a consumption-based income tax; give added support to the consumer through individual retirement accounts and family-based saving plains; and place limits on the ability of the Federal Reserve to manipulate money supply growth, the Federal Funds rate, and the exchange rate.

Numerous organizations recommend integration of policies across the technology spectrum to include trade policy, monetary policy, regulatory policy, human resources policy, investment policy, fiscal policy, national security policy, and environmental policy.

Everyone you talk to would call for the Administration and Congress to support reform of product liability law. Current laws tend to discourage innovation and commercialization, and need to be amended to reflect the reality of global competition. A uniform Federal law on product liability to help meet, rather than frustrate, US technology goals is long overdue.

While discussing product liability reform, we should not overlook the need for regulatory reform of antitrust laws for research, overseas marketing, and joint production. Much could be accomplished by having more reasonable interpretation of existing laws.

Conclusion

As we have stated in somewhat brief descriptions, the Federal government and US Industry are making a considerable effort to transform how we do business today. In recent years, the government officials have sought new goals for their research dollars. One of the most important emerging themes in the Federal programmes is international competitiveness. Large Federal expenditures are made to support R&D that will increase American productivity, thereby helping industry in global economic competition. This, in turn, will play a key role in absorbing a large quantity of resources affected by the end of the Cold War.

There are many who do not believe that a new competitiveness rationale will enhance the economy by reinvigorating the national R&D effort. These individuals believe that competitiveness is not a politically powerful substitute for the Cold War in forging a durable coalition for supporting R&D at the generous levels typical of the past decades. There are also those who believe that many of the new programmes are shaped by political necessity and many likely undermine the economic performance of the programmes when the political needs are shifted. In Contrast, the current approach to R&D and its technology is essentially economy-wide. Its appeal rests on the argument that it can help US industry boost productivity which will increase both its domestic and international markets. Almost every industrial sector has been a target for Federal support.

The new methods of technology enhancement taken by the government have caused two major changes to how Federal R&D programmes are formulated and managed. One change is greater privatization in the selection and results of research projects. This has given private industry responsibility for technical choices in the projects and essentially all intellectual property rights. The other change has been increased collaboration among industry and research organizations.

To some degree, failures should be expected because the outcome of an R&D effort is inherently unpredictable. What we haven't learned, thus, far is how to analyze, and rapidly terminate government programmes that are regarded as technical failures. Governments officials, unlike industry managers, are more sensitive because of political pressure to the effects that cancelling a project will have on employment. In short, the government has difficult completing successful projects and difficulty in cutting its losses on failures.[8]

No matter what the outcome of government/industry technology developments, we must believe that the possible benefits of a discovery can be realized only if people other than the discoverers have the opportunity and incentive to a apply new findings to their needs. This will ultimately determine the success of our defence conversion programme. In the meantime, the government can improve the performance of selected economic sectors by adopting policies that facilitate and increase investments in technology through research, development, and manufacturing.

NOTES

1. United States General Accounting Office, January 1994. "Defence Conversion; Slow Start Limits Spending" Washington, D.C. 20548 USA.

2. Bitzinger, Richard A. Defence Budget Project, April 1993, "Adjusting to The Defense Drawdown: The Transition in The Defence Industry" pages 3-4, Washington, D.C. 20002 USA.

3. Defence Technology Conversion, Reinvestment and Transition Assistance, March 1993 Technology Reinvestment Project, page 1-1, Arlington, Virginia 22203-1714 USA.

4. Advance Technology Programme, U.S. Department of Commerce, National Institute of Standards and Technology, Gaithersburg. Maryland 20899-0001 USA.

5. Manufacturing Extension Partnership, U.S. Department of Commerce, National Institute of Standards and Technology, March 1993, Gaintersburg, Maryland 20899-0001 USA.

6. Brown, Harold. Critical Issues in Defence Conversion, September 1993, The Center for Strategic & International Studies, pages 27-28, Washington, D.C. 20006 USA.

7. Listening to Industry: Business Views on Technology Policy, June 1994, pages 17-23, U.S. Department of Commerce, Technology Administration, Office of Technology Policy, Washington, D.C. 20230 USA.

8. Cohen, Linda, R. and Noll, Roger G. Privatizing Public Research, Scientific American, September 1994, pages 73-75, New York, New York 10017-1111 USA.

IMPACT OF DEFENSE CONVERSION AND US RESPONSE

PRESENTED BY

Nicholas Montanarelli

NOVEMBER 27, 1994

WORKING GROUP II

Round Table on Military Conversion and Science

UNESCO-ROSTE

Venice, Italy

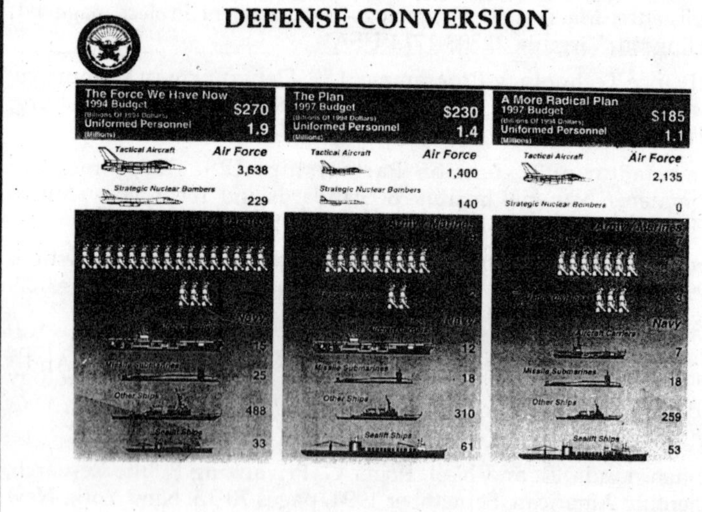

DEFENSE CONVERSION

Where The Defense Cuts Hurt Most

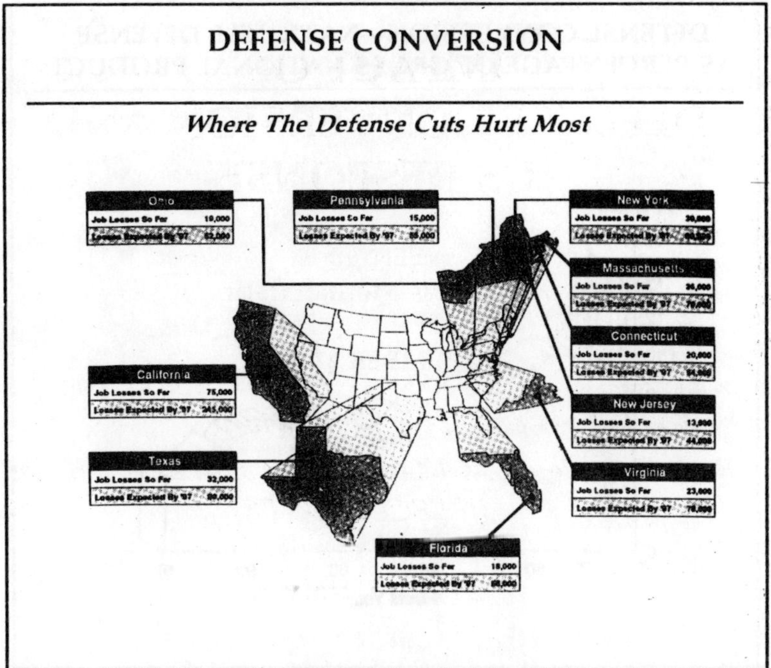

DEFENCE CONVERSION GOALS

- Facilitate The Transition By Encouraging Economic Growth
- Preserve Defense Capability
- Ease The Immediate Impact On Workers, Communities And Companies
- Improve Government Programmes (More Effective And Efficient)

DEFENSE CONVERSION—NATIONAL DEFENSE AS PERCENTAGE OF GROSS NATIONAL PRODUCT

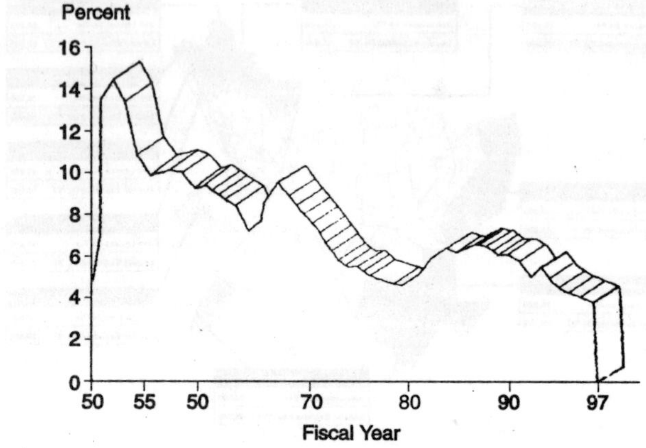

Percent
16
14
12
10
8
6
4
2
0
50 55 50 70 80 90 97
Fiscal Year

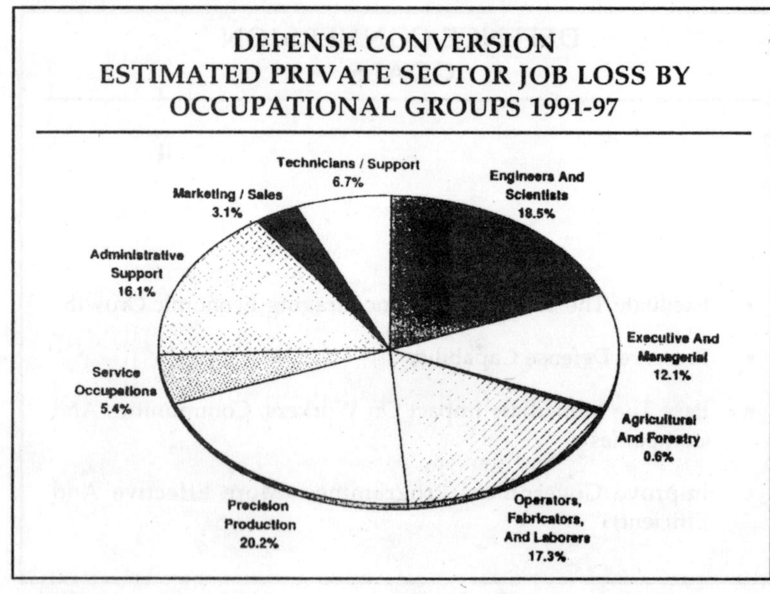

TECHNOLOGY REINVESTMENT PROJECT

PRESIDENT CLINTON'S TECHNOLOGY INVESTMENT PLAN

- **A NATIONAL INDUSTRIAL POLICY:**
  — Boost America's global economic competitiveness
- **APPROACH:**
  — Accelerate development/application of commercially viable technologies
- **TECHNOLOGY GOALS:**
  — Create jobs and protect the environment
  — Make government more effective and responsive
  — Obtain world-class leadership in science, math, and engineering
  — Start new initiatives to build economic strengths

TECHNOLOGY REINVESTMENT PROJECT

FEATURES OF THE TECHNOLOGY PLAN

- **EMPHASIS ON:**
  — Dual-Use technology commercial applications
  — Cost shared Government—Industrial partnerships
  — New Technology Demonstration (pilot) programmes
  — National "Information Superhighway" network
  — Access to existing and emerging technology "know-how"
  — Research and development/manufacturing extension canters
  — Flexible manufacturing processes
  — Enchanced basic science research
  — Permanent research and experimental tax credit

BUZE WORDS

- Strategic Partnerships
- Dual Use Technology
- Defense Conversion
- Industrial Consortia
- Regional Alliances
- Manufacturing Technology
- Technology Transfer
- Technology Applications
- Technology Utilization
- Technology Transition
- Spin-offs

TECHNOLOGY REINVESTMENT PROJECT

TECHNOLOGY REINVESTMENT PROJECT

MISSION

To stimulate the transition to a growing, integrated, national industrial capability which provides the most advanced, affordable, military systems and the most competitive commercial products.

STRATEGY

Invest Defense Conversion, Title IV funds in activities which stimulate the:

1. development of technologies which enable new products and processes
2. deployment of existing technology into commercial and military products and processes
3. integration of military and commercial research and production activities

TECHNOLOGY REINVESTMENT PROJECT

ACTIVITY AREAS

- **TECHNOLOGY DEVELOPMENT**

  Promote the development of dual-use technologies
  - Spin-Off Transitioning (activities that demonstrate commercial viability and have already been developed for defense purposes)
  - Dual-Use Development (activities that are applicable to commercial and defence)
  - Spin-On Promotion (activities that demonstrate defence applicability and have already been developed for commercial purposes)
- **TECHNOLOGY DEPLOYMENT**
  - Establish links between existing technology capabilities for small and medium-sized businesses
  - Manufacturing Extension Service Providers (outreach)
  - Extension Enabling Services (services to integrate service providers and technical sources)
  - Alternative Deployment Pilot Projects (in-reach)
  - Technology Access Services (brokering, "yellow pages," etc.)

TECHNOLOGY REINVESTMENT PROJECT

TECHNOLOGY DEPLOYMENT ACTIVITIES

TECHNOLOGY REINVESTMENT PROJECT

ACTIVITY AREAS

(Continued)

- **MANUFACTURING EDUCATIION AND TRAINING**

  Eastablish programmes for the retraining of defence workers and improve the manufacturing curriculum in the academic sector

  - Engineering education in manufacturing across the curriculum
  - Practice-oriented master's degree programmes
  - Educational traineeships for defense industry engineers
  - Manutacturing engineering education coalition
  - Supplementary education awards to ongoing centres and coalitions devoted to manufacturing
  - Individual/group innovations in manufacturing engineering education

TECHNOLOGY REINVESTMENT PROJECT

COST SHARING

- All programmes have cost sharing (match) requirements at least 50 per cent
- Match can include:
  - ▲ **Cash**
    - Can come from participants or third parties
    - May include IR&D under some circumstances
    - Includes license fees, royalties, fees for services
    - SBIR Programme
  - ▲ **In-kind Contributions**
    - Compensated services of personnel
    - Value of equipment, land, buildings
    - Technology transfer activities

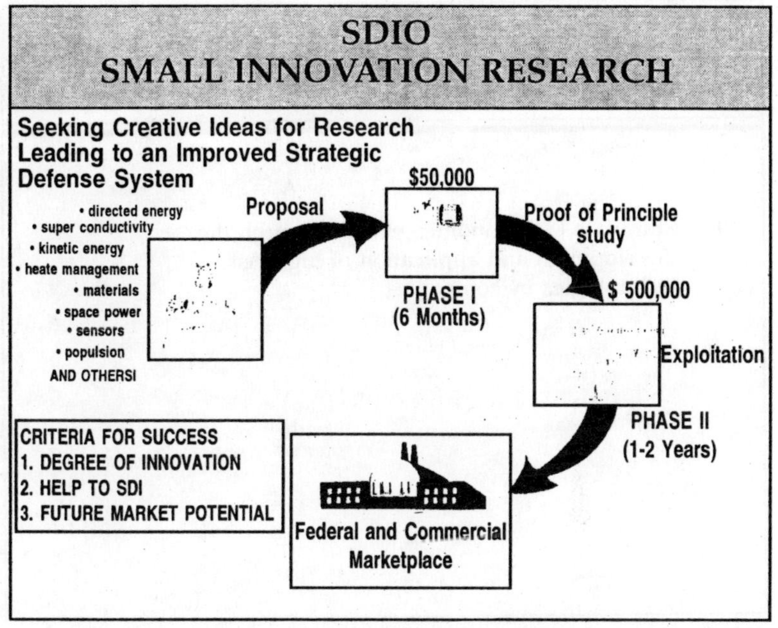

TECHNOLOGY REINVESTMENT PROJECT
INTELLECTUAL PROPERTY RIGHTS

- GENERAL POLICY
  - Government to acquire nothing if technology commercialized in a reasonable time
  - Restrict foreign access to technology
  - Encourage broad exposure to technology among consortium partners
- PATENT RIGHTS
  - Contracts, grants, and cooperative agreements
  - "Other transactions"
- RIGHTS IN OTHER INTELLECTUAL PROPERTY

Advanced Technology Programme MISSION

- Stimulate U S economic growth through the development and application of high-risk technologies by companies

ATP PROGRAMME SELECTION

PURPOSE IS TO:

- Define and implement high-risk, high payoff R&D programmes
- Establish a framework for industry and government partnerships to develop national R&D programmes
- Stimulate and facilitate public discussion and sharing of non-proprietary ideas for future technology and business directions
- Encourage industry to submit programme ideas

ATP PROGRAMME DEFINITION

PURPOSE IS NOT TO:

- Provide single companies or small groups of companies with a mechanism for funding research proposals that benefits only their companies and has little impact on the overall economy
- Force companies to cooperate with each other or with federal agencies or universities
- Provide federal assistance to carry out work that would otherwise be performed in a timely manner by the private sector

MAJOR CHARACTERISTICS OF THE ATP

- Development/application of high-risk technologies to stimulate economic growth
- Market oriented—industry proposes ideas, shares costs, and performs work
- Competitive selection process-technical and business merit Cost sharing
- Cost sharing

ATP ELIGIBILITY

- Individual companies
  - No more than 3 years
  - Up to $2 million total
  - ATP pays only direct costs
- Joint ventures
  - No more than 5 years
  - No limit on award amount
  - ATP share less than 50 per cent
- No direct funding to universities, government agencies or non-profit independent research institutes

Ballistic Missile Defence Organization

ADVANCED TECHNOLOGY PROGRAMME

- 4 annual competitions, to-date
- Total funds committed—$515 million ($247—government, $268 - private)
- Range of awards: $500,000 → $20M
- 89 awards (23 joint ventures, 66 single applicants)

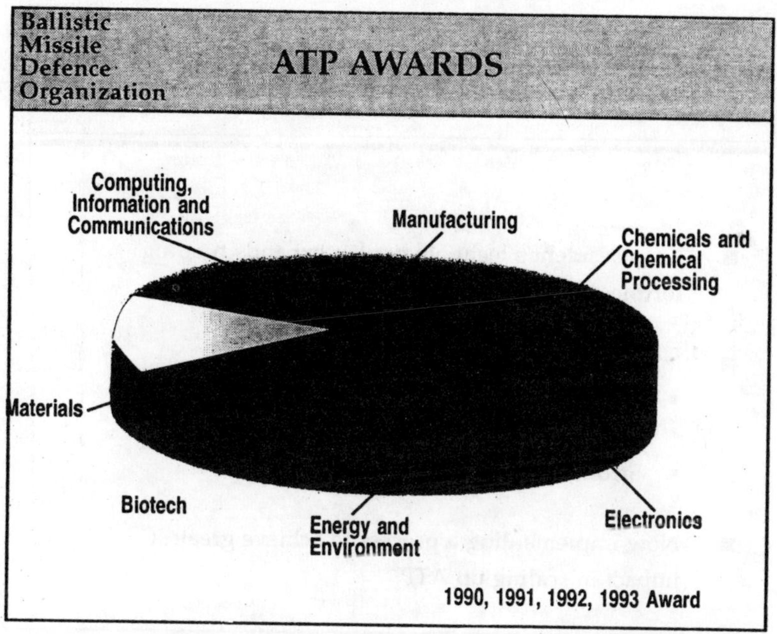
Ballistic
Missile
Defence
Organization
ATP AWARDS
Computing,
Information and
Communications
Manufacturing
Chemicals and
Chemical
Processing
Materials
Biotech
Energy and
Environment
Electronics
1990, 1991, 1992, 1993 Award

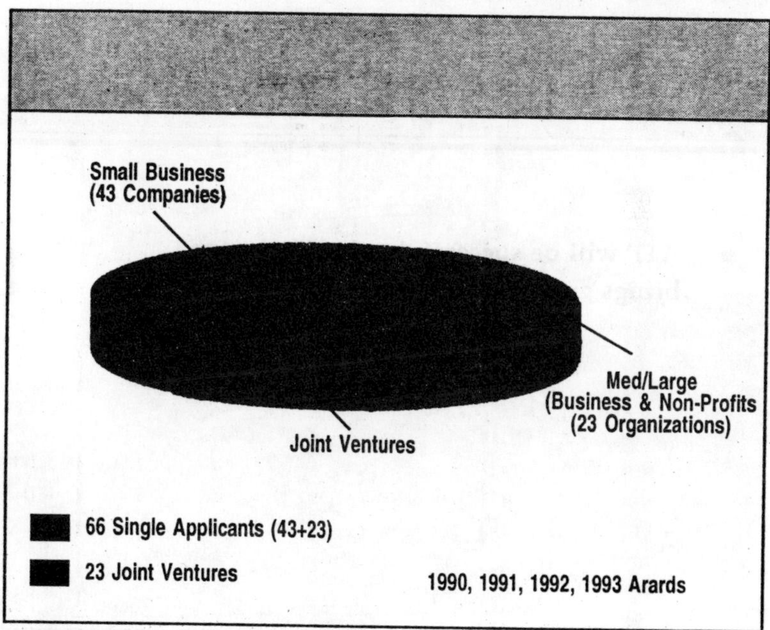
Small Business
(43 Companies)
Med/Large
(Business & Non-Profits
(23 Organizations)
Joint Ventures
66 Single Applicants (43+23)
23 Joint Ventures
1990, 1991, 1992, 1993 Arards

ADVANCED TECHNOLOGY PROGRAMME

- The President's technology plan expands funding for the ATP to $750M by 1997
- Initial ATP is a solid base to build on:
  - Competitive process
  - No political set-asides
  - Strong market orientation
- Now implementing a process to achieve greatest impact in scaling up ATP

BOTTOM LINE

- **ATP will be successful only if industry brings good ideas to the table**

THE

MANUFACTURING

EXTENSION PARTNERSHIP

OBJECTIVE OF MEP

HELP SMALLER MANUFACTURERS BECOME MORE COMPETITIVE

- Implement appropriate advanced technology—core
- Use best manufacturing practices—core
- Adopt modern business and workforce approaches—essential related services

. . . all these involve fundamental change in the companies

SMALLER MANUFACTURERS ARE IMPORTANT

- There are 370,000 manufacturing firms with under 500 employees
- Smaller firms make up 98% of all manufacturing establishments
- Smaller firms contribute more than half the value added in manufacturing in the US
- Smaller firms account for 75% of new jobs in manufacturing
- Smaller firms employ 65 per cent of all manufacturing employees (over 8 million jobs)
  . . . and
- Smaller firms supply many of the component parts needed by large firms

COMPONENTS OF MEP

- Manufacturing Technology Centres (MTCs)—grow to 30, each serving a large population of companies, regionally or sectorally defined
- Manufacturing Outreach Centres (MOCs)—grow to 70, each serving a lower concentration
- State Technology Extension Programme (STEP)—funding and technical support for planning by states, as well as continuing service delivery in sparse areas
- Links—the national structure of communications, data systems, evaluation, field agent training, tool development, and linkages with technology sources

WHAT EXTENSION CENTRES DO
(Examples)

- CORE
  - Assessment of company needs
  - Undertake fundamental company reshaping
  - Software demonstration/selection
  - Hardware demonstration/selection
  - Field agents working hands-on
  - Technology projects
  - Shared manufacturing/teaching factories
  - Extensive performance measurement
- ESSENTIAL RELATED SERVICES
  - Workforce training and workplace organization
  - Business system development
  - Marketing
  - Financing

BARRIERS FACED BY SMALLER MANUFACTURERS

- Lack of awareness of changing technology, production techniques, and business management practices
- Difficulty for owners and managers of small companies to find high-quality unbiased information, advice, and assistance
- Isolation of smaller manufacturers, which have too few opportunities for interaction with other companies in similar situations
- Regulatory environment which creates a disproportionate burden for smaller firms
- Difficulty obtaining operating capital and investment funds for modernization

From Learning to Change: Opportunities to Improve the Performance of Smaller Manufacturers, National Academy Press, 1993.

OPERATING PHILOSOPHY

- There are Federal, state, local, private resources and programmes in place which relate to the mission
- Establish linkages with existing resources and programmes
- Don't duplicate existing resources
- Work with excisting programmes

TECHNOLOGY REINVESTMENT PROJECT

Technology Development

Issues

- Increased Federal Financial Support for civilian R&D
  - Expand Advanced Technology Programme
  - Increase support for manufacturing
  - Eliminate low priority programmes
  - Ensure more private sector input
- More Federal R&D partnerships with industry
- Indirect support through tax incentives
  - Make the R&E tax credit permanent
  - Change to R&E tax credit
  - Strengthen the capital gains tax differential
  - Revise rules for allocating R&D expenditures

TECHNOLOGY REINVESTMENT PROJECT

Technology Diffusion, Commercialization & Use

Issues

- Technology Transfer
  - Orient Federal labs more to industry needs
  - Ensure more synergy between military and civilian technology and dual use
  - Emphasize technology transfer more
  - Ensure more private sector input
  - Ensure more state input
  - Streamline CRADA process
- Create Stronger tax and capital formation incentives generally
  - Restore the investment tax credit
  - Provide more accelerated depreciation
  - Reform the alternative minimum tax
- Business assistance
  - Support industrial extension programmes
  - Benchamark against foreign competitors
- Elevate manufacturing as national policy element
- Reform government procurement

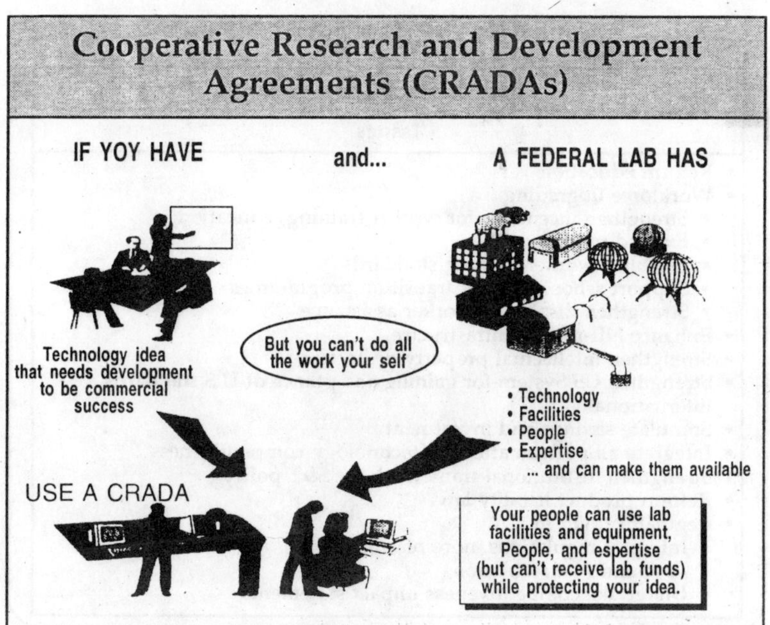

- **1980 Stevenson—Wydler Technology Innovation Act**
- **1982 Small Business Innovation Development Act**
- **1986 Federal Technology Transfer Act**
- **1987 National Defence Authorization Act (DoD Direction)**
- **1987 Presidential Executive Order 12591**
- **1988 Technology Competitiveness Act**

TECHNOLOGY REINVESTMENT PROJECT

Technology Infrastructure

Issues

- Reform education
- Workforce upgrading
  - Strengthen incentives for worker training/education
  - Expand training
  - Establish worker training standards
  - Support school-to-work transition programmes
  - Strengthen disolcated worker assistance
- Enhance NII-related infrastructre
- Strengthen intellectual property protection
- Strengthen US System for gaining acceptance of U S standards internationally
- Stimulate savings and investment
- Integrate all policies affecting technology competitiveness
- Strengthen institutional framework for S&T policy
- Reform product liability law
- Regulatory reform
  - Interpret regulations more reasonably
  - Ease antitrust restrictions
  - Undertake competitiveness impact statements

THE FEDERAL ROLE IN TECHNOLOGY

- How is the government investing in science and technology?
  - ▲ Total U.S. R&D>$150B/year
  - ▲ Federal government provides:
    - 45% of the funds for U.S. R&D
    - 60% for defence, mostly weapons systems development
    - 15% for health
    - 0.5% for industrial development
- What has changed?
  - ▲ Global competition has accelerated the rate of innovation and challenged US industry
  - ▲ Post Cold War-> opportunity to redefine our technology investment strategy

THE FEDERAL ROLE IN TECHNOLOGY

- **How is the government responding to change?**
  - ▲ Invest in civilian technology
  - ▲ Drive defence toward a dual-use technology base
  - ▲ Transfer technology from government labs
  - ▲ Continue commitment to basic science

9

Conversion Technologies of the National Academy of Sciences of Ukraine

ANATOLIJ SHPAK AND SERGEI BOROVIK

The establishments and institutions of the National Academy of Sciences of Ukraine like any highly qualified teams in the world have taken an active part in creating elements, technology, new kinds of military equipment and armament. Accordingly, there was successful and mutually beneficial cooperation among institutes dealing with problems of natural sciences and a number of defence enterprises. During this time scientific teams with highly qualified employees have been organized in order to solve scientific and technological problems of defence strengthening. Special fundamental research undertaken has made significant contribution to general development of fundamental science and scientific and technological advance in industry.

However, the present-day situation has caused dramatic reduction in orders for military purposes. That is why the future and the very existence of many highly professional teams is becoming an acute problem.

Fortunately, our Academy as opposed to other Academies of former Soviet republics, including the Russian Academy, has always been characterized as the paying special attention to practical application. Fundamental results was just the first step, followed by particular samples of mechanisms, machines, technologies.

Therefore, a number of scientific research elaborations carried out according to the orders of military enterprises could be used immediately or after certain improvements in national economy in creating new machines and mechanisms, equipment, as well as consumer goods and modernization of existing technologies.

I believe it would be appropriate to give several examples. Priority conversion directions of National Academy of Sciences of Ukraine include research in materials science, application of new composite, ceramic, thermostable materials in aircraft-, auto-, and ship-building industry.

First and foremost, we mean the following welding technologies:

- welded constructions transformed with transformation coefficient of 50, for space engineering;
- oil storage tanks, dry substances storage, pontoon bridges;
- welding of precise machine-building and radioelectronic products;
- underwater welding and cutting of metals;
- welding and cutting of refractory metals, tungsten, molybdenum, zirkon, niobium.

Then, the following almost completed research is worth mentioning:

- individual means of protection against fire-arms and cold steel weapons;
- materials for leser technology and communications. Ceramic mirrors (cooled and non-cooled) for powerful infrared lasers and space communications;
- soldering of metal-nonmetal units for space engineering;
- fire-proof construction ceramics;
- high-temperature superconducting coatings.

Attention should be paid to domain-acoustic processor, the device employing the effect of memorizing of high-frequency signal by micro magnetic structure of polycrystal medium. It is designated for long-term memorizing (for hours, days) of phase portrait of complex information signal and coordinated filtration of signals with complex structure.

Some years ago the institutes of chemical profile were to solve an important task: working out of processes for transforming liquid rocket fuel—heptile—into practically useful products.

Nowdays our scientists have elaborated the processes of transforming heptile into such products:

- inhibitors of hydrogen sulphfide corrosion;
- biologically active compounds for pre-sowing seed treatment during vegetation period (futicides and regulators of plant growth);
- surface-active substances for various purposes, in particular, for detergents;
- accelerators of epoxide resin polymerization;
- medicines;
- polymer materials.

We can give a lot of similar examples. They clearly demonstrate both great potential of our Academy and plenty of unclaimed scientific research and technologies created, specifically, for military industry.

From this follows our point of view concerning conversion problems of scientific teams that predominantly deal with matters of defence. Taking care of preserving scientific schools, actively working research teams with high scientific qualification, it seems logical to change emphasis, i.e. to somewhat reduce new fundamental research (at least, for the time being), and concentrate means and forces on transformation of military high technologies for civil purposes.

This would help retain highly qualified specialists, reduce anxiety regarding their future, and make less painful transition of scientific teams to market-driven economy.

Possible Ways of Cooperation in the Sphere of Conversion

1. Elaboration of methods of early prediction of natural disasters (hurricanes, sandstorms, volcano eruptions, ice hummocks) using space-based side vision radio locators.
2. Creation of general automated database of ionosphere parameters and a system of ecological monitoring of the Earth, specifically, earthquake prediction by using non-coherent scattering observatories.
3. Organization of joint venture concerning production of millimeter-range wavelength medical equipment for curing digestion organs.
4. Working out of data processing multiprocessor systems using databases with microwave technology for data exchange.
5. Creation of joint ventures association on developing modern sensor devices.
6. Organization of joint venture on elaboration of methods of transforming rocket fuels and explosives into raw material for chemical industry.

10

Military Conversion and Science in the Czech Republic

STANISLAV STACH

1. Introduction

The end of the Cold War and of the East-West confrontation, followed by the fall of communism, the break-up of the Warsaw Pact, the rise of new social order in the Central and East Europe, by unification of Germany and withdrawal of Soviet troops from the Czech and Slovak Republic, Hungary, Poland, former GDR and Baltic states, together with a long-term influence of the Confidence and security building measures and signing of Strategic offensive arms and Conventional armed forces in Europe limitation treaties, created an entirely new situation in Europe. The present huge armies and expanded weapon industries, built during the 40 years of the arms race, have lost their purpose and become in encumbrance to the newly formed states, building democracy and market economy. The global political context has always played a decisive role both in development and in reduction of the military production.

Particularly in countries to the East of the Iron Curtain the weapon industry was an example of centrally planned and controlled, state sponsored economy.

Though the processes of restructuralism are taking place parallely in the East and in the West, the revolutionary changes in the former Warsaw Pact countries have reflected themselves in the sphere of weapon industry in an unprecedented way. The key word for the whole period of the four last years became the term "conversion". The conversion of weapon industry, in spite of its particular character, has become an important phenomenon of the overall transformation of the society.

From the wider point of view we can include under this term:

- the limitation of the military budget and transfer of saved means to other peaceful ends,
- the release of military personnel, its requalification and inclusion into the civil sphere,
- the civil utilization of abandoned military installations,
- the peaceful application of some military equipment,
- the military industry suppressing and its transformation to peaceful programmes,
- the military research and development installation's transformation to peaceful programmes,
- the economic, social, environmental and other consequences of the withdrawl of foreign forces,
- the regional problems, including questions of the infrastructure, services, unemployment, stemming from the military industry conversion, armed forces down-sizing and relocation, and the foreign troops withdrawal.

The Czech republic's military industry is being influenced by many circumstances simultaneously, and it is not easy to decide which of them is the most influential. To the main factors, whose consequence is the limitation of the weapons production and the military industries conversion we can count:

- The Czech armed forces and its equipment down-sizing,
- The Czech Republic's military budget reduction,
- The Warsaw Pact and Eastern markets of the COMECON member states disintegration,
- The rise of insolvency in many of East European and Asian states,

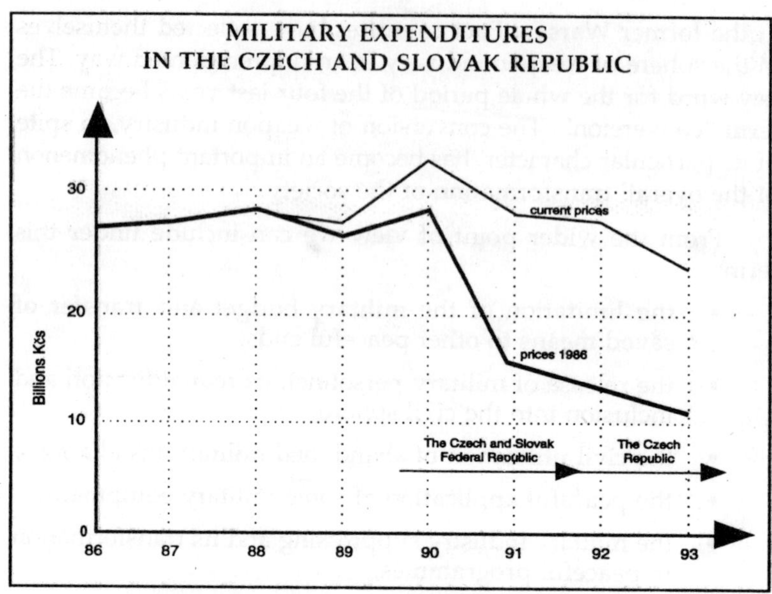

Fig. 1. Military expenditures in the Czech and Slovak Republic.

- The political decision of the Czech government not to support the weapons production and to end this production in the quickest way, not regarding the price paid, from humanitarian reasons,
- The necessity of a gradual improving of interoperability and compatibility of the Czech Armed Forces with the NATO countries.

The Czech Armed Forces was reduced from approximately 200,000 men of the former Czech and Slovak Federal Republic in 1989 to 65,000 men of the present Czech Armed Forces at the end of the 1994, that is to about 32 per cent, or to 42 per cent regarding the division of the Czech and Slovak Republic in 1992/93. The real military budget was reduced from 28 billions Kcs in 1989 to about 11 billion Kcs 1994 (in 1986 process) that is to 39 per cent respectively to 59 per cent as is seen from Fig. 1.

As a result of this trend the acquisition of any weapons and military equipment was stopped, purchases of spare parts were severelly reduced, and financial resources allocated to research and development programmes in the civil sphere fell nearly to zero.

The weapons and military equipment acquisition interrupting as well as closing of the opportunities of export and influenced the situation in the defence industry.

The conversion of the weapon production has taken place in complex environment of transformation of the economy, the liberalization of the system of prices, the privatization of state owned organization, the property restitution and transformation of external economic connections.

2. Conversion of Military Industry

The Czech Republic belongs to countries with a long-term tradition of military production. A rather modern industry was built immediately after the creation of Czechoslovakia in 1918, on the basis of companies Skoda Plzen, Scheillier and Bellot Praha, Zbrojovka Brno, CKD Praha, CZ Strakonice Explosia Semtin and others. Especially Skoda Plzen company has undergone the important development in this period. It owned, before the Second World War, the ship building company in Komarno, weapon factory in Brno, aircraft companies AVIA in Prague and Kunovice, car factory Laurin and Klement in Mladá Boleslav, machine and bridge works in Adamov, ammunition and gun factory in Dubnicen. Váhom and an export organization Omnipol. Most of these companies belong still to the basis of the Czech industry.

The Czechoslovak industry was one of the ten most important exporters of weapons in the between-the-wars period, and in 1934 and 1935 held the first place among them. The main items of the military export were infantry and artillery weapons, explosives, and later on special military vehicles, including tanks. Also the aviation industry developed well. Most of the companies, concentrated into robust syndicates, were private owned.

During the Second World War the Czech industry served to the fascist Germany. Many installation were further rebuilt and extended.

After the Second World War, the communists' victory, and beginning of the East-West confrontation the weapon industry started to grow again and concentrated on licensed production

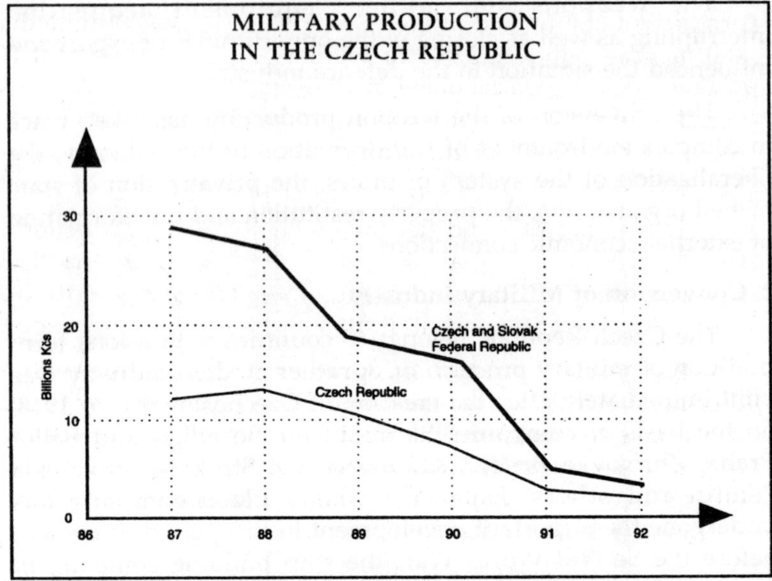

Fig. 2. Military production in the Czech Republic.

of Soviet equipment. The centre of gravity of military production began to move to Slovakia. New factories were built e.g.: ZTS Martin, ZVL Povázská Bystrica, ZVT Banská Bystrica, ZVS Dubnican. Váhom, Vihorlat Snina, Tesla Liptovsky Hrádock, Mostárna Brezno, VSS Kosice, PS Povázská Bystrica, ZVS Meopta Bratislava and other. Production delimitation was accompanied by transfer of expert of Slovakia.

The professional level of the aircraft industry grew substantially in after-the-war period, especially in the Czech Republic. The licensed production of Soviet Mig jet planes brought a technological breakthrough, and enable later an independent development and production of airplanes. The L29, L39 and L59 types of aircraft production represented 66 per cent of the world production of training airplanes, up to 1996. New factory for aircraft engines was built in Slovakia in Povázská Bystrica.

The core of the military industry specialized on production of tanks and armoured personnel carriers, was created in 1956-1992, and allowed lately for expanded production. The military production culminated in the CSFR in 1987-88, when more than 100 factories, about 73,000 of workers directly and about 50-60,000 indirectly participated in weapons production. About 70 per cent of the production was exported. The military factories were concentrated in the Vah region in Slovakia, in South Moravia and the Prague region in the Czech Republic.

The period of rapid decline of the military production in the Czech and Slovak Republic began after the 1989 revolutionary changes (see Fig. 2). The 1992 production comprises about 20 per cent of the 1988 production of weapons.

The severe restriction of opportunities to sell the military products both abroad and at home caused the necessity to seek ways have to transform the military factories to produce civil products. Such transformation was complicated by recession in other spheres of the internal economy, that showed no interest for new machine products.

The government, under the pressure of producers, decided to help financially during the first stages of the process of conversion, and realeased some fiscal means for this purpose. About 1.5 billion Kcs in 1991 (0.3 billion for the Czech Republic) and about 1 billion Kcs in 1992 (0.2 billion for the Czech Republic) was used for this purpose. Gradually about 100 conversion programmes were prepared, from which only part was realized. However, the producers were bound mostly to resolve the situation without much help, or simply stop the production.

The split of the Czech and Slovak Republic into two independent sovereign states, at the end of 1992, made the process of conversion in the Czech Republic more easy. The majority of non easily convertible factories, producing tanks and armoured vehicles, was concentrated in Slovakia. Only the more easily convertible industries were left in the Czech Republic: aircraft and electronic factories, production of hand-held weapons, precision engineering and optics factories, production of equipment for protection against the chemical, bacteriological and nuclear weapons etc. In addition, these factories were often technically equipped, staffed by qualified personnel, with good working discipline, and used to quality control requirements.

3. Conversion in the Field of Science, Research and Development

The military complex of the Czech and Slovak Federal Republic consisted, of course, also of the research and development facilities associated usually to production factories, or ministerial research institutions. Some of these institutions functioned within the framework of the armed forces. Some institutes of national academies of science and at the universities and colleges participated on long-term scientific programmes, financed by the Ministry of Defense. Comparatively modern research and testing institutes were built within the military forces.

The armed forces supported scientific programmes in civil institutions oriented particularly to the sphere of medical and veterinary sciences, chemistry, and protection against toxic and biological weapons, development of advanced materials and technologies, laser technology, infrared technology, millimeter electromagnetic waves, computer, communication and radar technology and new principles of navigation.

Some programmes in the field of armour, engineering, automobile technology, artillery, rocket technology, training and transport aircraft, reconnaissance and communication, fire control system, ammunition and explosive were in development stage. Some workplaces were specialized on adjustment of the licensed procedures to domestic conditions.

Basically, it should be mentioned, that the science and research in the Czech Republic were never fully militarized. The top scientists were never interested in working on classified projects, specially due to fear that their opportunities to travel and publish the result of research could be limited.

After the 1990, the armed forces gradually stopped to finance the scientific programmes in the civil sphere. The conversion of not too wide scientific teams became a constituent part of a wider trend of restructuralization of scientific institutions. The fall-down of resources allocated to military research is shown in Fig.3.

At present, even the state does not single out sufficient means for science and research. The salaries in research

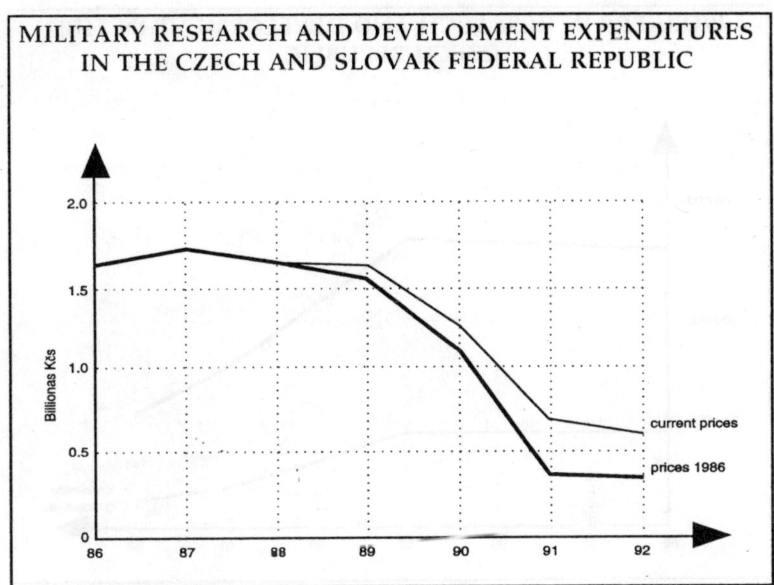

Fig. 3. Military research and development expenditures in the Czech and Slovak Federal Republic.

institutions are substantially lower than in sphere of private enterprise. The transformation of society prefers a quick pay-off. Scientific and research institutes are reducing substantially the number of employees, some inefficient programmes are wound-up, some institutes are dissolved. Though the process of privatizations involves the scientific institutions only marginally, majority of them have to earn their own living, at least partially. Resources are no longer provided globally, but selectively on specific projects, predominantly in the form of grants. Young, talented workers are often seeking and finding self-assertion in international and private companies, or in the sphere of entrepreneurship. Only smaller part of employees is succeeding in applying for foreign or domestic grants, that help them to maintain their standards of living.

But very small portion of scientific workers is leaving the country. If they are going abroad, it is mostly for a temporary stay, they usually return home. Fig. 4 shows the decline of number of workers in the field of research and development.

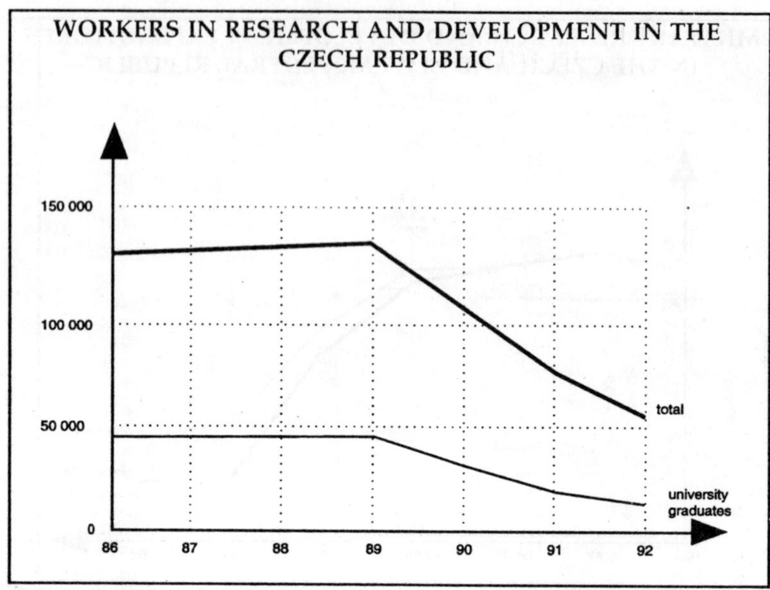

Fig. 4. Workers in research and development in the Czech Republic.

Among the positive factors of the present process of transformation we can count:

- closer contact with world science,
- higher requirements applied to scientific workers, accompanied by selection of the best,
- higher opportunity of self-assertion, not limited to the national scale.

There are, of course, some negative consequences:

- reduced financial means provided by the state,
- difficult financing of long-term projects, not bringing an immediate pay-off,
- outflow of young and talented workers into the private economy, which offers higher gains.

Especially, the exploratory research is most endangered, and as a result of scarce resources available, is stagnating. Short-term projects, linked to industrial and business needs, bringing immediate profit, are preferred.

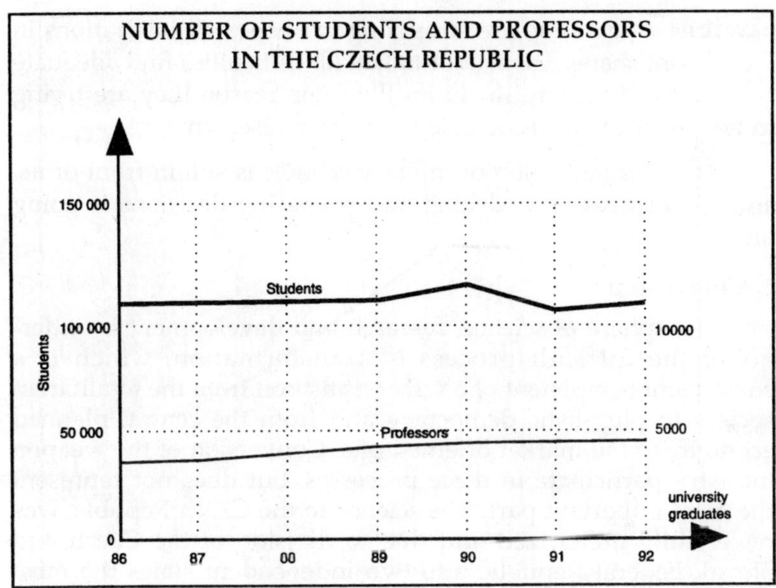

Fig. 5. Number of students and professors in the Czech Republic.

4. Conversion and the Sphere of Education

Civil universities and colleges only exceptionally participated on military projects. Officers, and even civil employees in the field of defense were educated mostly in military schools. The conversion of weapons industry concerns the civil schools and universities only marginally. The number of students has a steady, slightly increasing trend, uninterrupted by revolutionary changes of the last period (see Fig. 5).

The number of applicants, particularly in liberal arts, exceeds many times the number of vacant places available. It could be expected that the reorganization of the educational system will bring some changes, but only in coming period. It will probably result in higher financial burden put on students and their parents.

A different situation exists in the military educational system. The military schools are still too overstaffed, and the down-sizing and reorganization of the armed forces did not still influenced them. The older, highly qualified employees of military schools, and people specialized in purely military branches of learning, are struggling to keep their institutions in the present shape. The would only with difficulties find adequate positions in the civil life. From the same reason they are trying to take over the decision role in military research.

The reorganization of military schools is still in front of us, and the process of analyzing and preparing decisions is going on.

5. Conclusion

The sphere of science, research and development is undergoing the difficult process of transformation, which is a constituent component of a wider transition from the totalitarian society to pluralistic democracy and from the central planned economy to the market oriented one. Conversion of the weapon industry participate in these processes, but does not represent the most important part. The science in the Czech Republic was never fully militarized and due to division of the Czech and Slovak Federal Republic into two independent states the most difficult problems of conversion of the heavy weapon industry passed to Slovakia. The centre of gravity of the weapon industry in the Czech Republic is the sphere of the aircraft industry, electronics, hand-held weapons, precision engineering and optics, production of ammunition and explosives. The duality of the military and civil production was always presented in these branches, and it is why the factories and linked research and development institutions are comparatively successful in reducing the military production and in transition to the civil one. In addition, some new opportunities are outlining themselves in context of inevitable implementation of measures to improve the compatibility and interoperability of weapons and system with NATO member states. This building of compatibility is connected with modernization of equipment and with new request for research.

The transformation of society brings many positive factors, connected with an opening to the world, the exchange of information, and higher mobility of scientific workers.

Concurrently the reduction of resources allocated by the state to science development and to the armed forces brings many organizational, economic, and social problems. The number of workers in research and development is falling. There is connection to higher qualification requirements, and to higher attractivity of jobs in the private sector, especially for younger and talented people. The preference of quick pay-offs and short-time programmes brings stagnation into the exploratory research. New pieces of legislation are being elaborated.

The civil educational system is comparatively stable, system of military schools is waiting for a principal reform.

Any small nation, like the Czech Republic, has to make every effort to utilize all national resources in an optimal way. Even the integrated national resources are not sufficient for an effective development of science. A cooperation with the world scientific community is essential. The expected inclusion of the Czech Republic into the European economic, political and security structures, together with a wider share on common development programmes, would play an important role in consolidating the sphere of science and research.

Making use of the top level science and technology is a prerequisite of success in an economic competition. The independent, own scientific base makes possible the transfer of the scientific knowledge, and enables, at the same time, to contribute to solving the global and regional problems.

The armed forces should retain its position as an organization supporting the science progress and to continue in singling out resources for scientific programmes out of its budget. Military scientific and research institutions should have to try to build links with analogous institutions abroad. The participation in common projects should be discussed, within the framework of Partnership for Peace programme, with NATO authorities, and, within the framework of the associated partnership, with the WEU institutions. The military schools should try to be included into the network of NATO educational institutions.

Precondition of any cooperation is the knowledge of languages. Especially in the field of military the language barrier is more important than unified weapons.

At the same time, maintaining and edifying the cultural level of the nation means to allow as many young people as possible to get as wide education as possible, in spite of the risk that they will not work exactly in spite of the same field of activity they studied, including the wide opportunity to study in schools abroad.

11

Social Conditions for Science: Are there too Many Scientists and Engineers?

HORACIO MENANO

The political and socio-economic changes produced in eastern and central European countries in the last five years have had enormous consequences in local conditions for Science. This was firstly the immediate result of the decrease in funding for research and technological activities and could be seen as one of the most important factors in generating the massive brain drain prevalent in these countries.[1,2]

Another important consequence of the political changes have been the modifications produced in the industrial-military complexes of the two former blocs. It was to be expected that this would take a form of decreasing research activities either by particular decision-making or from diversion of funds. In either case consequences would follow:

It is necessary to distinguish the consequences of sudden decrease of the activities in state owned institutions engaged in defense research activities and the situation of private research institutions with large defense contracts facing the sudden disappearance of important funds. In both cases the non-availability of funds will in the end produce pressures for the dismissal of scientists and engineers. In the first case it seems that the purpose of the institution and even its existence can be put into question if there is no possibility to restructure it through some form of transition toward "civilian" objectives. In the second case the decrease in funds is more easily observed and the institution itself is, normally, not in danger. In both cases there is, together with the (brain) loss of scientists and engineers, a change in the internal (social) conditions for work and in many cases institutional deterioration.

From the year 1990 on both these situations were very evident in the former Soviet Union and central European countries but also became more and more prevalent in the other European countries and in the United States and Canada. The situation of conversion of military into civilian **R&D** is becoming very important everywhere.

On the other hand it is now clear that this important and specific surplus of scientists and engineers is developing in an environment where a general change in conditions for Science is felt almost everywhere.

This situation can be described globally as if the market for (new) scientific institutions and for scientists and engineers is not expanding anymore. It can also be described as a situation where there are **already too many scientists and engineers.** Some very dramatic examples show particular aspects of the general situation as can be seen in the case of the decision to terminate the Superconducting Super Collider (S.S.C) Lab. One year after the decision was taken from around the Lab's 1100 member scientific and technical staff only 100 remain. From the 200 physicists only 72% found new jobs and from those only about half found jobs in their own original field. Others found jobs in computer, electronics and even in financial industries.[3]

The question can be now asked: is this can extreme example specially related to the field of high energy and theoretical physics and also only seen in this very short term?

It seems on the contrary that the problems are very broad as many papers published in very recent months show.

Following the test case of the SSC collapse let us look at some of the discussions now being held in the USA not only because they are very openly being described in a rather well documented way but because, regarding our main theme on conversion and world-wide brain-drain, this country has always been one of the preferred places of attraction for scientists and also an inexhaustible reservoir.

Interestingly enough the series of papers on "**Science Careers: Playing to Win**" published on the Science issue of September 23 last 4 starts with the statement from David Goldstein of the California Institute of Technology saying **"The expansionary era of American Science has come to an end".**

As we described above the situations is related with the end of Cold War and in the last few years with recession induced corporate and government funding cuts. The figures of unemployment for scientists as a class were still rather low, in 91 around 1.4%, but in certain areas the figures were unprecedently high as was the case for recipients of new mathematics Ph.D., with an unemployment rate of 8.9%. This situation seems to have a tendency to be worsening in the last years. Certain fields are suffering less than others as is the case for biology. Nevertheless these descriptions tell very little as they do not reflect the very important dislocations of science posts inside the scientific institutions and industry with young scientist holding patterns of repeated "**postdocs**" and the rise of researchers holding temporary posts.

It is now not only a big challenge for the individual scientist to start or maintain himself in a scientific career in academe or in industry but also a great challenge for institutions themselves to adapt and change. As examples, there have been meetings on "reinvesting the research university" and on changing for a new-paradigm graduate student and also recommendations to the United States government to undergo a shift in the way it supports research, moving from a system dominated by grants for investigator-initiated proposals to one preferring contracts for targeted research. As could be expected there is no unanimity of these views. The need to further analyse the state of the Science and Technology system in the United States has now been translated into a very broad study to be conducted by a panel of distinguished scientists coordinated by the chairmanship of Frank Press former president of the National Academy of Sciences and to be finalized in December 1995. The report is to be seen as one to have objectives comparable to the report by Vannevar Bush titled "Science: The Endless Frontier" which laid the foundations for the growth of research in the United States after the Second World War. The report was requested by United States Senate and will deal with the setting of new **R&D** priorities and it will supplement the very recent White House report on basic science **"Science in the National Interest".**

When we now turn our attention to the general situation for Science in the European countries we will find, in spite of the enormous differences in institutional structures and constrictions related to specific national systems, many of the problems referred to above. Some of the difficulties can be seen in the very fierce discussion regarding the restructuring and funding of research centres that are now being pursued in Germany, Britain and France and probably in all the others. In all places there is, with the acceptance of a system of contracts for targeted research a clear demand for an increase for at least a maintenance of core funding from government sources. Simultaneously it is apparent that the great proportion, in European terms, of temporary posts for scientists and engineers are now producing concern for the build up of acceptable careers for individual scientists or scientists to be. Two interesting examples referring to science education come from Britain where there is a very great decrease in the number of candidates to science degrees in the British universities[5] and this has started a movement toward the reform of the A level system, the **"gold standard"** for admission. Another reform would be a change in the British Ph.D. system introducing a first year for a new **"Master of Research"** qualification that could also be used for direct employment in industry.

All those signs and symptoms to use a typical medical nomenclature, are sufficient to indicate the existence of not only a discomfort in the global scientific community but of a malady. This malady has been certainly aggravated by the acute political changes, local economic disturbances and rather general recession, but must have originated in a model that behaves as if there is no need for an increase in the number of scientists pursuing a career with some degree of stability.

I personally do not believe this is the case and that there is a great need to address ourselves to what is necessary to maintain progress in Science and what are its necessary social conditions.[6]

REFERENCES

1. ANGELL, I.O. AND KOUZMINOV, V.A., 1990, Report of the Working Party on Brain Drain Issues in Europe. Tech. Rep. nr. 3 UNESCO-ROSTE.
2. BIGGIN, S. AND KOUZMINOV, V.A., 1993, Proceedings of the International Seminar on "Brain Drain Issues in Europe". Tech. Rep. nr. 15, UNESCO-ROSTE.
3. ROUSH, W., Colliding Forces, Life After the S.C.C., Science 266: 532, 1994.
4. HOLDEN, C., Science Careers, Science 26: 1905, 1994.
5. The Economist. Science Education. 27th August, 1994.
6. GANELIUS, T., 1983, Progress in Science and its Social Conditions. Proceedings of a Noble Symposium, Pergamon Press.

12

Problems of Military Conversion and Science in Russia

NICOLAY MALYSHEV

The public cataclysms in Russia did not pass the sphere of science. First of all, the slump of its national and state authority, a sharp reduction of its financing give evidence for it. The expenses for science have come down from 5.1 per cent in 1990 to 3.1 of national income in 1993.

Did science find itself by chance in such a position?

The development of science was determined mainly by the political guidelines of the state. Science in the USSR was not always an ingenuous productive force, but till recent years it was a factor of national pride. In this sphere it was taken as a matter of course not to calculate the expenses and losses during the implementation of state objectives, such as the creation of the powerful research and experimental base in the sphere of nuclear physics, development of inter-continental ballistic missiles, the opening up of outer space.

The fall of financing in 1990 has shown that the state was not already able to play a role of a generous patron. The danger of destruction of many famous scientific schools, research teams, important scientific directions which represented both national and world pride had become the reality.

By this time the supply of science with the material and technical resources sharply worsened which was already insufficient. In this sphere we were always becoming detached from the industrial developed countries, and whereas science in the West had been technically re-arming, our lag was turned into difficult overcoming alienation. By the end of 1980 the main funds of science had put together less than 2% of the main funds of our economy. One of the main component of the general crisis in Russia is a disparity of the level of material, technical and information base to the objective of the modern science.

Science in Russia which had taken the path of reform, was from the first steps excluded out of the sphere of great attention form the side of high level leaders, authorities of all levels.

In 1991 the average strength of the scholars and employees was reduced to 55,000 men or by 1.8%; in 1992—to 768,000 men or by 25% and in 1993—to 407,000 men or by 17.6%. The scientific sector of military branches (more than 700 research institutes and labs) had lost about 18% of its strength together with the significant reduction of important R&D. As a whole during period of time the strength of scholars and employees was reduced by 1,230,000 men or by 39. 3%. According to the evaluations, in 1994 the strength of employed people in this sphere will be reduced by 10-12% and in 1995—still by 7-8%. The significant reduction of personnel had taken place during the past period in the branch sector of science.

The collapse of the USSR had brought heavy consequences which were connected with the rupture of not only economic but also scientific relations. In the sphere of galvanics, for instance, Russia was left with science but without appropriate manufacturers (they are now in Ukraine and Lithuania). In the sphere of welding, on the other hand, Russia had lost the main scientific centre of the former USSR—Paton's Institute, but Russia has a part of manufacture. And such examples could be continued. In the R&D sphere Russia had lost a part of its property including experimental bases and installations which were left out of Russia. Such situation has been seen also in the military sector of Russian economy.

Because of consumption reduction in renewal and increase in production quality, level of technology and equipment, the production demand for scientific and technical production was reduced. In 1993, 1382 new kinds of goods were produced in comparison with 2404 in 1990 what is less by 42.5%. Specific gravity of new goods in the total value of production came down in 1993 to 3.4% in comparison with 6.5% in 1990, including absolutely new goods—1.6% against 3%.

The value of direct treaties of industrial plants with the scientific bodies was sharply cut. The value of searching R&D in the sphere of creation of necessary scientific and technical surplus in common value of research works of scientific institutes and labs of machinery building was cut from 26% in 1991 till 0.8 in 1993. The quality of completed R&D and produced models of new technique in machinery building was reduced 11 times during the last 3 years.

The situation in military and political sphere had been also changed: the interest of authorities to the military sector, including its base of basis—military branch of science feeding many branches of knowledge, had become lower (Fig.1), see tables 1 and 2.

At present more than 45% of organizations network which implement the scientific R&D, are situated in the territory of some regions. They are: Moscow and Moscow region, S.-Petersburg and Leningrad, Novosibirsk, Sverdlovsk, Rostow and Nijnegorodskaya regions and some other republics.

Unfortunately, till nowadays Russia had not a regional scientific policy. Now the main principle of such policy is to avoid extremities: to shift off the responsibility of its realization onto the Centre or the local authorities that in both cases would lead to undesirable consequences in the development both of science and of regions.

For averting such irreversible process taking place in scientific and technical sphere, the measures on reorientation of the state scientific and technical policy are performed.

The special bodies were organized by the decree of the President of the Russian Federation. They are: Russian Fund of fundamental research for support of originating scientific projects, which are mainly performed by the institutes of Russian Academy of Science (it receives 3% of budget of civilian R&D), Russian nonbudget Fund of technological development for financing R&D and measures on production of new kinds of goods.

The Government of the Russian Federation had adopted a decision about creation of a fund of stimulation of the development of small forms of scientific and technical sphere. It has been investing into this fund 0.5% of allocations from federal budget for science development.

The analysis of effectiveness and utilization in 1992-93 of federal budget means for civilian R&D in military sector shows that the distribution of means through the great quantity of organizations and manufacture's has taken place instead of the concentrations of these means for the conservation and development of high scientific and technical potential of Russian science in the interest of national economy and using of it in the key scientific and technical directions which secure and consolidate the world level of home elaborations.

In 1992-93 in the Ministry of Science of Russia a huge work on organization of State scientific centres of Russian Federation was performed with the aim of conservation of leading scientific schools of world level, development of country's scientific potential in the sphere of fundamental, searching and applied investigations and also training of high qualified scientific personnel.

It should be noted that in 1994-95 preferential development will be given to the R&D which is implemented according to the programmes of the state scientific centres. Creation of such centres will lay essentially the foundation of strategic line of concrete support of the leaders of Russian science. The created centres can already now take under its tutelage the main branches of national economy, realize the elaborations not only non-yielding to international level, but in some directions overcoming it. In the framework of the programmes of such centres there is anticipated the development of investigations and elaborations in the sphere of aircraft and space technique, power engineering (including nuclear one), new materials, electrical engineering, electronics, optics, optoelectronics, laser technique, genetics, biology, microbiology and some other forward-looking directions.

At present accroding to the Decree of the President of the Russian Federation N 939 from June 22, 1993 and the resolution of the Government of the Russian Federation N 1346 from December 25, 1993 the status of state scientific centre was awarded to 48 scientific organizations more than half of which are related to the military sector. The interdepartmental commission on scientific and technical policy had recommended to award such status also to 8 scientific bodies. Thus, the total number of state scientific centres will reach 70-75.

The main priority will be given as usual to the fundamental scientific elaborations which are a source of new knowledge, a base for the development of applied R&D.

It is envisaged to concentrate the work of the branch academies on the priority directions.

The change fundamentally the situation we need to reach an activization of participation of Russian science and particularly its military sector in international technical co-operation, an access of Russian high technologies to the world market, to draw foreign investments for support of Russian science and participation in taking decisions in the sphere of science, engineering and economy.

All these measures need creation of an absolutely new system of legislation for ensuring the scientific and technical activity.

13

Culture of Peace and Transformation of Science

BORIS BORISOV

Science wars begin in the minds of men,
it is in the minds of men
that the defences of peace must be constructed

These are the first words of UNESCO's Constitution, written and adopted almost fifty years ago, just after the Second World War was over.

Ever since, the United Nations Educational, Cultural and Scientific Organization as the whole UN system has witnessed drastic and sometimes dramatic developments in world history.

Today, a unique convergence of historical facts has put the abolition of war on the agenda. This certainly does not mean an end to the violence of war, it means rooting out the culture of war that has come to dominate our institutions and therefore, our everyday lives.

Today, more than ever it is necessary to seek positive ways to resolve conflicts by working out our behaviour and attitudes.

Today, with the end of the Cold War and the dissolution of the superpower blocks it is necessary to involve everybody in the peace building process.

Today new peace-building structures are needed to help transition from a culture of war to a culture of peace.

It imposes a re-ordering of global priorities—financial, educational, scientific, cultural, social, human to tackle global problems—from social injustice to the environment that threaten our security and well-being.

In response to the challenge of peace-building, UNESCO, which has always undertaken long term actions to build the foundations of peace through its fields of competence, is to assume a new and dynamic role, aimed at encouraging and reinforcing a culture of peace.

As Federico Mayor, UNESCO Director General said, "It is time to get history to lay down its arms. To teach our children the history of power, but not of knowledge, the history of war but not of culture . . Therefore, change we must. We must learn to pay the price of peace just as we had to pay the price of war. We shall have to set fresh priorities".

It is, therefore, no surprise that UNESCO's Culture of Peace Programme puts so much emphasis on the ability of each individual, each community, from the grass roots up, to build and enhance peace. What is even more important is to persuade policy makers and leaders of states to adopt the attitude of culture of peace.

One of the documents that the Executive Board examined at its recent 145th session in October-November 1994 was entitled: "The culture of peace programme: from national programmes to a project of global scope". The very title speaks of the necessity to start from a given country. It supposes that any process becomes the object of national policy only if the state is interested in it.

If this is the case, the state should formulate an objective. A system of measures and activities, planned and implemented, represent the state policy towards this process.

Take the concrete case of Russia, in particular the actual state policy towards science, and more particular towards conversion.

Let us start from positive results. The state has removed all artificial ideological and administrative obstacles which seriously hindered international scientific cooperation.

Undoubtedly, science has become more open and democratic. At the same time in the changing social and economic formation science in Russia has faced dramatic difficulties, which could be overpassed only with a resolute and active support of the state and society in general.

At present the situation with science in Russia remains very alarming.

Some expert in Russia estimated that sums allotted by the State for scientific research have been reduced by some 30 times. The share of state allotments for science in the gross product in Russia has reached an extremely dangerous level—only 0.5%.

According to the State Committee for Statistics only 17% of scientists have salaries that exceed the officially established minimum, whereas the average salary of scientific worker occupies the 10th place out of eleven leading branches of economy.

A post-graduate grant in the prestigious Moscow Physics Technology Institute in August 1994 was 25,000 roubles, which means that it is at least 5 times less than minimum. This certainly does not correspond to the qualifications and complicity of work performed. And as a logical result—a large scale internal and external brain drain. To understand this situation it is necessary to go into history.

It is quite obvious that this situation has not occurred all of a sudden.

Fundamental science in Russia was developed in its own way and mainly with the help of its own resources. By the beginning of the twentieth century Russian fundamental science gained recognition in the world.

It is important to note that Russian science in spite of many difficulties and losses (emigration, arrests, ideological cleanings etc). managed to survive during the post revolutionary period and the time of Stalin dictature.

The rise of Russian science coincides with the period of Khrouschev when its rating was extremely high in the country and in the world. It was prestigious for sons of party leaders to choose scientific careers. The sixties were the period of "lyrics and physicists".

The situation changed during what we call "stagnation period", under Brezhnev's rule, when strategic decision of the development of science were taken by non competent administrators. At this period we witnessed the creation of many secret scientific institutions (so called "boxes") with numerous scientific staff but with very low input. Practically all of them were oriented towards research in one way or another linked with military unilization.

It is sufficient to say that Seventy per cent of the total budget of the country went to military purposes at that time.

On the other hand there was a policy to cover the whole spectre of sciences to show to the world that we had leading schools in all branches of science. Instead of concentrating on major disciplines there was evident waste of money, scientist's energy and output without visible results.

That was the reason why scientific and technical revolution in the western countries occurred in the late seventies and in the eighties left the Soviet Union scientifically and economically far behind.

At the same time science has become one of the most active social detonators which led the country to the collapse of the communist system and to the democratic revolution of 1991. Let us remember the role of Russian scientists in opposition to the official regime, just to cite Pyotr Kapitsa and Andrei Sakharov.

To sum up, many difficulties we experience now, are in many respect connected with military oriented science and with the abandon of so-called "defensive conception". Military oriented industry complex which produced fighters, tanks and guns and in which millions of people, including scientists, is facing the crucial problem: how to survive, converting the industry for production of consumption goods and to what extent.

I am personally convinced that a state like Russia with its enormous territory and thousands of kilometres of its borders and its geopolitical role in the world must have military oriented industry, probably several times smaller but several times more effective than the current one. But at the same time we must think of today and of tomorrow—so that converted branches of industry will have modern automation technologies which can be created only with the help of science.

These objectives can be achieved only when they become the object of state policy.

I consider that after a sort of "catastrophism" to use the expression of Russian Ambassador to France Academician Ryzhov, a depressive feeling which was characteristic for the years 1991-93 not only for simple citizen but also for many politicians we are coming now to the understanding of the necessity of psychological stabilization. To achieve stabilization it is absolutely vital to launch a national programme of culture of peace.

I think it is symptomatic that the main theme during the meeting of Mr. Mayor, Director General of UNESCO with President B. Eltsin was culture of peace in the minds of men. As President B. Eltsin stated, Russia is willing to cooperate in the development of the Programme "Culture of peace". Russia is interested in the creation of a national programme, which would include an all embracing system of education of the entire population for peace democracy and human rights. I believe that transformation of science, oriented to the peaceful conversion would constitute an important element of the programme.

It gives to all of us an optimistic view for the future.

As concerns the concrete proposals of cooperation of Russia with UNESCO in the field of sciences in would like to point out the following:

1. As a follow up the Memorandum of cooperation between Russian Academy of Science and UNESCO, the Russian Federation is disposed to conclude an agreement about realization in Russia of major innovation projects in the field of fundamental sciences.

They may present particular interest, for the proposal to make use of unique and costly Russian scientific stands, polygones and equipment, which in the west would cost a fortune. This could be realized by creation of a foundation for support of fundamental sciences under the auspices of UNESCO or with participation of western countries interested in it.

2. We consider it necessary to reinforce our cooperation in the field of protection of environment with due account of the conception of sustainable development adopted by the Rio Conference in 1992.

3. We are interested in cooperation in the field of monitoring and forecasting of earthquakes, especially regarding the measures of preventive character.

4. We would like to be associated with UNESCO initiatives in the field of ecologically safe, new and non traditional sources of energy and in drawing up of the conception of global energy strategy for the coming Solar Summit in 1995.

5. We are ready to share with UNESCO conceptual ideas and practical experience in the field of creation of ecologically clean settlements within the mandate of the Organization.

6. As a matter of particular interest we are looking forward to an integration of Russian universities and higher education institutions in the worldwide system of science and education, in particular by a wider use of UNESCO possibilities to offer short-term grants for young scientists to carry out common scientific research.

7. In view of positive experience of cooperation of Russian scientists and specialists with ROSTE in tackling major problems of military conversion and "brain drain" and carrying international expertise in the field of scientific and technological policy and defining the basic foundations of legislation on energy resources we consider important for us to continue our cooperation in the legislative and normative fields.

8. We are ready to make efforts to seek for budgetary and especially for extrabudgetary resources to initiate new projects and we hope UNESCO would take necessary actions to further develop cooperation with Russian science.

It goes without saying that these proposals are not exhaustive. To implement them successfully, Russia needs political and psychological stabilization and stability, and western states should be fully aware of these necessary and cooperate with Russia correspondingly for mutual benefit.

14

Intellectual Migration and Technological Innovation

JOÃO CARAÇA

1. About Knowledge, Language and People

The point about intellectual migration is to understand what is knowledge and where it resides. Knowledge can no longer be envisaged as a mysterious fluid, flowing in and out of countries and walls, sometimes embedded in machines, sometimes encoded in documents, sometimes even broadcasted electronically.

Knowledge resides in human bodies, like physical strength, and the whole issue is about capacities of human bodies, organized in groups, societies, nations, etc.

Unlike physical strength however, knowledge does not add simply, unfortunately. Take two men of equal physical strength. It is easy to understand that given proper communication between them they can combine their efforts to, say, pull a load of stones twice as heavy as one of them would be able to pull, alone. What about the knowledge of that couple of two men? Is it double of the knowledge of one of them? Clearly no. Suppose they are both unskilled workers speaking the same language. Then it is easy to admit that the total knowledge of the system of two men is equal to the knowledge of each one of them.

Take as a further example a legion of 10,000 soldiers. With proper training and coordination the physical effect of that legion is very close to 10,000 times the power of a single soldier. What about its total military knowledge? Clearly, it is bigger than that of the individual soldier and clearly also it cannot be obtained simply by multiplying by 10,000 the value corresponding to the soldier level. Here, we assume that the purpose of training, coordination, and command is to enable that legion to function collectively (through the use of proper communication channels) with a total knowledge corresponding to the military knowledge of its general.

Therefore, knowledge is not additive, unlike material things, such as energy. Further, knowledge resides in each human body (with different levels and values depending on each individual person) and can be represent by the language, or languages, each human being employs. It is tempting to ascribe a first measure of the "quantity of knowledge" words each individual human being is able to use in its own daily and professional life. In this case, the military knowledge of a general is maybe only 100 times bigger than that of each rank soldier (500 words for a soldier versus 50,000 words or "memory positions" for a general). But it is this immense language advantage that allows him to coordinate (if communication channels, i.e. officers, sergeants, corporals, function adequately) a physical power 10,000 bigger than, supposedly, his own.

We see, thus, the power of knowledge, language and communication. The role of language is not only that of a *medium*, enabling the human being to relate to the world around him, including his fellow human beings, but also that of a *repository*, representing the capacity of forcing and directing his interaction with it, and thus his ability to survive.

The purpose of organizations, of institutions, is to enable through communication the creation of higher, more complex languages, and the "election" to command of the person which generates and manages a higher repository of knowledge.

Several levels of knowledge (and of language) must be considered*.

---

* João Caraca and Manuel M. Carrilho "A new paradigm in the organization of knowledge", Futures 1994 26 (7), pp. 781-86.

First, *tacit knowledge,* governing the relationship of the human being with the world as a whole (the outside world and his own group) experienced particularly as the confrontation of two orders, the "objective" and the "subjective". It is the level of the organization of knowledge which corresponds to what can be defined as "common knowledge", the type of knowledge which is not taught explicitly to us, but which we learn by "exposure" in our own society. It is the level of knowledge of the unskilled worker. Clearly this level has evolved with historical times, but not in a simple linear progression.

Second, we have to define a level of *explicit knowledge* in which language emerges as its definite operator, through the creation of "specialized languages" leading to the affirmation of the identity and the diversity of groups inside a community, and corresponding to a growing level of complexity in the interaction between man and his world: that of "intersubjectivity". Explicit knowledge is associated with the regime of specialized information.

Third, emerging from the level of explicit knowledge through a permanent process of increasing complexity in the relationship between man and his world, the density and intensity of communication processes leads intersubjectivity to be replaced by an enlarged "interactivity", which in turn correspond to languages of higher precision. This is the level of *disciplinary knowledge,* the context in which disciplines, i.e. sciences, philosophy, ethics, aesthetics, appear. Disciplines are associated with larger and highly developed repositories of meanings.

It is in this light that we must treat the effect of knowledge and communication in any area. For instance, if we deal with economic activity, we have to understand what are the intellectual levels of the various segments of the population, how the diverse institutions are organized, and which rules of overall coordination and operation of the economic system are being used. High level repositories of knowledge are effective only if proper institutions are created, or are at work, which take full use of their specific meanings, values and perceptions.

2. About Migrations and Technological Innovation

Migrations are massive motions of people from one territory to others. When people migrate they bring along their language, which embeds their repository of meanings, i.e. their knowledge. People migrate in quest of better social and economic conditions of living.

The USA can be seen as the result of massive inflows of immigrants which already had a level of tacit knowledge of a quite advanced character (developed in the conditions of a highly sophisticated agricultural-commercial European society, experimenting with industrialization).

In the physical, material conditions of North America, those massive transfers of tacit knowledge strongly enabled explicitation processes which were then captured by burgeoning institutions. When the power of the State was finally installed after the Civil War the conditions for the functioning of a huge national market were then set. And intellectual migration or brain-drain (i.e. migration of highly specialized or disciplinary knowledge) only acquired an economic visibility in its aftermath.

The notion that science and scientists are "national" emerges only by the end of the 19th century* and is further accentuated by the 20th century World Wars. And massive migrations of scientists, in terms of the international scientific community, have arisen mainly in connection with political constraints, ranging from institutional repression to physical terror, like the massive transfer of German scientists of Jewish origin during the rise of the III Reich.

With the implosion of the Soviet block, concerns about massive brain-drain have again been voiced. But many misconceptions have also been diffused.

In a recent paper by researchers of the Russian Centre for Science Research and Statistics** it is pointed out that the

---

* Charles Halary "Les exilés du savoir", Editions L'Hasrmattan, Paris 1994.

** E.F. Nekipelova, L.M. Gokhber and L.E. Mindeli "Emigration of Scientists: Problems Real Estimations", Russian Academy of Sciences, Moscow 1994.

structure of the active population and that of the emigrants is very similar. This means that there is no specific brain-drain factor. Normal motivations (like ethnic ones, for sure) are at work when looking at emigration globally.

But of course one cannot minimize the loss of intellectuals and of scientists in a given country. The institutions they belonged to, if they were employed at the commanding level, will sure be retarded in their operation and severely handicapped if whole sectors are disbanded. A terrible issue is vested in the ability of the emergent new economy, with its new rules of the game, to cope with it.

Not all scientists leave the country though. Many of them simply leave the science and technology system to look for jobs in the fast-growing business sector and in administration. And this must be considered a as beneficial effect of this "supposed brain-drain". The level of languages (i.e. knowledge) and attitudes they bring into the economy and its regulatory institutions will have a very important effect in a quicker regeneration of wealth when conditions will become favourable.

As these reflections are concerned solely with potential effects in the field of technological innovation, no mention to related and crucial important security issues has been made.

But a final point should not be overlooked. The emigration of bright and eminent scientists has a devastating effect in the stimulation of intelligent young people for entering scientific careers; thus, the inflow of new and young personnel will probably sharply decrease. This may cause, a generation later, also a decrease in the sophistication of high-level languages and therefore, a slow-down in the peace of economic recovery.

15

Considerations on Socio-Economic Consequences of the Restructuring of Military Industry in Italy

ALBERTO TRABALLESI

All industrialized countries are experiencing considerable restructuring of the military industrial sector, following public spending cuts. Owing to the fall of the internal market, restructuring was further needed to maintain the competitiveness of this sector on the international market, which is also slackening.

The implication is a loss of jobs, but not necessarily an increase of unemployment, because jobs may increase in other expanding industrial sectors, while being reduced in the military sector.

In a developed country, military industry is only a small share of the entire industrial sector, so in a macroeconomic perspective a reduction of orders deriving from the military sector have almost non-existent repercussions in terms of employment on economic development. On the contrary, the effects on technological innovation are more visible, because these are largely technology intensive types of production.

Under the microeconomic and territorial viewpoints, however, it becomes apparent that military factories are unevenly distributed on the national territory, where concentrations are found in specific areas.

Consequently, the process of restructuring is extremely important locally and its socio-economic effects have a direct influence on regional economic systems, at least in the short to medium term, particularly in connection with the impact on scientific and technological development, which is certainly alsc affected by the degree of specialization of individual sectors and by the ensuing competitiveness in the face of sectors other than the military.

The case of Italy does not merely confirm this general picture, it even magnifies it, so a few data on the size of the sector may turn useful.

The Italian military industry accounts for less than 1% of employment in the national industry; it employs 40,000 workers for the production of military equipment and its turnover amounts to 7-8,000 billion Liras. In this context, the internal market absorbs 4,000 billion Liras, including imports, while exports amounted to 1,000 billion Liras in 1993.

The planning of military expenditure over the next few years, being approved by Parliament, and the expected reasonable increase of international market orders, which may occur after regulations on armament transfer is fully adjusted to those of the other European Union countries, indicate that the Italian military industry may rely on a market rapidly approaching an amount of about 6 to 7,000 billion Liras.

In this case, in Italy, the global size of diversification into civilian production would turn out to be limited, as it may involve less than 20 per cent of the labour force of the sector, that is to say from 6 to 8,000 people, as against 6.7 million people employed in the national industry, in which there has been an employment fall by slightly more than 100,000 jobs since 1990.

Territorial distribution of production and related specialization have been left out from the above comments, which outline the presence of a limited balance between supply and demand, in the light of planning made so far.

It is in this connection, however, that the problems of Italian industry are to be found, together with their repercussions on the local socio-economic situation.

Historically, the largest part of military industry has developed in northern-western and central-southern well defined areas of the country, where production became highly specialized and armaments were made to meet specific requirements. The indentification of their origin and location would require a study of its own and is not relevant here. In particular the aeronautical industry developed in the Turin-Milan-Varese area, the light armament industry developed in the area of Brescia; ship-building is to be found along the Genoa-La Spezia-Leghorn route; ammunitions are produced in the area of Rome, where electronics is also developed; finally the aeronautical industry is also present in the territory of Naples.

This territorial distribution has become so specialized since World War II that specific areas of reference were created: Varese for the helicopters industry, Turin for combat aircraft, Naples for transport aircraft, Genoa and La Spezia for ship building, La Spezia and Brescia for land vehicles and heavy armament, Brescia for light armament, Milan for avionics, Rome and Genoa for naval electronics, Rome for missilery and terrestrial electronics, Florence for electronics applied to land vehicles, Leghorn for the torpedoes industry, Milan and Rome for telecommunications and electronic warfare apparatus. This is only a general picture, that leaves out other smaller production site concentrations, in other areas, to which, anyway, our considerations also apply.

These specialization trends have both favoured the establishment of sub-contractors and part suppliers linked to specific production types and led the training of experts with secondary school and university degrees towards the specializations best suited to the local types of production. Consequently, local universities, national research institutions and local enterprises used to entertain relations and exchange research experience.

This system of interchange is particularly important, because the whole production-training-research system may be endangered in a specific area when a production activity is modified, or even interrupted.

In Italy, there has been a interruption of the flow and exchange of personnel and research between universities (mainly

Faculties of Engineering) and military enterprises, as a direct consequence of the above phenomenon, which in turn is linked to a specific situation, mentioned below. This interchange was important in Italy, where there are limited possibilities of financing public research directly within enterprises, by leading them towards the civilian sectors relevant to the military industry: new materials, advanced electronics, artificial intelligence, etc.

Furthermore, the financial crisis and the ensuing cuts to public orders prevented Italy from acquiring the professional skills that have become available following the world crisis in the other countries (including the East), therefore, there will be a delay in the production of technological innovation in terms of products and processes.

In short, the "Italian pattern" for the acquisition of new technologies has broken up; according to this pattern the interchange between universities and enterprises occurred unofficially: the enterprises employed graduates from the Engineering Faculties, which in turn adapted their curricula and guidelines of research to the needs of armament producers in the military and civilian sectors. This process used to take place informally, without an apparent transfer of financial resources.

From a general point of view, international experience and the existing literature on the issue of the restructuring have shown that one of the elements to be taken into account is what could be defined as the degree of "military rigidity" of the individual types of production. Within the military industry the least rigid branch is electronics, followed by ship building, the aeronautical industry, land vehicles, missilery, ammunitions and light and heavy firearms (ordered from the least to the most rigid).

A comparison between the above pattern of the sector and the territorial distribution of production types and their geographical specialization outlines the various problems to be encountered during the rationalization of the Italian military industry, including diversification and conversion. In the same way, it is possible to identify the consequences that restructuring will bring about.

Where diversification into the civilian market is relatively easier, on the basis of the above considerations, the local development pattern may be expected to remain effective, requiring adjustment without modification to its inherent structure.

Then there are two problems that must be taken into consideration.

The first problem is the stimulation of public demand for dual products, in that diversification is in any case targeted on the public market (civil defence, management of the territory, purification, health service, etc.). As regards Italy, a difficulty to be solved is that of a sizeable demand, managed by different subjects, often uncoordinated, and poorly standardized. To this end, specific studies and surveys are being developed, under the auspices of the Presidency of the Council of Ministers, to identify relevant solutions, in the framework of the industrial policy and economic planning of the Country.

The second problem is linked to the need to safeguard the planning potential, which is the most important asset of these enterprises. Diversification alone cannot fully replace the lack of good quality activity, arising from investments made by the Defence sector. So far, in Italy almost all military research was financed in the framework of acquisition programmes of the Defence sector itself. At present, on the contrary, it would appear useful to revert the trend and acquire resources to finance military research, regardless of production.

In this way, both civilian and military planning potentials would be maintained, so that enterprises with a low "military rigidity" could be diversified into an integrated production, to meet both military and civilian demand. This course of action has become compulsory, if their survival is to be guaranteed, also on amount of the crisis of the above mentioned Italian pattern for the informal interchange between enterprises and universities.

The three year 1994-96 research plan has been drawn up along these guidelines by the Ministry for Universities and Scientific and Technological Research, with a clear practical intent to promote technological innovation, to enable production sectors to rise up to the challenge of competitiveness in a modern economy, in which the limited available resources must be effectively exploited to finance research projects.

In areas where, on the contrary, the specialization of production hinders diversification, the whole pattern of development is bound to break up, so alternative solutions will have to be sought for.

When discussing restructuring, attention focuses exceedingly on plant characteristics and labour specialization, leaving out the characteristics of research activities and of vocational training institutions. On the contrary, the latter must be taken stock of when identifying a new pattern of local development, for two reasons:

1. for their very nature, research and training are more flexible, although they are linked to production, as mentioned above;
2. when acting in a medium term perspective, effective alternative solutions can be conceived on the basis of available qualified labour and research and development potential.

Besides, the problem of possible plant closures must be mitigated by adopting measures in favour of the staff employed at present. However, it must be taken for granted that the youngest part only of personnel can be retrained and employed in production activities that are extremely different from military ones.

Finally, as regards the general process of industrial concentration, now underway in the international military industry, its manifestation in Italy has acquired a specific pattern, also on account of events occurring outside the military market.

These events were the decision to dissolve EFIM, one of the two public corporations in control, among others, of industrial military enterprises, taken on the basis of its financial crisis, and the disengagement from the sector by the only large private group: FIAT.

These events, added to the contemporary drop of internal and international demand, explain why there were no alternatives to the creation of an industrial military aggregate within the FINMECCANICA Corporation, whose majority is at present publicly owned. Therefore, this industrial aggregate now includes former EFIM companies. For the same reason, FINMECCANICA is now participating in smaller private enterprises and is in control of about 70 per cent of military production.

The process of unification, however, has not improved the organizational effectiveness of enterprises as yet, but rather it brought about the overlapping of leadership, research and development among the various previously independent companies. Consequently the reduction of production was difficult to manage because after the merger, executives were engaged in obtaining the leadership for the personnel of the companies of origin.

This situation practically blocked any form of transfer of executives towards other (civilian and research) sectors, both nationally and abroad. In other words, effective procedure of redeployment in dual and civilian production sectors of personnel with high technology intensive competence has not been started.

This situation is quite the opposite of what happened in other European Union countries and in the US, where, on the contrary, the redeployment of technical executive staff on the market occurred rapidly and, in some cases, satisfactorily (within and outside the country of origin). This difficulty has also adversely affected the flow and interchange of personnel between universities and military enterprises, in the framework of the crisis of the system enterprises-training-research, as was mentioned in the analysis of the territorial situation.

To sum up what has been said so far, in Italy, at present there has been neither a brain drain nor a scientific innovation transfer from the military to the civilian sector, from large public corporations, to private ones, even of small and medium size. What is happening now, is the reduction by military enterprises of unqualified labour, while research and development functions are maintained as is technical executive staff, on the assumption that all process potentials can be used in the future and that only production levels are reduced.

However this is only a transition phase, brought about by the restructuring process; in the future a new balanced situation will come about, as a consequence of the completion of corrective interventions, suggested by the analysis of the territorial impact of the military industrial sector.

This new situation will be characterized by a more efficient and effective interchange among universities, research centres and military enterprises; furthermore, the "civilian" scientific technological basis will acquire more strategic value than that of the military basis, quite the opposite of what has been the case so far and following the modifications of the economic situation and international politics.